MUSLIM SOCIETY
AND THE WESTERN
INDIAN OCEAN

Muslim Society and the Western Indian Ocean explores the social processes through which practical reasoning is translated into meaningful collective action. Focusing on craft learning and religious practice, the study examines the ways in which the two kinds of knowledge are simultaneously transmitted between Muslim masters and apprentices in the traditional shipyards of Kachchh, Gujarat. The chapters of the book are loosely structured around the career trajectory of the typical apprentice, from his early years of labouring in shipyards to his later life as an accomplished sailor, experienced in the ways of the Indian Ocean. Apprenticeship is treated as a process that puts into stark relief broader social processes and concerns.

Given the rise of Hindu nationalist politics in Gujarat, and the increasing importance of 'religion' as a form of political identity, Edward Simpson explains how the masters of the shipyards have incorporated their rivalries with other Muslims and with Hindu nationalists into what the apprentices are taught. He demonstrates how migration and trade within the Indian Ocean can produce divisive and overlapping parochial hierarchies of corporeal, material and symbolic kinds. Based on substantial ethnographic research and further textual and archival research, this book offers a unique perspective on the anthropology of western India and the western Indian Ocean region.

Edward Simpson is Lecturer in Anthropology at Goldsmiths College, University of London. He has written on various aspects of both Muslim society and natural disasters in Gujarat, western India.

ROUTLEDGE INDIAN OCEAN SERIES
Editors: Ruth Barnes & Zulfikar Hirji
University of Oxford

There is a need to understand the Indian Ocean area as a cultural complex which should be analysed beyond the geographical divisions of Africa, the Middle East, the Indian subcontinent, and South-East Asia, as its coastal populations have intermingled constantly. The movement of people, goods and technology make it imperative that spatial concepts and the role of material culture be central in the study of the region by archaeologists, historians, ethnographers and anthropologists.

MUSLIM SOCIETY AND THE WESTERN INDIAN OCEAN

The seafarers of Kachchh

Edward Simpson

Routledge
Taylor & Francis Group

LONDON AND NEW YORK

First published 2006
by Routledge
2 Park Square, Milton Park, Abingdon, Oxon, OX14 4RN

Simultaneously published in the USA and Canada
by Routledge
270 Madison Ave, New York NY 10016

*Routledge is an imprint of the Taylor & Francis Group,
an informa business*

Transferred to Digital Printing 2009

© 2006 Edward Simpson

Typeset in Times New Roman by
Florence Production Ltd, Stoodleigh, Devon

British Library Cataloguing in Publication Data
A catalogue record for this book is available from the British Library

Library of Congress Cataloging in Publication Data
Simpson, Edward, 1971–
Muslim society and the western Indian Ocean: the seafarers of
Kachchh/Edward Simpson.
p. cm. – (Routledge Indian Ocean series)
Includes bibliographical references and index.
1. Shipbuilding industry – Employees – Training of – India –
Kachchh.   2. Muslims – India – Kachchh – Social conditions –
20th century.   I. Title.   II. Series: Indian Ocean series.
HD8039.S521485 2006
338.7′623820095475 – dc22   2005026801

ISBN10: 0–415–37610–6 (hbk)
ISBN10: 0–415–54377–0 (pbk)
ISBN10: 0–203–09951–6 (ebk)

ISBN13: 978–0–415–37610–5 (hbk)
ISBN13: 978–0–415–54377–4 (pbk)
ISBN13: 978–0–203–09951–3 (ebk)

FOR MY PARENTS

CONTENTS

ACKNOWLEDGEMENTS

When I left secondary school I failed to find an apprenticeship in a traditional Norfolk boatyard. Eighteen years later, apprenticed in the traditions of Social Anthropology, I have written a book about men who build and sail ships in the western Indian Ocean. Inspired by a series of travels in India, which took me on one occasion to each and every port of the Gujarat peninsula by bicycle, I returned in 1997 for a prolonged period of fieldwork, choosing this time the old mercantile town of Mandvi. During that time and on a number of subsequent visits to the district of Kachchh, I have inevitably incurred a great many debts as people aided and abetted me along the way. I am grateful to them all but aware of the fact that any inaccuracies in the text are of my own making.

I thank all of those at the University of Manchester and the London School of Economics who tutored me in the anthropological tradition and who taught me to use its conventions with both confidence and caution. Largely because of them this study is unashamedly based on the staples of a lengthy period of fieldwork, participant observation and what I consider to be an honest analysis of the facts as I collected and interpreted them.

The bulk of this work was funded by awards from the Economic and Social Research Council (R00429634237 and TO26271189). More recently, I have been funded by a Nuffield Foundation New Career Development Fellowship (NCF/00103/G), which, although primarily intended to allow me to conduct research on the reconstruction process after the devastating earthquake that hit Gujarat in 2001, has generously allowed me time to rework parts of this text.

Parts of Chapters 3, 4 and 5 have appeared as Simpson 2003. Parts of the Introduction and of Chapter 2 have appeared as Simpson 2006 and are reproduced with permission of (© 2006) the *Journal of the Royal Anthropological Institute*.

I would like to express my gratitude first and foremost to Christopher Fuller and Jonathan Parry. I would also like to record my debt to the late Alfred Gell and to others who have been in and around the LSE over the course of the last decade, namely, Peter Gow, Maurice Bloch, Martha

Mundy, Catherine Allerton, Manuela Ciotti, Luke Freeman, Peggy Froerer, Lucia Michelutti, Roseanna Pollen, Alpa Shah, Jason Sumich and Vernon Eichhorn.

I am also grateful to Brian Didier, Thomas Blom Hansen and Zulfikar Hirji for commenting on previous drafts of the text. More generally, I would like to thank Roger Ballard, Helene Basu, Francesca Bray, Stuart Corbridge, Rachel Dwyer, Katy Gardener, Anne-Marie Giard, Barbara Harriss-White, Andrew Holding, Farhana Ibrahim, Tim Ingold, Kai Kresse, Ian Lacey, Pierre Lachiere, Enrico Lepri, Pedro Machedo, Mattison Mines, David Mosse, Fillipo Ossela, David Parkin, Sandy Robertson, Abdul Sheriff, Jennifer Tanguay and Paul Towel for their encouragement and advice.

I am grateful for the support of the staff of the Centre for Social Studies in Surat and the Maharashtra State Archives. In Bombay, I was fortunate enough to meet and share long conversations about western India with Preeti Chopra, Chhayya Goswami, Aparna Kapadia, Mangala Purandare, Rusheed Wadia and Sally Warhaft. Among those whom I met and spent time with in Gujarat, I would like to thank Sukhet Bakali, Nirav Bhimani, Umesh Jadia, Pramod Jethi, Dinesh Katira, Anis Khatri, Majid Khatri, Makhrand Mehta, Daud Pathan, Haji Saleh Mohammed Pathan, Zainul Abuddin Pir, Vipul Sampat, Sukhur Thaim, Dilip Vaidya and Devendra Vyas. I thank the members of the Bhadala football teams, 'The Titanic' and 'The Seagulls', who played on the unrelenting ground of the Salaya pitch in the heat of the 1998 season and to all of those in the shipyards for whom friendship never quite managed to unseat ridicule.

Finally, I thank my wife Isabella Lepri, for all her patience, and my sanity.

NOTES ON LANGUAGE
AND TEXT

The number of non-English words appearing in the text has been kept to a minimum. I have only included local terms when an English equivalent is either unavailable or misleading. Diacritical marks are omitted and the normal adjustments to the transliteration system are employed. The principal languages referred to in this book are Gujarati and Kachchhi. Gujarati is an Indo-Aryan language (LSI 1908, Vol. IX, Part II: 322–377) spoken by some fifty-five million people worldwide. It has four principal dialects: Pani, Surati, Charotari and Saurastrian (Kathiawadi), with a fifth major variant spoken by the Parsis. A standard written form is used in government schools and in literature. In Kachchh, the first language for most people is Kachchhi; a distinct language, but classified by the *Linguistic Survey of India* as a 'Sindhi dialect' and part of the 'North Western' groups of the Indo-Aryan languages (LSI 1919, Vol. VIII, Part I: 183–206). Kachchhi has no formal script and where Kachchhi words are used in the text they appear in transliterated Gujarati form. It hardly seems appropriate to talk of 'loanwords' in the context of the Indian Ocean, but both these languages use considerable numbers of terms from Arabic, Hindi, Persian, Sindi, Swahili, Urdu and English. I make no attempt to trace the etymology of such words and they are transliterated as they are popularly used. Technical words, especially those associated with religion and social organisation, are derived primarily from the classical languages of Arabic and Sanskrit. In such instances the simplest form closest to colloquial use is provided. Words common to Indological literature, works on Hinduism and Islam, and the names of persons, places, communities and religious movements appear in non-italicised anglicised form. Generally, throughout the text priority has been given to the way words sound rather than to the conventions of Sanskrit or Arabic orthography. 'Kachchh' is consistently used, although this word also appears as 'Cutch', 'Kachh', 'Kutch' and 'Kacchh' in quotation and in the bibliography. Throughout, I have referred to Saurashtra not Kathiawad and Sind not Sindh. Bombay was renamed Mumbai in 1995; however, for simplicity rather than political malice I have stuck with the old name throughout because of the sheer number of times it appears in the text in quotation, in the references and as a pre-1995 territory. Primary sources have been cited as endnotes. The names of the seafarers discussed in this book are pseudonyms.

ABBREVIATIONS

The following abbreviations are used more than once in the text.

BJP   Bharatiya Janata Party (the main political party associated with Hindu nationalism)

CM   Chief Minister

FO   Foreign Office (India Office Library, London)

GBP   *Gazetteer of the Bombay Presidency* (various volumes)

GSG   *Gujarat State Gazetteer*

Guj.   Refers to texts written in the Gujarati language

LSI   *Linguistic Survey of India* (various volumes)

MSA   Maharashtra State Archive (Bombay)

PD   Political Department (of the British Government of the Bombay Presidency)

RSS   Rashtriya Swayamsevak Sangh (parent organisation of the larger Hindu nationalist movement)

VHP   Vishwa Hindu Parishad ('cultural' wing of the Hindu nationalist movement)

v.s.   Vikram Savant (also Vikramaditya Samvat) from a sovereign of Malwar who defeated Soka, a King of Delhi, and took possession of the chief throne of India some fifty-six to fifty-seven years before the date from which the Gregorian calendar commences.

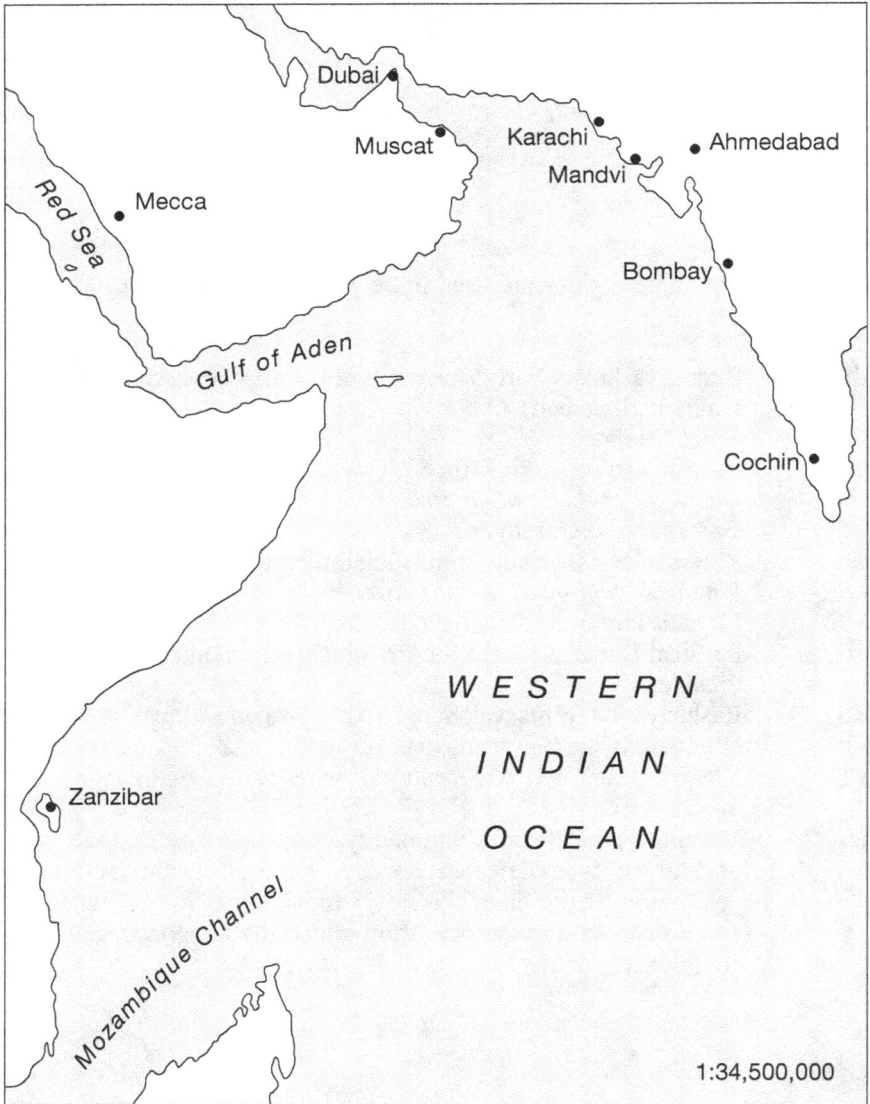

Map of the western Indian Ocean

INTRODUCTION

This study is concerned with changing patterns of power, legitimacy and wealth among Sunni Muslim seafarers from a port town in western India. The purpose of this introduction is to describe the object and aim of the study and to outline the logic of its structure. My aim is to show, ethnographically, how the structures of social organisation relate to patterns of religious thought and practice and how both emerge from particular economic and political conditions and are given shape and meaning by the very nature of these conditions – as well as by the larger concerns of nation-building, colonial history and ethnic and international affairs. The material demonstrates how migration and trade within the Indian Ocean can produce divisive and overlapping parochial hierarchies of corporeal, material and symbolic kinds.

Established as a trading post in the late sixteenth century, Mandvi lies on the western bank of the Rukhmavuti River on the southern shore of the district of Kachchh in the westernmost part of the state of Gujarat. A few kilometres inland from the coastal town is the village of Riyan, where back-fill shifting in the wind has revealed an ancient quay. Coins and shards from distant ports are regularly uncovered to reveal a tradition in trade that postdates the Indus valley settlements, but precedes the shape of today's coastline. The site suggests the area surrounding the Gulf of Kachchh has been cosmopolitan for millennia and that the social, architectural and religious fabric of the region has been constructed out of the exchange of population, trade goods and ideas. From the sixteenth century, if not earlier, Mandvi was a departure point for pilgrims bound for Mecca; and throughout the nineteenth and early half of the twentieth century it was the port of embarkation for migrants destined for Bombay, East Africa, Zanzibar and Muscat. A significant node within Indian Ocean and hinterland trade networks, up until the early nineteenth century, Mandvi had a quayside slave market and regular Arab trading partners.[1] The architecture of the town reflects a diversity that came with long-distance travel and trade. Roistering Dutchmen adorn the walls of the former royal palace which, later, under the patronage of a Hindu merchant, became one of the first modern schools in western India. Across the way, the internal ceilings of a decaying mercantile house, owned by a man fluent in Italian from trading ice cream and pasta in Somalia, are a series of murals depicting the ports of the East African coast. The population also reflects a similar diversity, with origin claims linking caste groups to places around the western Indian Ocean. To the east of the river is the village of Salaya, which is home to an endogamous group of Sunni Muslims known as the Bhadala (singular and plural, pronounced 'Bad-ela' and sometimes referred to in other literature as Bhodala). These Muslims have recently usurped the traditions of seafaring from their Hindu rivals. Today, the Bhadala employ a vast workforce to build the wooden cargo vessels (known as 'country craft') in the Rukhmavuti Estuary, which they use for trade primarily between India and the Emirates. In recent decades, they have invested their profits in the religious monuments that dominate the skyline of their village. This study focuses on the Bhadala and how and why they have discovered a renewed zeal for their faith. It also explores what form this faith takes and how they convey this to the sizeable number of non-Bhadala sailors who work in their shipyards and later on their fleets. In this sense, the study is a contribution to the analysis of vernacular Islam in South Asia and the ways in which knowledge is understood and, in turn, transferred outside the literate and privileged spheres of formal or *madrasa* (religious teaching institution) education. Exploring these questions allows us to understand further the nature and shape of religious belief and practice for ordinary Muslims in South Asia.

Object

I first met Rasheed at Bapu's teashop in an area of Mandvi popular with sailors whose vessels had returned home to take shelter from the monsoon winds during the summer months. Then, Rasheed wore heavy gold necklaces, pungent aftershave, branded t-shirts and replica jeans, which were always somehow too big for his hips. He walked with a conspicuous swagger and would laugh and joke confidently on the street even with strangers. We began to meet regularly at Bapu's in the evenings. He introduced me to many other sailors and together we talked of life at sea and of the problems they had re-establishing relationships with their families after such long absences. These men spent much of their time organising exchanges of gifts and finding buyers for this or that item they had purchased in Dubai. They would also act as brokers between employers and potential employees for work on ships and for employment agencies in the Emirates. They all wore their wealth conspicuously and clearly enjoyed the highly masculine sense of fraternity that came with seafaring. Central to their burgeoning sense of status were various social, economic, ritual and political relationships with kin, non-kin, strangers, friends and enemies. Rasheed led me carefully and sensitively through these relationships, knowing from many years of experience that foreigners of any hue or persuasion did not know the same things as he did.

In those early months, Rasheed and I drank whisky in secret and went on pilgrimage with tens of thousands of devoted Hindus to one of the most venerated temples in Kachchh. We were allowed to stay overnight in the temple compound; I was not the only foreigner to enjoy the temple's hospitality but Rasheed was certainly the only Muslim. In Mandvi, he arranged for me to meet local people who were known for their knowledge of shipbuilding and seafaring and encouraged me to ask questions he himself wanted answers to. Later, I understood he had mostly taken me to meet the former leaders of a Hindu community who were the perpetrators of violence against Muslim seafarers in the 1980s. He also took me into the estuary to meet Muslim shipbuilders, fleet owners and other sailors who were preparing their wooden vessels for the forthcoming season. One day, however, he did not show up at Bapu's for tea; days passed and there was still no sign of him. Eventually, one of the other sailors who was also inexplicably drawn to Bapu's shop told me he had heard that Rasheed had been badly beaten and fearing further violence had fled to Bombay. I did not see Rasheed again until he returned to Mandvi six months later.

We did not resume our friendship exactly where we had left off. Rasheed told me that before he fled for Bombay he had had an affair with a Hindu woman whose husband was away working in Oman. Their illicit relationship had been discovered and he had, indeed, been attacked by some men from her caste. He feared further reprisals and was keeping a low profile. Later in that year, however, he gathered a number of his friends and, armed with sticks, went to take his somewhat bloody revenge. He told me that he hoped the violence would escalate and draw in more and more people, turning his own indiscretions and punishment into a general problem of religious violence. Despite his intentions, and for all his talk, the violence did not escalate further, but the possibility of violence has never fully dissipated.

When he first returned to Mandvi after the six-month absence, for a few weeks we sat on the balcony of his house instead of at the tea shop. There, we talked without much distraction and gradually he told me the story of his life thus far. He had left school at the age of ten after completing fifth standard in Gujarati medium. At the time we were becoming friends he could speak Kachchhi and passable Arabic, and read, write and speak quite fluently in Gujarati, Hindi and English. He spent his early childhood with his parents and two brothers in a one-roomed house in the northwest of Mandvi, where we had gone to drink whisky at night. This house was owned by a local shrine to which Rasheed's father paid a small amount of monthly rent in return for a property with no running water or power. The family had kept the house and continued to pay rent for it despite the fact Rasheed had recently purchased a refurbished three-bedroom property, on the ground floor of which was an ornamental dining room, table and chairs, beds and a whole host of electrical gadgets, including a sophisticated Sony television. Rasheed claimed the upstairs front room as his own and decorated it with photographs he had taken of shopping malls and ships at anchor in Dubai and with commercial prints of the famous Sufi shrine in Ajmer and various mosques and pilgrimage sites in Saudi Arabia.

Upon leaving school, Rasheed had hawked sugared water to passengers in the local bus station where his father was a labourer. A year later, an acquaintance of the family offered the boy a job in a shop owned by a Kachchhi merchant in eastern India. He left Mandvi to make the journey across the country at the age of eleven. He returned all of his Rs. 250 monthly salary to his family. Working, eating and sleeping in the shop he contracted severe amoebic dysentery and had to return home to convalesce. In 1982, or thereabouts, he accepted a job in a provisions store in Bombay. On Sundays the store remained closed and, at a loose end, Rasheed started to explore the city, especially the areas around Dongri Channel where he had relatives. Here, he heard news of Kachchh and met with people who had recently seen his father in Mandvi. As his web of contacts expanded, he was introduced to the sailors from his home town, who today still congregate in the area while their ships are in Bombay harbour. Rasheed listened to the stories of foreign ports, exotic experiences and employment opportunities overseas. The sailors were evidently wealthier than Rasheed was ever going to be if he stayed working in the store and he admired their life-style and the sense of fraternity that prevailed among them. Inspired, on his next visit to Mandvi, he asked a senior member of his community to approach one of Salaya's ship owners on his behalf. At the time, the fleets were expanding and the Bhadala were recruiting increasing numbers of young men from Mandvi and so it was that Rasheed was offered work in one of the shipyards, the first step towards becoming a sailor.

Despite the obvious comforts Rasheed's career has brought his parents, they still talk about the anguish they claim to have felt when their son announced his intention to become a sailor. They say they spent a long time trying to dissuade him from going to work at sea. In their view, the Bhadala were not the kind of people Rasheed should be working for because, although poor, he was from a traditionally high-ranking caste. They regarded, and still do, the Bhadala as a dirty and corrupt people. That their son should become dependent on such people was an abomination of the prevailing social order as they saw it. They were also afraid of the ways in which the work and the experience overseas would change him. At the time, the family lived in an area of the town that was home to many sailors, and Rasheed's parents were only too aware of the arrogant and disrespectful attitudes of those who returned home after seasons at sea. In Rasheed's case, as we shall see, this concern was not ill founded.

Rasheed found the work in the shipyards to be hard and brutal. The other men in the yard bullied him and he recalled finding there was much to learn very quickly. He had to lift and drag heavy timbers around the shipyards in the heat of the day and run errands at the behest of others. He learned how to use rudimentary tools and how to avoid the persecution of the other men. He worked for three months without remuneration. It was not until the fourth month of his labour he started to receive irregular payments of between Rs. 25 and Rs. 50 per week – much less than he had been earning in the grocery store in Bombay. Many years later, Rasheed discovered that his father had secretly (Rasheed's mother still claims not to have known) taken a few thousand rupees from a ship owner as a bond on his son's labour. After five months, Rasheed was handed some official documents by his employer that legally entitled him to go to sea. He set sail in a particularly decrepit vessel some three weeks later. Onboard, he helped with the cooking, handled ropes and attempted to collect rainwater. After many days of making little headway, the ship's crankshaft broke and the crew had to use the auxiliary sail. One man fell overboard and was lost as the winds whipped up the sea; it was the closest Rasheed had ever been to death. The vessel's ancient sail quickly tore in the gusty winds. After the storm had abated they were left drifting helplessly towards the coast of Pakistan. They had passed a full day without drinking water before they were rescued and towed back to Kachchh by a passing fishing boat. Rasheed received no payment for the ill-fated voyage. His second experience at sea was no more lucrative or enjoyable than the first and he began to doubt the wisdom of his decision to become a sailor.

Back once again in Mandvi, Rasheed started to look for a position on another ship, but the captain of the ill-fated voyages refused to release his documents. He worked on repairing the same vessel for a further three months in dry dock before these papers were returned to him. Disheartened, in 1987, he returned to the provisions store in Bombay. From there he joined the *Al Karimi*, a ship with a contract to haul a regular cargo of melons from Bombay to Dubai. Rasheed received no salary, but was paid for loading and unloading the vessel. He soon found work on more prestigious ships and within a few years was regularly voyaging between the Emirates, India, Iran, Iraq and Somalia and his wages reached Rs. 1,000 per month. As he gained further experience at sea, he was able to earn increasingly large and regular salaries, until he was earning much more than he had been in the provisions store. He lost his virginity to a Russian prostitute in Dubai, tasted whisky for the first time and learned how to transport goods into India without paying import duties. As the seasons passed, Rasheed became wealthier, his status increasing exponentially with each return to Mandvi as he was able to bring more and more of his own trade goods from the bazaars of Dubai.

Now a competent sailor with strong connections to men in a number of ports, he was offered a steward's job on an international supply ship servicing the oil platforms in the waters off the coast of the Emirates. In this move, he left the permanent employ of the Bhadala. In the years to come, however, he frequently returned to their ships to work temporarily in exchange for a passage across the western Indian Ocean. He also started to broker contacts between them and potential sailors as well as with migrant labourers in the Emirates who were in search of a return passage to India. A few years later, in the early 1990s, Rasheed was offered legal employment in the Bombay High oil fields, for a salary of $250 per month. During his time, he was issued with an internationally recognised 'able seaman' certificate. The following year, he rejoined a country craft sailing from Mandvi and, on reaching Dubai, he jumped ship to find work elsewhere. He has worked on numerous supply vessels since that time, sometimes legally but more often not. In 1997, he signed a contract to work on a supply vessel based in Bahrain, his monthly salary increased to $450 and he received further internationally recognised certificates from the company.

In 1999, Rasheed took six months off work and got married. Unusually, he chose his own wife against the wishes of his parents, a distant cousin from Bombay with a college degree. She came to live in Mandvi for a while but could not get on with her mother-in-law. She found Kachchh to be provincial and boring and Rasheed's parents too trying. Rasheed and his wife returned to Bombay, where he tried unsuccessfully to start an employment bureau of his own, sending young Kachchhi men to work in the Emirates. Sensing failure, he once again stepped aboard a Kachchhi vessel and made several trips between Bombay and Sharjah. He stepped ashore again for a few months when his wife gave birth to their first child. Between 2001 and 2004 he held a lucrative contract to work six months out of every twelve on an international supply vessel, again in Bombay High. With his earnings he bought a tiny two-roomed house in a slum on the eastern shore of the Bombay peninsula. When his second son was born in 2004 he quit this job and, armed with a bundle of safety and proficiency certificates, found work on a service vessel operating off the coast of Scotland; where he was paid more than 1,000 dollars a month, a royal sum by the standards of Kachchh.

Aim

I introduce this study with an account of the early life of one of the seafarers of Kachchh for four reasons. First, Rasheed's story is typical of the fortunes of many of the men who, like him, first went to work in the Bhadala's shipyards some two decades ago. He has prospered and his horizons have broadened, but his networks remain firmly rooted in those he initially established through the Bhadala. His success and wealth are precisely what inspires new generations of young men to face the brutality of the shipyards. The study is thus structured by the stages of the career trajectory of a typical seafarer from his early days in the shipyards to his later life on the high seas. In this respect, each chapter explores in detail some aspect of Rasheed's experiences, transformations and battles and how he went about acquiring certain dispositions and opinions.

Second, Rasheed's example succinctly begins to illustrate some of the complex skills and dispositions seafarers must acquire in order to pursue their career with success. When I set off for Kachchh, I was interested in skill, learning and representations of technology in shipbuilding and to investigate these themes I was going to find work in a shipyard. I was interested in 'praxis', 'embodied knowledge' and how non-linguistic traditions and bodily techniques are conveyed between men of different levels of experience. Having laboured on and off for many months as an anthropologist in the Bhadala's shipyards, I consider myself reasonably adept at handling an adze and cursing like a longshoreman. However, it became apparent that in the shipyards technical skills were a fraction of what was learned. The Bhadala masters were equally devoted to revealing and rendering persuasive a particular view of religious and social worlds to the procession of recruits such as Rasheed who came to them for work.

Rasheed's example shows how the process of becoming a seafarer takes young men through a series of stages from labouring in shipyards, to the trade routes of the western Indian Ocean and, often, into other spheres of economic activity in the Emirates or further afield. The emphasis of my study is on the early years of the seafarer's professional training in the shipyards and less on the professional certificates that may come later. I treat this period of labour as a period of 'apprenticeship' in which young men learn a range of skills and social behaviours that allow them to become suitable crew on the ships they are working to construct. At all stages, apprenticeship involves disciplining bodies and minds into skills and hierarchies and inculcating a set of dispositions towards tradition, religion and politics that reproduces patterns of capital and creates a dependent constituency for the master. In this sense, apprenticeship relations are the short-term cycles of exchange that underpin the longer-term exchanges concerned with the reproduction of the social and cosmic orders. However, from the outset, I do not wish to give the impression that power and wealth are perfect in their methods or unchallenged in their aims. There is of course failure, disobedience and insubordination within the relationships of apprenticeship on the part of the apprentice; likewise, capitalists, on occasion, are prone to put favouritism and generosity before profit; they are also liable to crush those they take a dislike to rather than nurture them with a long-term gain in mind.

The literature on apprenticeship subsumes as many varied forms of human activity under the term, as it suggests ways of viewing its purpose and rationale (see, for example, Herzfeld 2004: 37–60; Lave and Wenger 1991). In the seafarers' case, their labour clearly inculcates and sediments certain dispositions into apprentices' habits as Pierre Bourdieu (1977) might have suggested. However, these impressions upon the apprentice do not always rest easy and, as in Rasheed's case, are expressed violently on the streets and reflected in domestic tensions focused on marriage partners and ways of life. Following Michael Herzfeld, I am primarily interested in the social context of apprenticeship as a 'device for opening up larger social questions' (2004: 50), in this case about the nature of Muslim society against the backdrop of seafaring and migration. Therefore, in the way I see it, the first act in the drama of apprenticeship presents a series of challenges to the apprentice's ideas about mundane things such as bodies, hierarchy and respect; in the second act the apprentice plays out the ensuing conflicts of interest between both the airs and graces of his intimates and those of the seafarers as well as between masters and apprentices within the shipping group. There are further clear parallels with well-known ideas in the anthropological tradition that can be made to further refine this point.

Studies of rites of passage illustrate how initiands are separated from their primary group by a period of liminality and reintegrated to the original group as complete persons (Turner 1969). As Maurice Bloch has discussed, 'the process of reintegration is not seen as a return to the condition left behind in the first stage but as an aggressive consumption of a vitality which is *different* in origin from that which had originally been lost' (1992: 6, original emphasis). These images of separation and integration are useful to think through the patterns of shipyard apprenticeship, especially Bloch's emphasis on the violence of return, and they can be seen in shadowy form in some of the ethnography that follows. The parallels between apprenticeship and rites of passage are alluring and have clear mutual resonances (see Coy 1989; Haas 1989); however, in this case, the relationship should properly be treated as illustrative rather than demonstrative. I think such caution is necessary for three reasons. First, in a simple sense most apprentices leave the town every day for the water's edge but return to their primary group in the evening. The frequency and repetitive nature of this journey means their transitions, while not altogether without consequence, lack the abruptness and stark contrasts central to rites of passage. Second, many apprentices are initiated through apprenticeship into another group, say, for shorthand, the 'shipping group', and not into the activities of the primary group (their families and so forth) who, for the most part, are not engaged in shipping. Finally, there is the question of degree. For apprentices many of the conditions of apprenticeship are not so dissimilar from those of non-apprenticeship. In both cases there is social and economic hierarchy, age differentiation and there are discussions about the practice of Islam; there is also cricket, humour, violence and walks in the park on Sunday nights. I emphasise these continuities to place them in an appropriate relation to the discontinuities I concentrate on in following chapters. Overall, the apprentice is burdened with a further set of expectations, which he absorbs into his repertoire of possible behaviours.

My third reason for starting with Rasheed's biography is to follow Timothy Jenkins' (1994) description of anthropological purpose and method and to take as my analytical point of departure, rather than the object of my study, narratives such as Rasheed's. Such narratives, as seafarers recount them, and as Jenkins vividly illustrates, desire to explain and eradicate conflicts; they freeze the picture and engage with the expectations of the enquirer through a logical sequence of events. These narratives are, however, mostly devoid of context; they leave out the obvious and the taken-for-granted passes without saying. In their telling, the complexities of the seafarers' lives become a linear discourse and thus a different beast to the contradictions and ambiguities inherent to those lives. For Jenkins, the antidote to the problems of the standard narrative is anthropological fieldwork. Through fieldwork, connections can be made and contrasts drawn with other kinds of activity that may or may not complement, undermine or even expose as false the 'standard narrative'. This seems to me to be a very important point, which, although obviously a central part of the tradition of British anthropology, has seldom been discussed with such clarity. It thus seems imperative to carefully distinguish between (i) narratives, (ii) ethnographic observations and conversations that take place outside or around such narratives, (iii) informants' analysis and inferences, and (iv) analysis and inferences undertaken by the anthropologist. These distinctions aid the reader to recognise what kind of data they are being presented with. They also allow the reader to see why narratives are often so problematic and the purposes they serve when held up against the habits, motivations and other domains of knowledge in the lives of informants. These things are often simply hidden from view by the 'standard' accounts of what happened or what is happening and, indeed, can often be used to critique those standard accounts. It is also the case that the seafarers of Kachchh, in common, presumably, with most if not all people, have their own reserves of substitute and rival descriptions and explanations for the same acts. It is also the case that they mostly know how to use this range of alternatives appropriately – sometimes with guile, cunning and deceit in mind – and always according to the context. It follows that there is no way of knowing in advance which factors, and which explanations, will come to the fore at times of social change. Therefore, given the basic career trajectory exemplified by Rasheed, the following chapters largely exclude further similar narratives (with the exception of Chapters 1 and 3 which examine other kinds of narratives) and look instead at the habits, motivations and areas of knowledge that are often hidden from view by the 'standard' accounts of what happened and leave the following kinds of questions unanswered. Why do apprentices find work in the shipyards so brutal? Why was the sense of fraternity among seafarers so strong and of a notably different character to other kinds of network? What are the roots of the conflicts engendered by apprenticeship? And, why was Rasheed so intrigued by Hindus?

I wish to dwell briefly on this final matter in order to highlight what I mean; I shall revisit the other questions in later chapters. When Rasheed and I went on a Hindu pilgrimage he used me to mask his identity. However, I do not believe he had any reason more sinister than curiosity for wanting to visit the temple. He also deliberately drank tea, despite the fact Bapu's brews were never great, in an area of Mandvi known for being a flashpoint in fights between particular groups of Hindus and Muslim seafarers. He also had affairs and fell in love with Hindu women. I have often asked him why he is so intrigued by Hindus. In both conversations and formal interviews his standard account is that Muslims need protecting from the chauvinisms and encroachments of Hindus, especially in the era of strong Hindu nationalism in Gujarat. Quite consciously, he sees his small acts of resistance and aggression as stemming the tide of Hindu dominance. This is a perfectly sensible and plausible answer under the circumstances, but over the years I have seen this is but part of it.

Without doubt, Rasheed likes to court controversy and to be the centre of particular kinds of attention but, caught up in a wealth of complex relationships, his actions are seldom as clear cut as he describes. Rasheed is, indeed, probably interested in stemming the tide of Hindu dominance but not in the way either his narrative or his aggressive actions at first appear to indicate. It seems to me that all of Rasheed's difficulties with Hindus (and there were further incidents in addition to his beating in 1997 and his retaliation in 1998) come from failed attempts at friendship and a desire to be closer to the object of his curiosity. Arguably, Rasheed is not, in fact, intrigued by Hindus as a social object at all but by one particular section of the population with whom he has class, experience and expectations in common (I shall return to the history and politics of these commonalities in Chapter 4). It is precisely the failure of these attempts at friendship that brings about violence; he (and others) then restore order through the re-imposition of the standard narratives of communal differences. He also knows that after violence there is reconciliation and that, too, allows for the creation of heroes. On other occasions, however, Rasheed simply does not see any connection between his actions and attitudes towards Hindus and the standard public narratives of religious difference and confrontation. For example, there is a persistent rumour in Mandvi that Muslims have agreed among themselves to seduce Hindu women in order to defile the Hindu population. This story is told by both Hindus and Muslims; Rasheed himself also told me this, but like most other people he did not know anyone who had been present at the meeting where this course of action was decided upon. Sensibly, I thought, I asked him if he was part of the plot and whether this explained his affair with a Hindu woman. Rasheed saw instantly the connections I had made and uncharacteristically found it difficult to respond; he was in fact befuddled. It had simply never occurred to him to connect this farfetched but powerful public narrative to the complexities, passions and intimacies of his own actions. For Rasheed, his affair started life as a romantic adventure and not a political act; it only turned into a political act once it started to go wrong and love led to violence. Yet, even as Rasheed worked on the symbolic barricades and replaced the word 'Hindu' with 'bastard' in his everyday speech, he never totally lost sight of the origins of this conflict. And, in 2004, he informed his wife that he was still in love with the woman and was considering taking her as a second bride. He tried to sugar the pill and told her that she, as his first wife, would have her own Hindu servant to boss around. His wife duly took this announcement in her stride and told Rasheed she would leave him if he ever mentioned this idea again.

The ambiguities and inconsistencies in Rasheed's opinions and actions reveal the frailties and frustrations of the common human experience. This sense of common humanity is stripped from much of the rhetoric and everyday understandings of the standard accounts of religious difference in India. In such accounts, the complex religious identities of others become a list of dehumanised, negative and politicised characteristics. Muslims, in particular, are widely thought of as being disloyal to the country and fostering political allegiances through religious networks with Pakistan and Saudi Arabia. They are said to be isolationist and conspiratorial while seeking political dominance through strategic terrorism and the creation of an electoral majority through high birth rates. Such myths are conflated with the very real political concerns of Kashmir, the status of Muslim personal law and the rivalry and skirmishes between Pakistan and India – let alone the scars left by the division of the sub-continent into India and East and West Pakistan in 1947 (later to become Bangladesh and Pakistan respectively). These political issues and the popular myths that enliven them are also conflated with the more pragmatic issues of daily life such as differences in diet, ghettoised residential patterns, parallel religious economies, varying ritual cycles and the rivalry inherent to the gang culture of young men whether it revolves around criminality, competitive kite flying or cricket. It seems to me, however, that the falsehoods and simplifications of the standard narratives are able to masquerade as truths because the majority of Hindus in Gujarat simply do not have relations with Muslims intimate enough to disabuse them of the impression that all Muslims are bootleggers, polygamous and gorge on beef. Of course, this is not to ignore the fact that for many people there is little or no incentive to be disabused. I hope the tone of my ethnography goes some way to counter these images.

I have benefited from reading the excellent historical literature on Muslims in South Asia (including Eaton 1978, 2001; Metcalf 2004, 2005; Robinson 2003; Zaman 1999a, 1999b) and recent ethnography (Ahmad 1978, 1984; Assayag 2004; Blank 2001; Didier 2004; Ewing 1984, 1988; Gardner 1993a, 1993b; Hansen 2001: 160–193; Werbner and Basu 1998). This literature notwithstanding, the focus in the study of Muslims in South Asia remains most strongly on 'religion' as texts, scholars and Urdu couplets. The corpus as a whole gives a much clearer impression of elite debates taking place, primarily in North India, in the late nineteenth century than it does of what daily life was or is like for the vast majority of Muslims in contemporary India. This is unfortunate and does little to dispel the idea that Muslims are necessarily dogmatic, textually pragmatic and put theological and sectarian interests above all else. Many of my informants consume alcohol from time to time despite the fact it is 'forbidden' to Muslims and Gujarat is technically a 'dry state'; others conscientiously abstain on Thursdays, Fridays and during Ramadan. Likewise, the majority attend the mosque erratically but most attend Friday lunchtime prayers. Generally, my informants also have quite different ideas about what being a Muslim means to the scholars of Deoband or the other elite metropolitan *madrasas*. I turn to address this matter and the cosmologies of belief in Chapters 2 and 3 but for now I wish to provide a few examples of a more worldly kind. Some of the most pious men I know will, in certain contexts, send and receive Western pornography and images of seductive Indian actresses on their mobile phones and have flirty text message conversations with non-related women. Many enjoy cricket and net fishing on the beach on Sundays and group picnics in the remote hinterlands of Kachchh. Furthermore, most of the Bhadala men at the forefront of *re*forming their religious and social practices were primarily schooled in English-medium Christian boarding schools in Maharashtra rather than in *madrasas*; they went on to pursue graduate studies in commerce rather than theology. I do not mention these things to suggest that they are hypocrites or to undermine their legitimacy or the importance of being a Muslim. On the contrary, I do so because they very simply reflect what life is like for the seafarers of Kachchh and the sorts of issues with which they, as Muslims, and as men, engage on a daily basis.

Finally, I start with Rasheed because his example also illustrates that opinions can change over time and in response to other, seemingly unrelated, demands. Take, for example, the question of whether saint worship has a legitimate place in Muslim practices. This issue reveals another important story concealed within the standard narrative of promotions and successes Rasheed recounts when asked about his life. During his career as a seafarer, Rasheed has slowly, but not imperceptibly, adopted both the political and religious attitudes and the enemies of his former Bhadala employers, which brought him increasingly into conflict with his family –

and not simply because he had chosen his own wife or because he suffered in the world in ways his parents could not understand. This change was reflected obviously in his more assiduous observation of prayers, in his clothes, his veneration of the words of the Quran, his deliberate attempt to learn more Arabic and his disavowal of what he considered to be public displays of false and immodest ritual during some festivals. Likewise, these days Rasheed no longer wears gold, considering it unsuitable against the skin of a Muslim. He has also abandoned the designer clothes and rests content for most of the time with the cotton pyjamas many older Kachchhi men wear. In the late 1990s, however, the most notable difference between Rasheed and his family was in the relationship they maintained with the cults of Muslim saints. His parents and brothers were regular visitors to the shrine that owned the house in which Rasheed was born. Then, Rasheed refused to visit this shrine or have any dealings with its attendant saints because as he had been told in the shipyards the saints were not behaving like 'true' Muslims. As Rasheed's remittances had increased, however, his mother started to send daily parcels of food to the shrine. The constant tension between mother and son on this issue provoked some remarkable and angry exchanges. She would accuse him of 'forgetting where he came from' and of 'ignoring those he owed'. Rasheed would counter by saying she was giving her (he perhaps really meant his) money to 'beggars', adding it was wrong to think the saints were divine figures to 'whom she could never give enough'. Even then, the tension between Rasheed and his family was somewhat lopsided because his mother also respected Rasheed's 'new' religious ideas because they carried certain seals of authenticity. One of Rasheed's brothers, an apprentice goldsmith, was, however, less careful in his criticisms of his brother. In one of the many frequent bouts of shouting to erupt in the household because of Rasheed's 'wayward' attitudes, his brother said that Rasheed had simply replaced the cult of saints with the cult of ship owners because he was utterly dependent upon them in a similar way for his success. The ship owner's status, he said, was simply based on money not on the glorious history of Islam. Rasheed became apoplectic and his brother moved to rented accommodation shortly after this incident. Although the brother was angry and spite-ridden at Rasheed's successes, he also had a genuine point because whenever Rasheed was invited for prayer or to a social function in Salaya, upon meeting those on whose ships he worked he would stoop before them and touch his eyes and mouth against the hand they offered him, much as his non-seafaring brothers did when they called upon a saint.

In sum, I saw Rasheed shun saints and talk about them in highly negative terms in 1997. Aside from the arguments with his mother and brother I have just mentioned, in 1998 I also saw an extremely protracted argument over Rasheed's refusal to go on a trip with his parents to visit a notable shrine in search of blessings for his own protection at the start of the sailing season. In the course of this argument Rasheed repeated, as he often did, that making visits to saints was wrong; he needed no intermediary to pray to Allah; in Islam all men were equal and although the saints were of noble birth there was nothing intrinsically special about them. The argument with his mother then started all over again in the terms outlined above. Perhaps it was just coincidence that in the end Rasheed's family departed without him, leaving him alone in the house, free to invite his lover to resume their affair. The arguments he had with his mother about donating money and food to the saints were over the legitimacy of the same saints who had tried to teach Rasheed to read the Quran when he was a small boy. These arguments notwithstanding, Rasheed, however, has always held Ajmer Sheriff (the tomb of the Sufi Saint Khwaja Moinuddin Chisti in Rajasthan) in high esteem and, although he has never visited, he keeps a small picture of the shrine in his wallet wherever he goes. Furthermore, it was Rasheed who pointed out to me, after the terrible earthquake that destroyed the northern parts of Kachchh in 2001, that the reformist Muslims of the Tablighi Jamat and the Ahl-e-Hadis in the nearby towns of Bhuj and Anjar had suffered the highest mortality rates because they had forsaken the traditions of protection offered by local saints and their shrines. These changing perspectives on such an apparently fundamental issue bring me to the chief theoretical concern of the study.

Of all the philosophical and methodological traditions to emerge from the anthropological study of Muslim societies not one seems more profound yet problematic than the pervasive division between 'high' and 'low' forms of religious practice or 'type' (Gellner 1969: 7–8). This is typically seen in contrasts between 'universalist' and 'particularist', 'Great' and 'Little' traditions, 'sharia-minded Islam' and 'mysticism' (Eickelman 1981: 202–203; also Geertz 1968) or the 'High Islam of the scholars' and 'Low Islam of the people' (Gellner 1992: 9). In a recent reformulation of this dichotomy, David Parkin (2000: 12) has argued for a soft distinction between ontological dualists and monists; the former see an unbridgeable gap between themselves and Allah; the latter see themselves as being at one with Allah or other forms of divine power such as cults of saints. In all cases, the former 'type' is generally thought of in terms of the following words and things: mosques, scripture, literacy, monotheism, social egalitarianism, ritual sobriety, and the absence of mediators and graven images. The latter is characterised by hierolatry, personalised relationships with the divine, social and religious hierarchy, elaborate ritual practices and a general proliferation of sacred objects, such as shrines and special trees.

The history of this dualism can be traced in various ways through the literature but it was given a particularly strong and dynamic form by Ernest Gellner. In doing so, he brought together with characteristic boldness the main currents of thought to have influenced modern anthropological understandings of social change (1964, 1988) and in Muslim societies in particular (notably, Gellner 1969, 1970, 1981, 1992). He drew repeatedly upon the political economy of Ibn Khaldun and Fredrick Engels, the religious philosophy of David Hume and, perhaps less explicitly, the work of the Islamicist Hammond Gibb (1972).

It is worth pointing out that the works of these scholars were rather well known to other alumni of Oxford University where Gellner was himself a student of philosophy in the 1940s. In T.E. Lawrence's *Seven Pillars of Wisdom*, for example, which was first published in 1926, Lawrence observes:

> It was a natural phenomenon, this periodic rise at intervals of little more than a century, of ascetic creeds in Central Arabia. Always the votaries found their neighbours' beliefs cluttered with inessential things, which became impious in the hot imagination of their preachers. Again and again they had risen, had taken possession, soul and body, of the tribes, and had dashed themselves to pieces on the urban Semites, merchants and concupiscent men of the world. About their comfortable possessions the new creeds ebbed and flowed like the tides or changing seasons, each movement with the seeds of early death in excess of rightness. Doubtless they must recur so long as the causes – sun, moon, wind, acting in the emptiness of open spaces, weigh without check on the unhurried and uncumbered minds of the desert-dwellers.
>
> (2000: 152–153; also 40 and 68)

Lawrence makes no reference to his sources of inspiration, but perhaps he had read what Gellner was to read a few decades later. Gellner took as his starting point the fourteenth-century work of Ibn Khaldun (1967), notably his analysis of the economic and ideological dependence of peripheral populations on the civilised political realm of the city. For Ibn Khaldun, the city was indispensable but ultimately incapable of military dominance in outlying areas (cf. vom Bruck 2005: 257) and thus, as Engels summarised in the late nineteenth century:

> the townspeople grow rich, luxurious and lax in the observation of the 'law'. The Bedouins, poor and hence of strict morals, contemplate with envy and covetousness these riches and pleasures. Then they unite under a prophet, a Mahdi, to chastise the apostates and restore the observation of the ritual and the true faith and to appropriate in recompense the treasures of the renegades. In a hundred years they are *naturally* in the same position as the renegades were: a new purge of the faith is required, a new Mahdi arises and the game starts again from the beginning.
>
> (1957: 448, emphasis added)

In order to balance the political focus of this analysis, Gellner turned to Hume's *The Natural History of Religion*, first published in the mid-eighteenth century (1998). In this work, Hume presents two arguments concerning the nature of religious development in human society. The main part of the essay describes the historical transition from polytheism to monotheism. He suggests polytheism emerged from the unknown causes of human misfortune being ascribed human characteristics. From this condition monotheism emerged because particular gods became increasingly important and eventually lost their anthropomorphic qualities as powerful men associated themselves with particular gods. The second, subtler part of Hume's argument, is that as deities emerge as unified and infinite they become too abstract for vulgar human nature, which turns once again to intermediaries and lesser gods. So, having elevated a deity to a level above and beyond common comprehension, mediators are called upon to act between people and their supreme deity. In turn, such mediators become the focus for devotion. Yet, this process is again reversible, and, as polytheism mutates, a shift towards monotheism will be evident. These shifts from monotheism to polytheism and back again are what Hume called 'flux and reflux'.

Concerned that Ibn Khaldun was simply political and Hume 'psychologistic', Gellner attempted to show that the 'pendulum swing' (rather than 'flux and reflux') was given momentum by competition between different tribal groups variously uniting under the banner of 'pure' Islam in order to gain power (Gellner 1981: 11). His resulting composite model can be summarised as follows. Social mobility occurs at the level of the tribal unit, but, however violent change might be, the basic pattern on which society rests is not transformed (Gellner 1969: 5–6). Only tribes can provide the basis for political order, but as they do so they destroy themselves and leave space for the rise of new elites. Peripheral tribesmen need spiritual intermediaries between themselves and the ultimate deity of the type Hume describes. This is because the tribesman is illiterate and has no means of apprehending the disembodied word, as generations of theological flatterers have painted the deity in unassailably transcendental colours and because he uses the sacred, albeit with a human voice, to arbitrate disputes (Gellner 1970: 240). The people in Ibn Khaldun's town, for a while at least after having taken the city walls, tend towards Hume's transcendental deity without intermediaries (Gellner 1970: 241). This is not merely a reflection of competitive flattery but because town life is literate, more anonymous and there are no stable personalities towards whom piety would take the form of loyalty (ibid.). Yet, as time passes, the political cohesion and religious puritanism, under which they were so effectively united, disintegrates; among a distant nomadic tribe a new form of puritanism brews under the influence of a charismatic leader (Gellner 1969: 9). Under this new banner, the outlying tribe puts aside its differences and marches on the city walls; the process starts again.

At the inception of change among the outlying tribe, however, Gellner parts company with his intellectual patriarchs. Hume saw, at least as monotheism waxed, how the patronage of powerful individuals brought them closer to the deity and, in turn, it was they who became intermediaries to the god they had created. In contrast, for Ibn Khaldun the outlying tribe united from the bottom up, as it were, under a leader. However, in Gellner's view it was a charismatic individual who united the peripheral tribe under the banner of religion, from where they derived enough power to take the city. By combining Hume, Ibn Khaldun and his own interpretation of Weber on charisma, Gellner could have drawn a less functional picture in which powerful individuals jockeyed for positions of influence around their selected leader, real or symbolic. Why did he part company with Hume at this point? While we will never know for certain, one possibility lies in Gellner's interpretation of his sources.

Ibn Khaldun generalised this model and Gellner (1964: 142) rightly thought he was wrong to have done so. Gellner (1970: 235) also saw the two main strands of Hume's argument as contradictory – or at least the former part of the treatise was a mere historical observation rather than a point of sociological or philosophical note. In my view, Gellner perhaps misread Hume at this point because sensibly, given the zeal of the period in which he was writing, Hume veiled his renegade critique of the orthodox Christian establishment in order to protect himself from its vengeance. As John Robertson ironically, and brilliantly, notes in an introduction to a late-Victorian edition of Hume's essay:

> the ostensible draft of the treatise . . . is to make out that whereas ignorant people cannot rightly conceive the power interpenetrating an infinite universe, more cultured people may; but that is a thesis which for any thoughtful reader serves to refute itself. He, at least, who in these days can suppose that the scanty knowledge possible to the wisest of mankind will serve to bridge the gulf between finity and infinitude, is already past all misleading.
>
> (1889: xxiii–xxiv)

These observations, I think, get to the heart of Hume's thesis in which he points towards the 'irrationality' of all belief in terms of the structure and limitations of the human mind and the error of the Church's unidirectional view of theological progress or 'evolution'. Hume does this through a presentation of a common Christian view of the evolution of religion, from polytheism to monotheism, and then turns this subtly upside down by concluding with 'flux and reflux', where monotheism has the capacity to create polytheistic religious orders. Gellner's neglect of the first part of Hume's essay perhaps led him to understate the differences between Hume's position and that of Ibn Khaldun, Engels and himself. Significantly, it perhaps also led him to assume, as Ibn Khaldun and Engels also appear to do, that the role and status of the intermediary in Islam is an intrinsic and predictable part of the system rather than being a sociological variable equally susceptible to the vagaries and shifting winds of social change – a point not made explicit in relation to Islam by Hume but one that is there for the taking if applying his work outside the context in which it was written.

Some of the more recent work on Muslim societies, however, has been critical of this dualistic model. The universality of the idea has been questioned by the observation that the ritual, political and social content of either form varies historically and geographically (Das 1984; Eickelman 1976). Likewise, Katy Gardner has shown there are numerous cross-over points between the different modes of faith and both are poles of a continuum towards which different social groups tend to gravitate (1993b: 233). The idea of a continuum suggests the distinction between the two forms is gradual and does not congeal in a clearly defined boundary. One form can also appropriate the other such that under certain circumstances the elements of the low form may be reinterpreted as a legitimate part of a higher form. It is equally possible for saints, generally considered typical of the low form in South Asia, to appropriate the high form in order to grant themselves further legitimacy. Additionally, as Dale Eickelman (1982: 1) has suggested, any analysis assuming the existence of an ahistorical Islamic essence, arguably the 'high' form, is a strangely parallel venture to those unitarian Muslim fundamentalists who regard their interpretations of Islam as definitive. It is also notable that the model relies on the fact that the revolution in the countryside needs the 'high' form to succeed – as if no social cohesion or zeal were possible under the auspices of the 'low' form.

The Bhadala are the latest group in a long line to have risen to dominate the local shipping industry. As with their Hindu and Muslim predecessors, economic success has been accompanied by a renewed zeal for their faith. They are clearly influenced by formal Indian reformist movements, the growth of anti-Muslim sentiments among Hindu nationalists and their own personal experiences on pilgrimage and business in the Emirates. However, these macro processes are given local meaning as they are projected on to the Bhadala's neighbours in Mandvi. In their rhetoric, the aggressive Hindu nationalist becomes the Hindu sailor with whom they used to compete and Rasheed now fights; the wayward Muslim becomes the hierarchy to which they were subordinate in the past and about whom Rasheed argues relentlessly with his family. The structures of these relationships are largely constructed through the collective biographies of the

Bhadala protagonists as well as drawing upon idioms of movement both as contemporary migrations and as Muslim history. Although many may regard Gellner's work as over-determined in its empiricism, I suspect that is often because few people read further than the title of his well-known 1981 publication. In my view, the clarity and persuasiveness of his analysis continues to place it on a high peak from where the complexities of these processes can be scrutinised. Before I lead the reader into this landscape, I wish to address two important inadequacies in Gellner's account, which, although significant, do not lessen the validity of his conclusions.

First, Gellner's account (here, I am thinking first and foremost of his 1969 work) appears as if in a sociological vacuum where the concerns of nation-building, colonial history and ethnic competition are absent and play no role in either the rural revolution or in the parallel accusations of decadence. This absence can be countered by looking to the work of others who have seen the re-interpretation of Islamic practices as a reaction to political inequality, ranging in scale from colonial encounters (Evans-Pritchard 1954; Lewis 1961) to competition with other religious groups (Benson 1983) as well as to status competition between Muslims themselves (Mines 1975). These anthropological traditions, including Gellner's, have drawn on Weber's sociology (see Turner 1974), which has led to the emergence of two further themes in the literature. The first focuses on the ability of economic elites to define 'proper' religious practices and to manipulate charisma for their own ends (for example, Caplan 1987; Gardner 1993a, 1993b); the second seeks to situate charismatic individuals within a wider economic, social and political milieu (for example, Gellner 1969, 1981). There is also, of course, the rather more vexed question of reform as an exercise in belief rather than material or political gain.

Second, Gellner's account of the rise and fall of urban elites (a cycle both Engels and Lawrence described as 'natural') has an almost mechanical quality. He uses the idea of a swinging pendulum to visualise the process but never indicates from where the pendulum is suspended; nor, for that matter, does he really outline the intricacies of the mechanism that gives it motion. In my study the focus is primarily to continue the metaphor, on the tiny moving parts (forms of material and symbolic exchange) that let the pendulum swing and, thus, allow Gellner's model to work. In other words, here the focus is on the short-term cycles of exchange as seen in apprenticeship, learning and seafaring, which underpin the longer-term patterns of exchange concerned with the reproduction and transformation of the social and cosmic orders as described by Gellner and which are clearly evident in Gujarat.

With these comments and the Hume corrective in mind, I take the religious syndromes I have discussed above (pp. 14–18) out of the vacuum and examine them as they are formed within the bodies of the seafarers of

Kachchh such as Rasheed. My argument is that the transmission of ideas about the world from masters to apprentices is not a generic expression of religious identity or the consequence of an internal purge along predetermined lines; rather, the content and direction of the reform process are products of relationships between the protagonists, capital, patterns of material exchange, Hindus and other Muslims. Gellner's dualism is clearly fundamental to the process. However, it is not running around untamed in the world, bits of it resting awhile with either this or that group; rather, as the example of Rasheed's shifting perspectives on saintly charisma indicate, it is disciplined within the bodies of individuals and appears differently in economic, ritual and political relationships with kin, non-kin, strangers, friends and enemies.

Structure

Chapter 1 describes the geography of Kachchh in a broad sense and aspects of the past and of the seafaring traditions that developed to make Mandvi a cosmopolitan, yet conservative, town. This material falls short of being a comprehensive account of the history of Kachchhi seafaring. In part, this is due to a lack of sources but has more to do with some indefatigable standard narratives about the past and its heroes and villains. Many of these narratives are plainly false; others have elaborated the kernel of truth on which they are based to the point where the truth is unrecognisable. Either way, I have largely had to forgo what might have happened in favour of what people say happened. Rather than looking in the past to hazard a guess at the truth, I examine the consistencies in the structures of what people say about the past. This leads me to identify three tendencies in the narration of the past, which together also form a lens through which the present is understood. First, there is a tendency to see local society through the prism of the macro narratives of nationalism and religious history. Second, in myth and practice, foreigner invaders are transformed into sources of domestic prestige. Finally, it is necessary for those returning with wealth to domesticate their spoils. That the past is structured around such tendencies suggests, to me, that the social fabric and thus the logic of such narratives are predicated on the experience of travel, the culture of international migration and the two-way exchange of populations and ideas. Resources from the 'outside', such as Islam and cosmopolitanism, are brought to intersect almost cyclically with 'domestic' resources such as land, military power, autochthony and historical depth. The result is that over the last few centuries various communities, attaining positions of mercantile prowess, have drawn upon the external resources they have encountered or imagined overseas in an attempt to consolidate and domesticate their status in Kachchh, which, in turn, made them vulnerable to fragmentation and decline.

A number of those commentating on corporality and society in South Asia (Marriott 1976; Marriott and Inden 1977; McGilvray 1982) have suggested that actions, such as profession and speech, and intangible influences, such as perception, desire and posture, embody and convey essential qualities or 'substance-codes', which act against each other to continually transform the (in)dividual and, in a more general sense, the caste body. At the transcendental level, all combinations make up continuous and graded-ranked beings ranging from the divine through the human to the immoral and the inanimate. Much of the material presented in the following chapters is similarly based upon the assumption that the Muslim body is the conjunction of 'reproduction' (as physiology) and morality (as part of the physiological condition), in particular 'bio-moral' combinations. However, the terms of the debate here are less to do with food and ritual transactions than they are with conceptions of the balance of the body on scales weighing qualities of descent and the transformation of individual propensities and substance codes.

This theory of corporality and transformation through the transaction of substances is adopted here in a wide sense. The moral persons of seafarers are transformed through their associations with particular places and their ability to absorb either positive or negative aspects of their history and sociality, especially those places that have a significant role in their interpretations of Islamic social history. In a more specific sense, this model has a genealogical inflection. Substance is provided by inherited blood, which provides propensity for certain kinds of action; action modifies substance within the limits of the dictates of substance. The mechanisms of this relationship are explained in an explicitly Islamic idiom. It is argued that people are formed from a soul (*ruh*) of two hierarchically ordered elements: a lower level (*nafs*) dictates desires, potential for violence and other base instincts, and a higher level (*aql*) determines intellectual, spiritual and moral faculties. Together, various combinations of these levels act against each other to form human mind and body actions. More generally, the distribution of these elements determines the attributes of the caste body and of the distribution of castes in a ranked hierarchy, which is in itself dependent on the presentation of a genealogical inflection.

There is, however, an apparent contradiction here because, if a sailor can be meritoriously transformed through his association with particular places, such as the sites of pilgrimage, how can this model also explain caste hierarchy as a distribution of different sets of people with a given nature? Jonathan Parry suggests that the protean representation of the person, as characterised by Marriott, is a Marxist ideology in the classic sense because it actually sustains and reinforces the static ideology of caste as a symbolic elaboration of the louring disorder that creates and sustains the world of order and regulation (1994: 114–115). Parry's argument is that vigilance is required to uphold the balance of the body and the larger bodies of caste and kin; the best way to ensure this is through the maintenance of tried and tested patterns of hierarchical caste interactions in order to postpone chaos and disintegration.

Although these debates refer to Hindu conceptions of the self and ritual transactions, like many debates in the anthropology of Hindu South Asia, they also accord well with the ethnography of Muslim seafarers. Thus, vigilance over the body is a central theme in Chapter 2, which examines the flow of practical, rhetorical and cosmological ideas and practices between masters and apprentices in the shipyards. Apprenticeship engenders a healthy knowledge of a ship's constituent parts and how to perform correctly within a social hierarchy, but its details also explicitly reveal the theory of practice at the heart of the Bhadala's attempts at social and religious reform. The analysis sets the scene for the following chapters on the Bhadala's relationships with other Muslims and Hindus and how their vision is successfully conveyed to their economic dependants. The ethnography shows how the Bhadala, as charismatic individuals of sorts, construct personal relationships with the past, with other Muslims and with Hindu sailors, and how these relationships have structured the polity and performance of their reformist drift. These narratives present Islamic practices as offering salvation from the chaos and immorality of other religious traditions and suggest an alternative vision of the social order and appropriateness as they attempt to overturn the traditional forms of hierarchy in which they occupied positions of servitude. The rhetoric of reform often acknowledges the existence of Hindu cosmology in order to posit it as antithetical to the form of Islam they promote. Hinduism and Islam are presented to neophytes in a hierarchical relationship. Hinduism is described as corrupt, polytheistic, idolatrous and impure; Islam, as a form of discipline and practice, offers the path of salvation.

Inscriptions of order on and through the body and as a reflection of the genealogical reflex are the subject of Chapter 3. It is argued that traditional Muslim caste society is ordered by putative regional origins, claims to centrality in the social history of Islam and conceptions of race and descent. The picture described resembles a living recreation of social order from the early days of Islam, with those claiming a plausible moral, ethnic or racial stake in the original narratives through descent or some other kind of connection, ranking over those who are attributed with more mundane origins. Here, qualities and propensities of the body and of the collective body of caste are clearly ideological in the same classic sense, maintaining the hierarchical and material orders of symbols and practical reason. However, as ideology, it is also subject to attack and criticism. The brave young lords of the shipyards appear to be aware that their lowly position in this hierarchy will not improve given the corporeal rules that lay within.

Their attack on the rationality of the social order that oppresses them focuses largely on the bodies of the saints (Saiyeds, putative descendants of the Prophet) at its apex, which, in my view, is also necessarily an attack on the premises of the social order as a whole, as well as the conceptualisation of the body on which it is based.

Since 1995, Gujarat has also been the showcase state for the Bharatiya Janata Party (BJP), the political party of Hindu nationalism in India. This sometimes firebrand and intolerant form of nationalism has not only met with success as a strategy of rule and electioneering, it has also found a place in the popular imagination. Government reconstruction programmes following the earthquake of 2001 have polarised residential patterns and left many Muslims feeling isolated from the techniques and strategies of rule. In 2002, between one and two thousand Muslims were killed by vengeful Hindu mobs, mostly in the east of Gujarat. The controversial Chief Minister of the state, Narendra Modi, described the killings as a reaction to a Muslim action, as if religious violence was as inevitable as Newton's laws of physics. Muslims had apparently attacked and burned a sleeper carriage of the Sabarmati Express outside Godhra railway station at the end of February. The train was carrying a large number of activists from an organisation that promotes the causes of Hindu nationalism. They had been to Ayodhya to agitate for the construction of a temple dedicated to the deity Ram on the site of the now infamous Babri Masjid. The 'reaction' against Muslims in and around Ahmedabad and other cities continued until June. Violence only broke out in two different locations in Kachchh and both incidents were rapidly and fairly controlled by the police.

Given these events, Chapter 4 turns to examine the growth of Hindu nationalism in Gujarat and the Muslim response to this political force. Recent events have been dramatic enough to have reordered and, to some extent, supplanted the ways in which communal relations were discussed in the late 1990s. However, it is with data from that period that I start as a way of tracing the recent local history of religious polarisation through changing ritual practices and material conditions. The second part of the chapter focuses on the rise of political Hindu nationalism in Gujarat and widespread religious violence during 2002. Data from both of these periods suggest that neither political nationalism nor the rise of violence against Muslims can be simply explained as an elite conspiracy or as an expression of alienation of the poor from a rapidly expanding economy. In the first instance, violence erupted, between the Bhadala and Hindus from Mandvi, at a time of divergent fortune. The Bhadala were prospering through trade while their former Hindu rivals were forced into the fragmented market for international labour. In the latter case, the rise of Hindu nationalism in Gujarat, I suggest that, rather than this being a simple case of antagonism between Hindus and Muslims, the central factor behind the violence against Muslims of March 2002 was competition between urban and rural Hindu elites for control both of the ruling party and of the reins of power in the longer term.

These examples also highlight two of many possible Muslim responses to aggression. In the first case, the Bhadala were prompted to refashion the class inequalities that placed them in a position of conflict in the first place, by creating new economic dependants (the apprentices in their ship-yards and the sailors on their ships) to cushion them against future violence. In the second case, the Bhadala have actively sought strategic alliances with other Muslims (including those they formerly opposed), in an attempt to foster a sense of unity to withstand attacks of the majority (broadly speaking the Hindu population) enchanted by the Hindu nationalist government. Together, these examples illustrate the ways in which Muslims have been ushered into positions of social and economic independence and self-reliance and marginalised from the democratic process.

Chapter 5 turns to analyse the parallels between conflicting ideologies and what, I suggest, is their inseparable corollary: the material exchanges of seafarers. The logics behind the material exchanges and patterns of brokerage that so preoccupied Rasheed and his friends reveal how the masters of the shipyards are so effective in inculcating their vision to others; by so doing I outline, and thus disenchant but not decommission, the mechanisms that allow Gellner's pendulum to swing. I suggest that the different values attached to various kinds of mythical origins described in Chapter 2, which seemingly gave life to the traditional orders of hierarchy, also find expression in the contemporary exchange of gifts, ideas and social and religious practices. Here, however, the persuasive capacities of this logic are being used to usurp the traditional sources of power – with the body of the apprentice at the nexus of the antagonistic relationship between long- and short-term patterns of reproductive exchange and thus religious and social *re*form.

The conclusion of the study turns to address the consequences of this material for the literature on the Indian Ocean and the historian's vision of the region as a unified space or 'world'. Michael Pearson has suggested the Ocean is best approached through littoral society (1985) and that it is not bound together by some nebulous notion of commonality (2000, 2003). He points to regionalism as one expression of this and to the bonds of similarity shared between Muslims to the exclusion of others as another. Although Pearson is painting with a broad brush, throughout this study, the argument follows his example and suggests the diversity evident in the littoral society of western India is structured primarily by movement in the Indian Ocean. However, to move beyond this position, the analysis enlivens the gamut of social loyalties and preferences that lie behind the simplifying mask of a regional or national identity. The thesis is that travel and migration in the Indian Ocean are more socially divisive than congealing and that, rather than diversity being evidence of a tangible unity, as some historians have it, idioms of unity, such as religious value and wealth, apparently drawn from the Ocean (although by no means restricted to it), are fluid and susceptible to manipulation and appropriation, which, in turn, produces a flux and reflux of diversity.

1

TEXTS, MACHINATIONS
AND THE PAST

'Our culture is wet with the sea', wrote the late Manu Pandhi ([Guj.] 1976–1977) to evocatively express the relationship between Kachchh and the western Indian Ocean. Pandhi was a Kachchhi who had a keen interest in the seafaring heritage of the lands he loved. Like his writing, society in much of Kachchh is strongly orientated towards the sea and is heavily laden with stories, phrases and songs derived from lives spent afloat on the churning ocean. Generous men are said to have hearts as wide as the ocean (*dariyadil*) and sailors are quite literally described as 'sons of the sea' (*dariya chhoru*). The myths of the many deities and saints entombed along the coast attest to the Ocean's power, mystery and hidden treasures. Pandhi's analogy also suggests two further aspects of the relationship between the sea and the land that run throughout this study. First, water is a scarce resource in Kachchh and is firmly associated, like the monsoon itself, with wealth, joy and fertility. In this respect, the sea has brought riches to Kachchh from trade, compensating for the withering agricultural lands that it is said, during the nineteenth century, drove Kachchhi people from the hinterlands to the coast and out to sea by ship. Second, these ships did not simply set sail for foreign shores never to be seen again; they returned with people, ideas and wealth saturating life in Kachchh with the effects of seaborne migration and trade.

Kachchh is a remote and archaic land in the north-eastern corner of the western Indian Ocean – or in the westernmost part of Gujarat, depending on the vantage. For centuries it was a royal kingdom, with its own language, currency and courts. The territory was only readily accessible by sea from the south because of the vast expanse of saline land, known as the Rann of Kachchh, lying to the east, north and west. Today, Kachchh is one of the largest (second to Ladakh) but most sparsely populated (around 1.6 million according the census of 2001) administrative districts in India. It is a land of ecological contrasts, ranging from barren salt flats in the north to lush agricultural lands in the south. The administrative headquarters are at Bhuj, itself one of the ten bureaucratic subdivisions that govern the 900 or so villages. Modern roads and rails run into Kachchh but there is no through traffic as it shares the heavily militarised border with Pakistan. The partition of the sub-continent in 1947 separated Kachchh from its close neighbour Sind, divided families and severed age-old ties between the two regions. The politics of nationalism in both India and Pakistan has re-imagined this boundary as the dividing line between the great traditions of Hinduism and Islam. The boundary thus obscures the multiple historical connections between the people and places to either side of it and because of the continuing sour relations between the two countries there is very little empirical scholarship on the relationship between Kachchh and Sind.

Without doubt, however, there were once vibrant spiritual and trade networks between Mandvi and Sind, dubbed the 'North-West Link' in the most recent *Gujarat State Gazetteer* (GSG 1989: 210) and the 'flow of history from West to East' by the Government of Pakistan in its submission to a boundary tribunal (Gupta 1969). These networks have largely been destroyed by the effects of the Partition. However, their obstinate ghosts continue to shamelessly haunt, and the idea of Sind, as a place of origin and as a place where important things happened that explain how things are today, continues to loom large in life in both Mandvi and Salaya for both Hindus and Muslims. Therefore, in order to give voice to what was, and to locate Kachchh within broader patterns of spatial and political geography, the following provides a glimpse of what relationships might have been like between the two territories.

There were of course the wandering armies of Alexander the Great, the Arab conquest of Sind, the influence of the Moguls from the cities of the north and activity around the many mouths of the Indus to connect the two territories, but I wish instead to focus on an account written as part of the British expansion into Sind along the Indus. This river carries tributary water from the mountain ranges to the north through a massive valley formed between the Thar Desert to the east and the Harboi Hills and Sulaiman and the Toba and Kakar mountain ranges to the west. The towns in and around the valley are, in part, creations of British commercial and military expansion in the region during the nineteenth century. Karachi became the entrance point to the land from the Ocean, replacing older native ports, and was linked by rail to Hyderabad, the start of the permanently navigable waterways that stretch upstream from there to the north of Multan. As trade expanded, Karachi, along with Bombay, was to become home to hundreds of merchants from Kachchh who moved west in search of profit. The Bhadala themselves claim that 150 years ago their ancestors ran vessels in the shifting channels of the delta waters to the south of Hyderabad; they later migrated eastwards towards Kachchh; a historical shift also recorded in the Gujarat section of the *People of India* survey (Part 1, Vol. XXII: 234). While the British designed methods of transporting goods upriver, with the intention of tapping into the markets of Central

27

Asia, the flow of the Indus continued, as it had done for centuries, to allow the movement of people up and down its course and into Kachchh.

Aside from the well-documented movements of the caravans of the silk routes and their tributaries, the creation of British ports and the subsequent availability of new kinds of goods appear also to have created new kinds of population movement or, alternatively, older types of population movement assimilated the new trade goods or 'notions' into their rhythms. Take as example the following extract of a letter from the young Bartle Frere (later to become the first governor of Bombay) to William Andrew (then Chairman of the Scinde Railway Company), on the topic of 'Lohanee merchants':

> These men are the great carriers of the Afghan trade. They have their houses in Guzni [Ghazni], where they spend the summer. Since trade, via Tatta and the Indus, was extinguished in the latter end of the last century [eighteenth], these people have supplied themselves with seaboard goods, via Calcutta. They descend from the passes before they are blocked up by snow, between Guzni and the Indus, in vast caravans of eight or ten thousand souls – the whole tribe moving bodily – men, women, children and cattle – their goods being on camels and ponies. Arrived in Derajat [the strip of land between the main Indus watercourse and the Sulaiman Range], they leave the aged men, women and children in black felt tents, with their flocks and herds in the rich pastures bordering on the Indus, while the able-bodied men push across the Punjaub [Punjab] with their goods for sale either in that province or on the banks of the Ganges. The leading merchants precede the main body on dromedaries, taking with them a few samples, letters of credit, &c. &c., make their purchases at Delhi, Agra, Allahabad, Cawnpoor, Mirzapoor, and even Calcutta, and return with them express – collect their families and flocks, and force their way up the passes.
>
> (Frere quoted in Andrew 1859: 155–156)

This remarkable account is followed by a report that the 'Lohanees' have turned their attention to Karachi, bringing wool by caravan from Ghazni to Dera Ismail Khan from where it was shipped down the course of the Indus. According to Andrew, the same traders journeyed to Kabul and Bokara where goods entered a trade network stretching from the Caspian Sea into China. While such movements on land illustrate the depth of connection between the west coast of the sub-continent and the hinterlands to the north, they also suggest a connection between the land trade routes and those of the seas, and the scope of the space incorporated into the Ocean region.

To my mind this material shows, after Ferdinand Braudel (1972), that the frontiers of physical, political and human units are not coterminous and the relationships between them shift over time. Today, it is extraordinary to think that British cotton, exported to Calcutta, made the long journey along the Ganges, across its watershed and into the Indus valley, before being shipped to the bazaars of Kabul and Bokara by Lohanee merchants. If regions are also given meaning by human activities such as the journeys, exchanges, and the cultures of the merchants, sailors and caravaneers who traversed water and land then, as Kirti Chaudhuri (1999) suggests, analysis of the Indian Ocean region should also account for the trans-Himalayan areas and the T'ien Shan as much as it does the waters of the Red Sea, the Persian Gulf and the Mozambique Channel. While Frere's account does not describe an empirical connection between these north–west links and Mandvi, the town does boast a sizeable population of Lohanee (Lohana) merchants with deities and migration myths that link them firmly to Sind and to the 'historical flow' from west to east. The majority of the people in Mandvi, along with the Lohanas and the Bhadala, claim their ancestors hailed from Sind but were either driven out or left for Kachchh in order to pursue seaborne trade.

If we turn our gaze now from the dusty hinterlands and out to sea we can see that from Mandvi by ship it is little further to Muscat than it is by land to New Delhi and this fact, too, has had a dramatic influence on the nature of society in Kachchh – on the periphery of India and on the shores of the Indian Ocean. The traditional Kachchhi sailing vessel was able to leave home and circle the entire western Indian Ocean within a season. This was possible because of the monsoon winds: the cooler airs over the sea are sucked northwards towards the warming Asian landmass and then, in turn, southwards from the Himalayas and the plains of northern India and out to sea as land cools. These winds allowed a dhow to set sail from Mandvi in September for the ports of western India before heading south-westerly to Zanzibar or even as far as Madagascar. When the southerly winds started to blow the same dhow could head up the East African coast towards the Arabian Peninsula and back to Mandvi. However, it was not simply the proximity of Kachchh to Sind or the generosity of the monsoon winds that allowed Kachchhis to profit; their successes also coincide with the expansion of the British Empire, most notably in Bombay but also in Zanzibar, East Africa, Oman and Aden. These historical connections have also left a firm imprint on the political and geographical orientation of life in Kachchh today. Very few natives of Mandvi have ever visited Delhi; conversely, it is rare to meet anyone who has made it to their teens without a trip to Bombay to visit relatives. Furthermore, given the rapid economic expansion of the economies of the Emirates in the last few decades and the enormous demand for labour this has led to, I also think it is safe to assume that many more men from Mandvi have been to Dubai than have been to Ahmedabad, Gujarat's principal city.

Today, Mandvi is a bustling town of around 40,000 people. The troublesome sand bar across the entrance to the port has, for a long time, prevented the smooth passing of even the smallest vessel at low tide no matter how skilled the pilot – even the country craft have to wait for the highest tides before they will attempt to enter or leave the estuary. The general silting of the creek, as the sub-continent slowly obeys the principles of gravity and attrition, has made matters worse. The inefficient dredging equipment, optimistically brought in to deepen the channel, proved too expensive to be properly maintained. Mandvi has been all but abandoned as a commercial port. The only large ships to call there drop anchor a couple of kilometres out to sea to wait for tugs, towing dumb barges by the brace, to trans-ship low-value dry-bulk goods to their holds. Such ships, having called at Kandla, Kachchh's modern container port, unflatteringly to Mandvi's heritage, load cargoes of nitrates or bentonite (a clay mineral) rather than making the passage home without ballast.

The town, however, remains prosperous and is well served with buildings dedicated to the education, health and religious requirements of its population. Mandvi's core is dominated by mercantile activity, which is mirrored in the more prestigious parts of the town by elaborate housing, places of worship and social congregation. There are two centres of commercial activity: the agricultural products market adjacent to the port and the consumer bazaars within the walls of the town. The majority of streets in the main town are too narrow for cars and a series of new housing colonies has been constructed away from the centre. As with many Indian towns, pollution and congestion at some times of the day reach critical levels, as more and more people own motor scooters equipped with sharp, ear-piercing horns and smoky two-stroke engines.

The road that runs south from the town towards the port is flanked by decaying rest houses. These buildings were constructed by various mercantile castes, either for the exclusive use of the members of the donor caste or as a gift to the general population for the use of all bar the members of the donar caste. The names on the plaques set aside and above the grand doors record the magnanimity of those donating money towards the building's construction. The lists of philanthropists belonging to the Memon, Khoja, Vohra, Bhatiya, Lohana, Jain and Gosain communities tell of times long past and of times when Mandvi was a gateway for migrants seeking fortunes and shelter in other ports of the Indian Ocean. These crumbling buildings now house the poor; their verandas host the conversations, chess games and reflections of the elderly, who look, often melancholically, out to the seas where they once risked their lives. In 1997, a solitary teashop was the only thriving business to remain in this part of the town where mercantile houses had once stood.

Over the previous two centuries, the human geography of the town developed around the social organisation of shipping. The language and traditions of the sea are to be seen in all areas of social life and in the caste iconography of the Hindu merchants and sailors. The legacy of commercial activity and maritime trade is evident in a pervasive class division between merchants (*vepar*) and labourers (*mahjur*) or sailors (*khalaasi*). These social categories transcend religion and sect, and ethnicity and race (also see Varadarajan 1991: 2). Traders and sailors are divided historically by their occupational specialisation within a very particular commercial structure. Simply put, merchants traded from their offices in ports; merchants employed – either directly or on contract basis – a captain and crew, on whose loyalty they relied; and sailors conveyed goods and occasionally merchants between ports. The simple division of labour was cemented through patron–client type relationships, tying individual sailors to a particular merchant's loyalties. The idioms and connotations of this class division reverberate throughout the whole town despite the fact that the majority of the population are not engaged in seafaring. Broadly, the town is arranged loosely around the central bazaars and an invisible line drawn from the south-east to the north-west. At the base of this line (in the south-east) are the areas traditionally inhabited by sailors; at the far end of the line are the mercantile houses, temples and social institutions. Despite the modern expansion of the town, this division remains in place and also broadly encompasses the less pronounced divisions between Hindus and Muslims within both areas. The result is a society broadly composed of mutually dependent, yet socially distinct, patrons and clients.

Within this division Hindu and Muslim groups form parallel hierarchies. The Hindu mercantile classes cluster around guild-type organisations where their community and commercial interests coincide with religious interests, which are commonly represented by a private priesthood. These castes are known as *mahajans*. The term is typically interpreted to mean a body representing a group of people engaged in the same commercial activity and a governing council with an elected or, occasionally, hereditary headman. In this context, the term refers primarily to a self-administering mercantile community organisation, its institutions and its members. The term literally means 'great man', 'great life', 'magnate' or 'great procession'. In Kachchh, *mahajan*-type organisation is found among the aggregate of Hindu (Bhatiya, Lohana and Banusali) and Jain (Dasa Oswal and Visa Oswal) castes engaged in trade. In Mandvi, the *mahajan* represents an endogamous caste population rather than the nature of the group's commercial activity. From the middle of the nineteenth century these community organisations developed legal codes relating to expulsion, marriage and inheritance and started to run small presses publishing journals and pamphlets detailing and elaborating the history and traditions of the community. In the Hindu case, the sailing class is formed by the single largest caste represented in Mandvi, known as Kharvas.

Among Muslims, there is no such formal distinction between mercantile and service caste organisation; yet, there is an entrenched division of labour, which reproduces the division more subtly. The major historical schism in the Muslim population is between Shias and Sunnis and this, with the exception of three Sunni communities (Memons, Khatris and Saiyeds), reflects the traditional division of labour between merchants and service castes. Among the Shia mercantile groups, the central sectarian division is between Ismailis (or Seveners) and Ithna-Ashariyas (or Twelvers). Prior to the nineteenth century, the two principal groups of Ismailis were Khojas and Daudi Vohras. The Khojas divided in the nineteenth century between those who remained followers of the Aga Khan (still called Ismaili Khojas or Aga Khanis), a small section of which converted to Sunnism in the 1860s (Sunni Khojas), and those who broke away to become Ithna-Ashariya Khojas from the 1870s. While many of these successions were famously orchestrated in the courts of Bombay (Masselos 1978; Shodhan 2001), they were also played out on the streets of Mandvi and in the hinterland village of Kera. Although both groups of Khojas played a significant role in the development of Mandvi and in trade in the Ocean, most have left the town, migrating to the point of local extinction. All that remain are their graves and the monuments to their success and generosity. For the Daudi Vohras that remain, as with Hindu merchants, the boundaries of caste, sect and guild are practically coterminous. The many Muslim labouring castes (see Chapter 3) are not so sharply defined and generally do not have the communal buildings, written community codes, laws and guilds of their patrons.

Most families, regardless of class or religion, have active contacts with kin overseas, mostly in Africa and the Emirates but also with the 'twice migrants' who left Africa in the 1970s for Europe and North America.[1] It is generally said that for the resident population of Kachchh as many again live elsewhere. There are constant flows of people between Mandvi and the communities elsewhere. Therefore, almost every aspect of modern life is conditioned by the fact that so many people reside outside its borders at any given time. Consequently, land prices in the town are very high, as people have invested in property, mostly with wealth derived from commercial enterprise conducted elsewhere. Given the ambiguities in patterns of ownership and the unknown whereabouts of many of those holding the deeds to certain plots, disputes over property ownership are common and competition to possess the decaying buildings is intense. Despite the high prices, perhaps as many as a quarter of the town's houses are unoccupied and are boarded up, their owners overseas. Many of these buildings are precarious and, in 1998, a man who had recently retired to Mandvi from Muscat was sliced in two by falling masonry as he turned around to pay the barber who had just shaved him.

The objective of the following sections of this chapter is to sketch the rise and fall of some of the connections between Mandvi and Salaya (described more in later chapters) and other places (such as Muscat) and to outline some of the imaginative frameworks through which these connections are understood.

Historiography

Over the years, I have been introduced to a wide range of local experts who have studied and written about the traditions of Kachchhi seafaring. Strangers frequently came to my house in Mandvi, having heard I was interested in shipping. They would often be laden with dusty tomes, unearthed from attics and cupboards. In most cases, these men willingly shared with me their collections of newspaper clippings, logs, models, paintings, photographs, caste journals and books as well as their own research. I was fortunate, I guess, as an outsider, to be entrusted with such prized artefacts and to witness hours of enthusiastic discussion about them. Locally, there was incredible competition between these men to establish what passed as the truth. Books in the Mandvi's municipal library had pages torn out to prevent others from quoting them and disputes about 'history' raged in the pages of local newspapers. I was delighted to find so much genuine local interest in seafaring and was intrigued by the lively debates it provoked among amateur scholars. As time passed, however, I began to notice something a bit fishy about this preoccupation. First, none of the experts had any relationship with the Bhadala or any of their Muslim sailors. Second, most of these experts seemed oblivious to the fact that the shipbuilding and sailing traditions were continuing right under their noses, preferring a nostalgic approach to what might have been in the past. Third, all of these discussions were based on texts and other secondary sources.

I can explain my first two observations simply by saying that the experts were high-caste Hindus or Jains from local intellectual families who would not countenance Muslims or the mud of the estuary. Much of the competition between them was simply for intellectual reputation and fame and such a reputation was gained largely through popularity. Popularity comes at the price of being populist, which involves exaggerating Kachchhi endeavours and writing history with the contemporary concerns of Hindu nationalism in mind. My third suspicion is, however, harder to explain away but its effect, in view of what I have just mentioned about the motivations of these experts, is that there is an impenetrable body of material that claims to represent what happened in the past. This is a first class example of Timothy Jenkins' (1994) 'standard narrative' I discussed in the

Introduction (pp. 9–10), but in this case, because it refers to the past, it cannot simply be fleshed out by participant observation. This standard narrative is largely characterised by repetition and exaggeration and is based on very few sources. It appears in newspaper articles with titles such as: 'The glorious past of Kachchh', 'The flags of 84 nations fluttered in Mandvi port', and 'Mandvi we remember your past'. The narrative presented in these articles, books and so forth is practically impossible to navigate around and has left an indelible mark on even the most naive or illiterate of local storytellers. The texts on which this impression of the past is based are in short supply. Therefore, representations of these texts, similar to what Sheldon Pollock (1993) calls 'object-texts' (that is, not the text itself but what people claim the text says), are common knowledge, play a significant role in the creation of what might be described as an 'ethno-historical imagination' and dictate, in various ways, how the history of seafaring and, indeed, the history of Kachchh, is narrated. This picture of the past is transparent enough for me to see that it is bold in the isolation and prioritisation of some incidents, periods and characters and conspicuously silent on other issues. However, adequate resources or oral traditions at variance with the standard narratives are not available to fill in the gaps or to counter them. Therefore, most of the material in this chapter cannot claim to directly struggle with the contingencies of history; rather, it is merely a description of a description of the past. Or, in other words, this is an ethnographic account that pieces together the ways the past has been honed to represent certain kinds of truth.

The most comprehensive ethnological, historical and archaeological surveys of the region were published as gazetteers during the period of British rule. Primarily published between 1880 and 1914 by the British administration in Bombay, they are compendiums of different sources, sometimes commissioned, but mostly drawn from pre-existent materials – although this debt is not always acknowledged (see Blank 2001: 306–307). In chronological terms, either side of the gazetteers, travellers and historians wrote about what they saw and heard in Kachchh. Most notable among them were Marianne Postans (*c.*1810–1865), who travelled to Kachchh in the 1830s, and Laurence Rushbrook Williams, a Quondam Fellow of All Souls College, Oxford, and one time adviser on Middle Eastern Affairs to the Ministry of Information under Churchill, whose visits to Kachchh spanned more than thirty years and culminated in the publication of an English-language history of Kachchh in 1958. By way of sources for *Random Sketches* (1839), Postans had at her disposal the personal papers of the early British officials in the region; many of these documents no longer exist. As was common for the period, she wrote for an English audience fascinated by the bizarre lands of the Orient. Focusing on some of the more unusual myths, social practices and customs that prevailed in Kachchh at the time, she succeeded in producing a personal account of the history and ethnology of the region that has had a long-lasting effect on

the ways the past has subsequently been understood. Rushbrook Williams'
monograph, *The Black Hills* (1958), is written in disarmingly simple prose
and traces the history of Kachchh from the earliest times, narrating battles,
political resolutions, murders and conspiracies. Writing from the political
perspective of post-Partition India, he pieces together a valuable account
of how the rulers of Kachchh maintained their independence and distinct
identity and how they brought innovation and change to the land.

Alongside this British scholarship is a parallel Gujarati corpus, among
which the works of Dungarsi Dharamsi Sampat and Douleray Karani have
arguably been the most influential. Sampat was an amateur historian
who had a keen interest in trade and the history of Kachchh. He published a lengthy series of articles in the caste journal *Bhatiya Yuvak* in
the 1930s and a number of books of which *Kachchhnu Vepari Tantra*
(1935, *Business Systems of Kachchh*), *Saagar Kathaao* (1940, *Sea Tales*),
Saahshik Sodaagaro (1950, *Great Merchants*) and *Kachchhni Lokvaarta*
(1943, *Folk Tales of Kachchh*) are the most relevant. In contrast, Karani
was a descendant of the bards who had mnemonically preserved the traditions of the ruling families of Kachchh. His compendiums of these
traditions, *Kachchh Kaladhar* (1988a), *Kachchhni Rasadhar* (1972) and
Kachchhna Santo ane Kavio (1988b, *Saints and Poets of Kachchh*), are
catalogues of the fantastic events and characters in myth and legend. This
work is very clearly based on the standardised traditions of the royal court,
which can also be seen in Rushbrook Williams (1958), who used Karani
as one of his main oral sources.

Many of these, and other English and Gujarati texts, have been reprinted
in the last two decades, reflecting the keen interest in the past and what
these authors had to say about it. While these texts are not exhaustive of
writing on the traditions of Kachchh, they are the best known and among
the most coveted as sources of evidence and legitimacy for particular social
claims and have been central in the creation of particular kinds of ethno-
historical imagination. Sampat's writing, for example, is indicative of
the kinds of resources that are used to create different pasts in Kachchh.
His texts are mostly codifications of oral traditions, family histories and
origin myths. Passing into print, they were widely read and, to a significant degree, became *the* oral traditions through which the Hindu mercantile
castes imagined themselves in history and myth. In other words, they came
to resemble the rhetorical invocation of the past that Bronislaw Malinowski
(1922) described as 'charter', which is to say, as shared, expressed and
ideologically charged versions of the past. These days, the fact that the past
is open to debate is taken for granted in the social sciences. However, as
Arjun Appadurai has illustrated, there is 'an assumption that the past is a
limitless and plastic symbolic resource, infinitely susceptible to the whims
of contemporary interest and the distortions of contemporary ideology'
(1981: 202). In order to counter this tendency, he shows that all societies

have some substantive provisions to determine how the past is authorised, given continuity, consistency and interdependence with other pasts. Thus, treatments of the past are an aspect of politics that involves competition, opposition and debate. The Kachchh case, however, reflects more on the 'inventive power of traditions' (Sahlins 1999) than on the notion of 'invented traditions' (Hobsbawm and Ranger 1983).

The types of resources people have at their disposal to describe, to embellish or to ignore the past obviously affects the type of history they can construct and how inventive they can be. Throughout this study, I refer to the texts mentioned above, as well as to many other comparable publications, not simply as sources of empirical evidence but as ethnographic artefacts (object texts), which have been incorporated into the traditions of Kachchh. Many of the events they narrate are fantastic and incredible and such mythic elements have clearly absorbed actual events and have transformed over time. Anthropological work on the relationship between text and oral traditions or myths has tended to assume that writing is the death of myth (Goody 1968; Lévi-Strauss 1978). From this perspective, myths, a series of movable mythemes, are free to transform just as they exist to be told; writing codifies and objectifies the myth and provides language with a material correlative (Goody and Watt 1968). It follows that writing is the defining factor of historical consciousness (as opposed to mythic) and writing introduces similar changes in the transmission of the past just as it does in other walks of life.

Are myth and writing (as a form of history and as artefact) really so opposed? Many parts of South Asia have had literate traditions for thousands of years and a vast corpus of religious, historical and philosophical texts has emerged. Additionally, some of the most comprehensive historical texts on western India were written by Persian and Arab scholars (for example Khan 1928; Manjhu 1961). During the period of British colonial rule, many of these texts were scrutinised, modified and cross-referenced notably by British and German scholars. As a consequence of these types of process, Appadurai claims, the politics of discourse concerning the past have become 'severed from the language of myth and ritual, in a traditional sense' (1981: 204). But is the 'traditional sense' perhaps the wrong way of looking at things given such a history? Indeed, in Kachchh, the narration of the past frequently appears as a series of linear narratives of events organised around datable texts, such as the travel accounts and legal and administrative documents. If this is the case, then how are 'charters' constructed, contested and evaluated and what are their 'substantive provisions'?

In this case, charters rely on textual evidence, the more authoritative the text the better, and such evidence should be documented over time and, ideally, into antiquity. Such charters narrate Kachchhi prowess in seafaring, explanations for particular tragedies and successes and, most vigorously of all, the origins and hierarchical and ritual relationships between different social groups. In Kachchh, elements of all oral charters share a striking resemblance to the published accounts. However, most published accounts (with the exception of the recent spate of reprints) appear in rare antiquarian books that are hard to find in India. Furthermore, not everyone in Kachchh has the inclination or skill to spend time rummaging though library catalogues, or the ability to read the language in which they were printed, let alone understand lengthy footnotes given in Greek, French or Arabic; nor does everyone have the skills in English to separate actual connections from inferences made in subtle prose between, for example, things Herodotus observed of the ancients and what Postans saw in Kachchh (see Postans 1839: 96, 246). Some of the charters I am discussing have passed in and out of print a number of times and, yet, they continue to have a life of their own outside the printed page. Sometimes, although a charter is based on a particular text, it may not reproduce the content of the text in its exact form and, at other times, it may have no correspondence whatsoever. Yet, textual authority is superior to any other kind, but the relationship between the text and the 'charter' cannot be assumed to be straightforward. And, in this sense, it could be said that the texts have become a necessary structural element for the construction of any charter and, as a mytheme of sorts, the text is free to transform as the charter is retold and reordered. Therefore, in Kachchh, Pollock's object-texts are not static repositories of order and sequence, or the antithesis to myth; rather, they can have a life of their own as what they tell of is imagined and ordered afresh as the facts of their existence enter the realm of public narratives in the form of newspaper articles, caste journals, books, paintings, oral accounts and so forth.

The legacies of colonial thought, and the often politically motivated desire to create a cohesive sense of identity and pride in the traditions of Kachchh, lead some people to go to extraordinary lengths in their quest to prove their tradition was superior to others, especially to that of the Europeans. In this way, the material so carefully compiled in the gazetteers by administrators schooled in Latin and Greek has become integral to Kachchh traditions. Most books and newspaper articles written in Gujarati on the history of shipping start by cribbing a list of ancient sources such as *Periplus Maris Erythraei*, Pliny, Hiwan Thsang and Ptolemy (for example, Burgess 1971), which are said to attest to the glory of Kachchhi shipping. Some of the consequences for patterns of governance and thought in India of the classificatory practices of the British (Dirks 2001; Peabody 2001; Zaman 1999b) and their hegemonic typefaces (Blackburn 2003; Robinson 2003: 66–104) have been well documented. However, there also seem to have been some more prosaic consequences of British activities on patterns of thought in western India. The most commonly cited sources in the standard narratives of Kachchh are held, and have been so for at least a century, in the library of the Asiatic Society of Bombay. I know this because at the end of my first major period of fieldwork in Kachchh I spent a few weeks visiting Kachchhis in Bombay. Some of them referred me to the Society's library, which, among its treasures, houses the very same books that were so often quoted in Kachchh. The object-text character of these tomes had presumably made its way back to Kachchh by ship or train in the notebooks of scholars such as Rushbrook Williams and Sampat. In a very literal sense, the history of seafaring as seen in the standard narratives is little larger than the Asiatic Society's collection, replete with all the peculiarities of any collection of books amassed over the period of 200 years or so as librarians came and went and tastes and styles changed.

Thus it is that in ancient times the Greeks, Menander and Demitrius, and peoples of putative European origins such as the Juan-Juans, the Avars (or Avares) and the White Huns are supposed to have held sway in Kachchh (see also GBP 1896, Vol. I, Part I: 492; Howorth 1873). They were followed, apparently, by the scurrilous Bawarij and Medh pirates and the Chalukiya, Gujjara and Sama dynasties (see also GBP 1896, Vol. I, Part I.). There are, indeed, ancient inscriptions littered the length and breadth of Kachchh but most of the sources appear to indicate that prior to the fifteenth century Kachchh had no separate existence as a political unit, and seemed to have been regarded as part of the dominions of whichever dynasty chanced to rule over the territories now known as Sind and Saurashtra. However, this period of comparative detachment also seems to have incubated many of the traditions that make Kachchh distinct today as the predecessors of contemporary religious traditions took hold, temples and places of learning were established and seafaring and long-distance trade became part and parcel of coastal life.

I turn now to one example of how the 'history' of ancient times is constructed from inferences from texts before I move on to discuss a few more recent events in the standard treatment of the past in Kachchh. To attest to the longevity of the Kachchhi seafaring traditions, the work most frequently cited is Vincent's (1805) obscure and convoluted edition of *Periplus of the Erythrean Sea*. The book is a merchant's travel account, generally thought to have been composed during the first century after Christ. If I recall correctly (I did not think to make a note of it at the time) the edition in Bombay is bound in green or blue board, has wide margins and contains a few anonymous pieces of marginalia. This work is commonly used to make strong claims such as: 'According to Vincent (Periplus, I. 25, 35, 254) in the time of Agatharcides (BC 200) the ports of Arabia and Ceylon were entirely in the hands of the people of Gujarat' (GBP 1896, Vol. I, Part I: 492). More recently, Hourani's (1951) interpretation of Vincent (1805) and Hollingsworth's (1960) interpretation of Schoff's *Periplus* (1912) have become popular. Hourani suggests that, around two millennia ago, merchants from 'Ariaca' conducted trade with the Somali coast. Hollingsworth claims that the 'Ariaca' of *Periplus* is the region around the Gulf of Cambay comprising Kachchh, Saurashtra and Gujarat. By combining these two sources it is possible to conclude that Kachchhi merchants were trading with East Africa at around the time of Christ (see Sakarai 1980: 300–302 and 330). This kind of speculation finds some support in the archaeological record, but it is of dubious historical worth and is not directly evident in any of the social traditions of Kachchh (also see the monumental footnote in GBP 1896: 492–496 for much more of the same); yet, many Kachchhi scholars have dedicated portions of their lives to unearthing evidence from such sources to vindicate the ancients who settled the land to trade from its shores.

The standard narrative links the seafaring traditions of Kachchh to Rajput rule and patronage from the sixteenth century onwards – although there is plenty of evidence to suggest relations between the landed and mercantile estates were often strained (see below). The Jadeja Rajput Kengar is the first king attributed with having some degree of autonomous rule in the region, and as having established the towns that were to become the main centres of mercantile enterprise in subsequent centuries. He is said to have founded the port town of Mandvi in 1581 with the aid of Topan Seth, a Bhatiya merchant from Nagar Thatta in Sind. He is also reputed to have called upon skilled shipbuilders to come from the same city (Sampat [Guj.] 1935: 7–8), a plausible claim given that the conditions of trade had worsened and Nagar Thatta was in decline following its sacking by the Portuguese in 1555 (Rushbrook Williams 1958: 118). Rao Bharmul took the throne in Bhuj succeeding his father in 1586 and continued to develop trade in Mandvi. Sampat claims that at this time trade was so extensive to and from Mandvi port that Kachchh became known as the 'nose of Saurashtra' ([Guj.] 1935: 8), a metaphor that, I presume, suggests that Kachchh was leading the way rather than admitting effluvium to the region. Towards the end of his reign he is said to have met with the Mogul Emperor Jehangir in Ahmedabad. In the exchange of gifts that took place, Jehangir conferred the right to Bharmul to mint coins in Kachchh and abolished annual payments of tribute to the Moguls. In return, Bharmul was to allow pilgrims bound for Mecca through Kachchhi ports and on to Kachchhi ships. Rushbrook Williams claims that this agreement reflects the prowess of Kachchhi shipping at the time when the Portuguese were preying on pilgrimage vessels in an attempt to embarrass the Mogul authorities (1958: 121). Sampat, however, suggests that the state did not have its own ships and the investment they made in building and equipping armed ships for the pilgrims gave a boost to the industry ([Guj.] 1935: 9). Either way, this agreement made Mandvi a principal port, behind Surat and Veraval, for haj pilgrims in the centuries to come.

In the early eighteenth century, the rulers built the characteristic fortifications of Bhuj, Anjar and Mandvi, and constructed a military outpost on the coast of Saurashtra known as Kachchhi Gadh as a deterrent against the pirates of Okha who regularly plundered ships entering the Gulf of Kachchh. God II came to the throne in 1761 and according to Rushbrook Williams, when the ruler was not defending Kachchh from Sindis, he was a 'keen amateur of shipbuilding', personally presiding over work in the yards in Mandvi (1958: 163). He was also a great patron of traders and merchants and Mandvi became famous throughout India for the products of its shipyards (ibid.). Under his patronage, a three-decked ship called *Victory* is said to have been constructed that sailed to England (Sampat [Guj.] 1935: 11). Whether these dates are accurate or these events actually occurred in the way they are reported is simply beyond the scope of my investigation. However, these stories are clearly intended to inculcate a sense of pride in the tradition and to flatter the rulers; in these regards they make perfect cultural sense in the Kachchh. Yet, taken as a whole, within the standard narratives there are a number of myths that are atypical in western India in that they are dominated by idioms of travel, invasion and the power of knowledge. I now turn to two such tales as examples.

First is the tale is of the Jakhs. Shipwrecked at Jakhao in the south-west of Kachchh, the seventy-two men (incidentally, the same number of verses as in the Yasna of the Zoroastrians who as Parsis in India also claim to have been shipwrecked off the coast of Gujarat) and a single woman (together the Jakhs) made their way inland on horseback, mounts we are left to presume they saved from the wrecked ship. In some oral versions of the myth I have heard, the Jakhs emerged from the waves on horseback, miraculously appearing without ships. From Jakhao, they headed inland to save the local population from the depredations of either King Punvro or a 'demon'. Gifted in warfare, and benevolent with their knowledge of medicine, they became popular and venerated figures and images of the seventy-two riders are to be found in numerous temples both inland and along the coast. Postans noted a troubled holy man 'called his god Jakh to his assistance. Jakh with his 71 brothers and a sister . . . came from Damascus and seated himself on a hill . . . the hill however unable to sustain so much purity began to sink' (1839: 156). Over 100 years later, in Rushbrook Williams' account, this had become: 'the weight of their combined sanctities flattened the top of hill after hill' (1958: 84). Speculation as to the origin of these fair-skinned foreigners attributes them to Anatolia or Syria (Kramrisch 1964: 55), or to Greece, Turkey or Central Asia (Rushbrook Williams 1958: 84–86). Whether Muslims or Zoroastrians, local renditions of the myth do not stress the religious identity of the invaders or the exact period in which they arrived. The popular tale of the Jakhs seems to have been recorded by Alexander Burnes (1879), a colonial official, in the 1820s; copied with minor variations by Postans (1839) and later writers before it was embodied in the fifth volume of the *Gazetteer of the Bombay Presidency* in 1880. Loyally reproduced, with some elaboration by Rushbrook Williams (1958: 83–85), the same account later appeared with some modifications in Karani ([Guj.] 1988b). More recently, the gazetteer version was reproduced as part of the *Census of India* (Chandras 1961), which became the basis of Kramrisch's (1964: 55–56) rendition of the story, which, in turn, became the principal source for Wendy Doniger's (1999) presidential address to the American Association of Asian Studies.

In this address, Doniger argues that the Jakh myth is an inversion of history as the 'Muslim' invaders are the heroes and the natives are villains and not, as one might expect, the other way around. The myth speaks of the assimilation of the values of the conquerors by natives; and, as Doniger suggests, it is probably a foreign myth that has taken root in local folklore, where invasion is transformed into a source of liberation and prestige (1999: 952). In other words, ungoverned and alien knowledge is domesticated and turned into a source of local power and glory. This form of imaginative and narrative structure is common throughout the traditions of Kachchh and oddly divergent from the more familiar and somewhat insular myths of Hindu nationalism, where native is hero and invader is villain.

The second example is of a sailor called Ramsinh Malum, whose portrait in the annals of Kachchh has been painted with unassailably flattering colours. His story was recorded by Postans (1839: 14–15) and by Rushbrook Williams (1958: 43, 137–142, 148) and has been reprinted many times by the local media. In the most commonly known versions of Ramsinh's story, he was shipwrecked and rescued by a passing Dutch ship, although Postans asserts that he was kidnapped from Saurashtra by Dutch mariners (1839: 14–15); either way, he so impressed the Dutch crew with his courage against the attacks of pirates that they took him to the Netherlands. Once there, he learned a bewildering array of craft techniques that he brought with him on his return to Kachchh. At first, he sought the patronage of the rulers of his native Saurashtra but to no avail. Later, he found patrons among the prosperous merchants of Mandvi at the direction of some of his Kachchhi relatives. It was not long before his skill came to the attention of the king (Lakhpat), who installed him in a workshop in the palace and granted him leave to train gold- and silversmiths to enamel their pieces. According to Rushbrook Williams, Ramsinh was sent twice more to Europe, the final time with a number of Kachchhi apprentices, to perfect his glass making and iron founding techniques (1958: 139). Ramsinh's most famous legacy, badly damaged in the earthquake of 2001, was the Aina Mahal (Hall of Mirrors) in Bhuj: a greying white marble structure decorated with Venetian glass at the centre of which is a pool irrigated by elaborate fountains.

It is possible that the myth of the Jakhs speaks of events in the mists of time when Kachchh was a submarine land, gradually populated as the forces of plate tectonics forced it upwards through the waves. While I obviously cannot say for certain why such a tendency (native is bad, invader is good) runs through these myths, one distinct possibility is that this speaks of forces in a society that has been cosmopolitan for *la longue durée*, in Braudel's sense of the phrase.

In contrast, Ramsinh mastered a staggering array of crafts and techniques in just twelve years in the Netherlands: tile work, glass blowing, enamel work, clock making, architecture, stone carving, foundry work, gun-casting and shipbuilding. It is possible, as Rushbrook Williams (1958: 140–141) subtly implies, that his role as overseer of many apprentices and craftsmen is understated or, indeed, that many of the finer works of craft commonly associated with him were simply imported from Europe. These imponderables aside however, to my mind the story is important for two reasons. First, it suggests that prior to the British arrival in Kachchh the local rulers had developed a taste for European art and artefacts. Second, along with the myth of the Jakhs, Ramsinh's tale also speaks of the assimilation of the values and technologies of the conquerors by natives; however, unlike the Jakh myth, Ramsinh ventures abroad to appropriate the secrets of the foreigner, returning with them for the greater glory of Kachchh.

If the truth, as I have suggested of what happened in the past, is masked by an impenetrable series of standard narratives then, alternatively, we might ask what truths lay in these standard narratives. To my mind, these tales are powerful imaginative instruments that reflect the fundamental social and historical processes that have defined the character of Kachchh. On the one hand, there have been invasions and the assimilation of people, ideas and practices; on the other, there have been endless forays overseas and returns home with wealth and status for the greater glory of Kachchh. These two imaginative instruments run throughout the following account of the 'past' from the turn of the nineteenth century as well as in the material in the chapters that follow.

The past and trying to see through it

Historians are confident that 'Gujaratis' were present in East Africa from the fourteenth century onwards (Alpers 1976; Pearson 1998a). However, in the Kachchh case, trade and its counterpart migration are most clearly evident and documented during the modern colonial era. This period can roughly be defined as stretching from the turn of the nineteenth century, when Europeans moved from sea to land in their colonial endeavours, to the middle part of the twentieth century and India's Independence from British rule. During this period, the European interest in exotic goods gave way to the pursuit of Asian commodities for mass consumption in Europe (McPherson 1995: 198). Also during this period, Kachchhis made a similar transformation to the Europeans as they moved from a predominantly transient, although cyclical, seaborne trade to settle more permanently overseas. Although the East India Company openly encouraged indigenous trade, it was the suitability of indigenous credit networks for the new types of trade that really gave the impetus for the expansion of indigenous capital enterprise (Subramanian 1987). Throughout the nineteenth century, the volume of trade in the Indian Ocean grew markedly as Europeans demanded raw materials, laid railway tracks and developed safe harbours to allow for the transportation of these materials. Kachchhis, drawing largely perhaps on their knowledge of markets and pricing derived from trading in agricultural surplus, moved to supply the British with raw materials, notably cotton, and into other niche markets. The vast majority of this trade was by sea, connecting with the caravan routes that came into Kachchh from the Thar Desert in the west to Palanpur, Ahmedabad and Ujjain in the east (Sampat [Guj.] 1935: 13) and to the ancient trade routes of the Indus. Later still, a great many Kachchhis became industrialists, mill owners, contractors and engineers in the cities of the British, especially Bombay (see Purandare 1997), as well as traders, petty currency brokers, moneylenders and dockworkers in the other ports of the Indian Ocean.

The turn of the nineteenth century had also brought the British to Kachchh from Bombay in response to the repeated acts of piracy off the coast inflicted on Dwarka and haj pilgrims, and on British and Indian merchant ships (MacMurdo 1856: 441). Their arrival not only heralded new patterns of diplomacy and political intrigue, it also marked the beginnings of records that are still housed in the colonial archives in Bombay, Delhi and London.[2] The British had acquired Bombay from the Portuguese in 1661; before that Surat had been the principal station of the East India Company over Cambay, Bunder Abbas, Basra, Nagar Thatta and Baruch. By 1685, Bombay was the seat of the western presidency, but it was not until sometime between 1801 and 1804, when a vessel belonging to a merchant from Bombay was attacked and a man and a woman were allegedly flung overboard, that the colonial administration began to take a serious interest in the affairs of Kachchh. News of this incident reached Bombay and armed vessels were sent to Okha to seek redress (LeGrand 1856: 447); on this occasion they were unsuccessful but their efforts paved the way for British officials to be permanently stationed in Kachchh. In 1809, the rulers of Kachchh signed a treaty with the East India Company. Bothered by piracy, troubled by events in Sind, and irritated by the incessant raiding between Kachchh and Saurashtra, the East India Company decided it was time to act. Kachchh however honoured none of the terms of the treaty and, in 1812, James MacMurdo was again sent to petition for the suppression of piracy; this time he met with more success. In 1813, King Rayadhan died and was succeeded by Bharmul II, who, in 1816, signed a treaty of alliance with the British. An annual tribute of 200,000 Koris (the Kachchh currency up to Independence) was agreed. In 1819, the infant Desal II succeeded Bharmul and Kachchh was placed under Regency rule until the child came of suitable age in 1834.

MacMurdo read one of the first English descriptions of Mandvi to the Literary Society of Bombay in 1818. He noted the town, 'a mere gunshot from the beach', was the most populous in Kachchh and engaged in brisk trade with Arabia, Bombay and Malabar (1820a: 217–218). He claimed that this trade employed upwards of 800 boats ranging in size from 40 to 500 *candies*, bringing annual revenue of Rs. 250,000 (ibid.: 218).[3] The exports he recorded were of cotton cloth and thread, silk, alum, ghee and crude piece goods. The imports were bullion, ivory, horn and hide of rhinoceros, dates, coconuts, grain and timber. Of the population he guessed (probably overestimating) to be around 50,000, upwards of 15,000 were Bhatiyas, 10,000 Vanias, 5,000 Brahmins and the rest composed of Lohanas, Muslims and the low castes.

A couple of decades later, in the 1830s, Thomas Postans (also see Burnes 1836) reported that the opulent and busy port of Mandvi conducted inland trade with Malwar, Sind, Gujarat and Jaisalmer, and by sea with all the ports of western India, the Red Sea, the Persian Gulf, East Africa and occasionally as far as Mozambique (1839–40: 169). He also observed that the principal export of the port was cotton cloth of English thread, sometimes woven in Malwar but mostly in Mandvi (ibid.: 171–173). He noted that vessels left Mandvi port to enter into two kinds of regional trade. The vessels that ploughed the seas to Berbera and Mogadishu were known as 'Buradur'. This trade was conducted with Somalis who traded with the interior. The second trade route was known as the 'Suwallee' and took ships to the ports of Lamu, Mombasa and Zanzibar. These two trades were clearly connected as, for instance, the staple import at this time was ivory brought directly from Zanzibar or trans-shipped via the ports of the northwest corner of the Ocean. In all of the ports associated with the 'Buradur' and 'Suwallee' trades, Postans (ibid.: 170) reported Hindu brokers from Surat as well as 'Banians' and Bhatiyas from Mandvi. Marianne Postans also visited Mandvi in the 1830s. She was impressed with the bustle, the appearance of wealth, and the gaiety of the people in what was otherwise 'a town of second rate importance' (1939: 10). She noted that: 'the population consists of two distinct classes: the military class; and those who reside in towns, and follow trade, or other civil occupations. The former devote themselves to luxurious sensuality, whilst the latter are . . . grasping and avaricious' (ibid.: 268). She also observed (ibid.: 12) that Mandvi principally exported cotton cloths; and in return received dates, coffee, dried grapes, antimony, coloured mats from the Red Sea, and the teeth of elephants and rhinoceroses from Zanzibar and East Africa.

The year 1819 was an eventful one for Kachchh as the kingdom was also rocked by a powerful earthquake. The standard narratives of Kachchh tell the well-rehearsed story of how farmers downed tools in response to the ensuing ecological disaster. They moved to the coast from where they successfully took to the sea and to commerce. Unfettered by communal or religious divisions, they successfully moved into respectable forms of commerce with the assistance of their highly benevolent rulers. In my view, this story relies too heavily on the drama of the earthquake, which serves as a convenient moment into which the complexities of ecological disaster, political insecurity and the fledgling growth of opportunities within the colonial cities can be collapsed. However, the coincidence of ecological failure and new opportunities clearly lay behind the large-scale migrations from Kachchh that occurred at this time and in subsequent decades. The beginning of Regency rule was marked with a serious outbreak of cholera (LeGrand 1856: 448) and the subsequent famine, pestilence and 'intestinal broils' were cited as the reason for why so many Kachchhis were appearing in the streets of a rapidly expanding Bombay.[4] In the following decade, invaders from Sind repeatedly plundered much of western and northern Kachchh (Rushbrook Williams 1958: 214–215). In 1823, it was reported that further crop failures and rumours of an imminent military invasion from Sind further reduced the population (GBP 1880, Vol. V: 165); in the following year there was severe drought and famine (Masselos 1996: 29–32). In the next decades natural calamities continued unabated and, cruelly, in 1862 excess rain destroyed the harvest; cholera once again struck in Mandvi in 1866 (GBP 1880, Vol. V: 173). In 1862, it was reported that 25,000 people emigrated from Kachchh and, in 1863, the number was as high as 35,000.[5] There was a widespread famine during 1888 and 1889 (Masselos 1996: 33–37) and endemic plague between 1896 and 1905. The series of disasters that struck Kachchh over the course of the century must, literally, have forced the population off the land. Coupled with the rise of Bombay as a relatively safe haven, and the development of port facilities, rest houses and charitable trusts for the poor and dispossessed in the city, tens of thousands of Kachchhis immigrated to Bombay, or overseas by dhow.

The nostalgia inherent in the standard narrative turns the nineteenth century into the dominant past and stresses cooperation and the lack of communal or religious divisions, and how the merchants' successes came with the assistance of their benevolent rulers. Again, it is impossible for me to scrutinise these claims accurately, but I do wish to present some evidence to suggest that things were perhaps not quite as they are commonly described. I do not present this evidence as a definitive correction to the standard narratives of 'history' or as an authoritative intervention in debates popular among historians but to tease out the kinds of fissures, contradictions and disputes that are concealed by the standard narratives.

First, there is compelling evidence to suggest that patterns of migration and trade were strongly influenced by caste and kin networks (Allen 1978; Burton 1872; Campbell 1981; cf. Markovits 2000), rather than being determined by the appeal of a generic and undifferentiated Kachchhi identity. This is not to say that only caste and kin defined the boundaries of their mercantile endeavours but that these forms of organisation were central to the organisation of credit, the distribution of profit and the reproduction of the mercantile houses. Today, in Mandvi, this can be seen simply in the specialisation of some castes in particular trades, the Daudi Vohras in ironmongery for example. It can also be seen in the clear association of particular castes with certain places, the Kharvas and Bhatiyas with Muscat and the Bhadala with Dubai, for example; as well as in both Bombay and Mandvi with concentrations of the properties belonging to particular castes clearly clustered around their communal buildings. It is also the case that travel and the organisation of commerce made various interest groups, including caste organisations, more aware of their differences and more protective of their religious identities. I return to this matter again below and more explicitly in the final chapter of this study.

Second, the rulers of Kachchh appear to have acted primarily in their own interests to secure revenue from trade, rather than simply promoting the creation of wealth among the trading communities. For example, throughout the nineteenth century, as is well known, Zanzibar was entrepôt for the East African slave trade and home to thousands of traders from Kachchh. The role of Kachchhis in this trade has been the source of some controversy and is understandably a sensitive issue for descendants of merchants reputed to have been involved. The reports of the explorers Richard Burton, David Livingstone and others may have exaggerated their role in slaving. Bartle Frere was, however, more cautious, suggesting that the Indians in Zanzibar were implicated as they drew revenue on each slave that passed through the customs house.[6] But even Frere admitted that Indians, mostly from 'Gujarat', financed half the traffic in slaves between Somalia and Madagascar. Writing in the late 1960s, a time of political sensitivity for Indians in East Africa, the historian, J.S. Mangat, was also keen to underplay the role of the Indians in the Zanzibar slave trade. He goes as far as to suggest that 'the adverse criticisms of the Indian community were to provide a precedent for ... the tendency to use the Indians as a "scapegoat"' (1969: 24–25). Given the number of prosecutions and references to Indians holding and selling slaves in the colonial records it is impossible to countenance this view (also see Clarence-Smith 1989: 11–12; Tominaga 1996). As customs master in Zanzibar, the Kachchhi merchant Ladha Damji, himself representative of the well-known firm of Jairam Shivji, subcontracted his gang of stevedores to other merchants; he is also known to have controlled a number of plantations that were cultivated primarily with slave labour. Abdul Sheriff, a leading authority on the history of the island, suggests that in the 1860s Damji possessed more than 400 slaves (1989: 142). This figure is significantly less than the 7,000 attributed to the firm in a popular Kachchhi account, but nonetheless represents a significant investment not only in terms of the quantity of slaves owned but also in the general economy of Zanzibar.[7] Gwyn Campbell is more forthright on the role of Indians in the trade, claiming that the success of the *karany*, the Indian community in Madagascar, most of whom were Khoja or Vohra Shia Muslims, was based on the slave economy (1989: 171–172). With their transoceanic network of capital they were able to advance credit to *antaloatra* (Muslims of Arab and Swahili origins), Merina and Mascarene traders. The *karany*, establishing a customs post in Mahajanga, are also reported to have maintained close contact with the firm of Jairam Shivji and the 'Banians' who controlled the slave trade from the 1840s in Mozambique.

The Government of British India's diplomatic and naval efforts to suppress the trade and holding of slaves led to Britain and Oman signing a series of treaties between 1822 and 1886 that were aimed specifically at regulating the activities of 'Indians'. In response to such political efforts, the traders variously claimed to be British Indians or subjects of the Sultan while they were in Zanzibar, as slave holding by Sultan's subjects was not outlawed until later. The British representative treated the Kachchhis as the former and, throughout the 1860s the traders were prosecuted accordingly for violation of anti-slaving laws. Appellate jurisdiction came from Bombay, but if any case made it that far the defendant would claim to be a citizen of Kachchh and therefore not subject to British Indian law.[8] Similarly, Kachchhi traders flew different national flags depending on the destination and cargo of the vessel.[9] Traders also claimed rights of protection and jurisdiction of the Sultan of Oman, the courts of British India, the French in Mauritius, and the Kachchh Durbar. Each 'penal code' carried different restrictions and penalties. Traders switched legal identities while remaining loyal to their own caste protocol and law.

The Durbar made a series of attempts to bring traders in Zanzibar under its jurisdiction. It issued a proclamation in 1869 encouraging Kachchhis living in Zanzibar to adopt British-Indian citizenship.[10] In the early 1870s, Kazi Shahabudin, the chief administrator (*diwan*) of Kachchh, visited Zanzibar with Frere. In Shahabudin's possession were letters from his King warning the Kachchhis to desist from holding and trading in slaves, with the threat that if they did not then their property in Kachchh would be confiscated.[11] It was evident to the Durbar that it did not have the power, influence or resources to assert Kachchhi law in Zanzibar, despite having sent representatives to negotiate with the merchants there. The rulers of Kachchh turned to the law of British India, personified by the Governor of the Bombay Presidency. Consequently, British attempts at regulating slaving were 'welcomed' by the Durbar. However, the application of

British law outside the immediate realm of the Bombay Presidency seemed to be a matter of the local political agent's personal integrity – with vague reference to statute. In the early part of 1873, a Bhatiya, Kanji Lalji, was deported from Zanzibar to Bombay, having been found guilty by the political representative of the British in Zanzibar of holding slaves.[12] In Bombay, he was acquitted on the grounds that he was a resident of Kachchh. If Kanji was not a British citizen (Kachchh was a protectorate and not under direct British rule) then he could not be subject to the laws of British India. When he was arrested in Zanzibar, Kanji had claimed to be a citizen of the Sultan and was, therefore, entitled to hold slave labour, but the political agent had ignored this plea and tried him regardless. Later in the same year, the case of 'Regina versus Haji Omar', a Khoja, came to the attention of the High Court in Bombay.[13] Omar was convicted on three violations of the Indian Penal Code relating to capturing and holding slaves. Between the two cases the Durbar had issued a second proclamation stating that Kachchhis in Zanzibar were prohibited from holding slaves and were to take up British citizenship.[14]

This proclamation, unlike earlier ones, was held to be legally binding on the grounds that there was no naturalisation act between Kachchh and Zanzibar. The ambiguity that had for so long been exploited by the traders was now beginning to work against them. When Omar came to court in 1873 the Bombay Court had appellate jurisdiction over Kachchhis, and the Durbar's actions had fragmented the solidarity of the powerful Kachchhi cohort in Zanzibar. By placing them under British law (probably illegally), the authority of the individual caste courts and mercantile guilds was undermined and disputes fell to the petty consular court. In short, the Durbar used the moral issue of slaving to gain assistance from the British to destroy the unity of merchants in Zanzibar and Oman. I suspect it is no coincidence that after the Kachchh Durbar brought the traders under its own jurisdiction, albeit through the agency of the British, many traders left Kachchh with their families to settle overseas, notably in Zanzibar and Oman, on a more permanent basis. The sometimes predatory activities of the rulers seem to have created a sense of difference and separation among the littoral communities as they attempted to avoid the demands made upon their wealth.

Third, the standard narrative of the past denies religious differences played a role in the organisation of commerce. Again, another well-known incident in the history of Kachchh suggests that religious identities were perhaps part of daily life and therefore also influenced patterns of commerce. King Rayadhan II came to the throne in 1778 and converted to Islam shortly after under the influence of the Muslim fakir, Mohammed Saiyed. According to Rushbrook Williams (1958: 170), the king roamed the streets of Bhuj, accompanied by a band of Pathan followers, demanding that everyone he met should profess Islam, regardless of their position or creed. Later, he turned his attention towards Mandvi, where he slaughtered animals and announced his intention to destroy the Rameshvar temple. Enraged, the people of Mandvi are said to have attacked him, forcing him to return to Bhuj. While Rushbrook Williams' account was written after the bloody events of Partition, which clearly changed relations between Hindus and Muslims dramatically, I tend not to be inclined to dismiss this account in its entirety. Rayadhan's conversion to Islam and the antipathy he displayed to Brahmans and merchants (Rushbrook Williams 1958: 170) suggests there were clear social fault lines through which such antipathy could be expressed. But, compare the following three statements from British sources relating to the early nineteenth century. The gazetteer of 1880 states that: 'At the beginning of the present [nineteenth] century, so progressive was Islâm, that it seemed as if another hundred years would see the last of the Hindu faith' (GBP 1880, Vol. V: 39). This observation was made of the same period of which MacMurdo wrote: 'of late the religion of Vishnoo has become so prevalent in Cutch, that some of the Jharejas [sic] even have adopted it, with all its peculiarities' (1820a: 224). Finally, M. Postans notes: 'The Rao [king] himself says that out of about two thousand Jharrejas [sic], he does not think three of them know what their religion is' (1839: 133). The first two statements imply that religious identities were strong and were actively being proselytised, while the final statement suggests that religion was not an important marker of identity among the elite. The validity of these statements may also be of dubious worth as historical evidence, but I am not inclined to think that they are wrong either because although these statements initially appear to be contradictory, in fact, they probably refer to different sections of the Kachchh population.

In the aftermath of the earthquake, MacMurdo observed that:

> The Moosulmans were equally alarmed [as the Hindus] . . . and an abundance of threats of punishments to the wicked were fulminated from the musjeeds [mosques]; and a paper asserted to have come from Mecca, with the usual seals attached, foretold of the day of judgement.
>
> (1820b: 106)

This response was reportedly matched among Hindus with the rise of millenarian movements. The community responses to the event were clearly very different and emerged from distinct patterns of sectarian organisation. None of these observations indicate the nature of religion in the construction of social segmentation, but they do suggest religion was an important and competitive part of social life. The paper supposedly arriving from Mecca intrudes into the image of India as a pre-colonial, syncretic social synthesis, reminding us of the outside world.

Generally, it appears that the most profound social division throughout the nineteenth century (and up to the present day) was between those who routinely travelled outside the kingdom and those who did not, and that differing conceptions of space and location clearly had much to do with the perceived importance of religion as a marker of social identity. The seemingly contradictory statements of colonial officials presented above probably refer to such a division in the population. Those who travelled the most were the same sections of the population that adopted refined forms of Islam and the exclusivist Vaishnava movements. Those who did not travel, or travelled much less, were the rulers and dominant landholders – whom Postans referred to as 'Jharrejas' – who were vague about their religious affiliation.

The three examples discussed above suggest a truth that might lie behind the standard narrative of the past from which most traces of social diversity have been drained. What kinds of truth are evident in this part of the standard narrative? This account, it will be recalled, saw farmers move to the coast, undivided by caste or religion, in order to pursue commerce with the assistance of their rulers. This narrative reflects a yearning for a golden age of shipping and communal harmony that has emerged as a response to alienation from the natural and social worlds as Hindus, to whom this narrative predominantly belongs, have gradually been marginalised from the seafaring and mercantile traditions so central to Kachchhi identity. The account is also communal in its nature as it writes the class of sailors and Sunni Muslims, in particular, out of the picture, and contrasts the glorious past, when Hindus were in charge and there were no communal tensions, with the evils of today, when Muslims control shipping and communal tensions have divided the population. This observation brings us into the twentieth century.

Of the decades either side of the turn of the twentieth century, Rushbrook Williams laconically observed:

> A far-flung network of commercial connections linked the country to Zanzibar, East Africa, Somaliland, Aden, the Persian Gulf and Egypt, as well as to the great ports of Bombay, Madras and Calcutta and to India's inland marts. . . . Abroad, they were enterprising, progressive, and, indeed, 'hustling'. At home, they loved the old ways and clung to them with tenacity, just as they revered the deities and honoured shrines which had become hallowed to their forefathers throughout the centuries. Thus, for many decades, time was almost at a standstill in Kutch, while tranquillity began to pass imperceptibly into stagnation.
>
> (1958: 237)

The large numbers of people travelling overseas brought a new kind of nostalgic conservatism with them on their return and the growth of a politicised regionalism that had one foot firmly in the past. The first few decades of the century brought a new wave of migration from Kachchh to East Africa, prompted in part by a virulent outbreak of plague and a disruption of agricultural activity. Kachchh entered a period of stagnation and community decline – at least in terms of the expansionist trade at which the mercantile communities had excelled in previous decades. The descendants of the great trading families lived from the wealth of their ancestors and from income from property bequeathed to them. The Second World War brought its own profits and casualties as around twenty Kachchhi ships were lost to Japanese submarines.

After the war, shipping further declined and the ties of the overseas populations with their homeland began to weaken. On the eve of Independence, Kachchh was one of around 565 semi-independent kingdoms in India. Ruled by the Jadeja Rajputs more or less continuously from the sixteenth century, it passed to rule from Delhi in June of 1948. For the next eight years, Kachchh was ruled as a Central Registered State from the national capital by a Chief Commissioner and two local advisers. In 1956, Kachchh, along with Saurashtra and Gujarat, became part of the bilingual state of Bombay, which was subsequently divided into Gujarat and Maharashtra in the 1960s. During the 1960s and 1970s political nationalism and xenophobia, particularly in Africa, further restricted the movements of Kachchhi enterprise overseas.

The 'oil boom' of the early 1970s, however, led to a new period of expansion for Kachchhi shipping modelled on the traditional pattern of merchants and sailors following the monsoons. This expansion went hand in hand with the dawn of a new wave of migration to the Emirates of young men in search of menial work in new industries and in the long-established Kachchhi firms; it also led to the rise of a new mercantile elite, the Bhadala. Initially, the rise of Dubai in the 1970s provided the initiative for the resurgence of indigenous shipping technologies. Today, international diplomacy continues to create alternative arenas of profit. Despite several attempts at constructing a pan-Asian highway in the 1970s, relations between Pakistan, India and Iran have precluded the development of a transport infrastructure between western India and a road or railhead at Bunder Abbas or Jask for trade with the Emirates. While the absence of overland routes ensures a constant supply of relatively small and low-value bulk goods for the country craft, for a number of years the sanctions imposed by the UN against Iraq provided the most lucrative avenue to profit for the Kachchhi vessels. Running the significant capital risk of having their ships impounded if detected by patrol boats, the traders shipped a wide range of goods through the shallows of coastal waters to the smaller ports of the Iraqi coast. The invasion of Iraq by American and British troops in 2003 brought a halt to this practice, initially because of the war and more recently because of the lack of security along the coast. For the time being the seafarers of Kachchh have fallen upon hard times and have returned to transporting their staple cargoes of foodstuffs, construction materials and livestock. By the 1980s, mirroring their patrons of the previous century, they had started to build grand new mosques, schools, hospitals and communal buildings in Salaya. They also started to dress differently, introduced more Arabic and Urdu words to their dialect, and sponsored luminaries to talk on theological matters. In time, many of them ceased to go to sea on their ships and they started to employ other Muslims, such as Rasheed, as crew.

The Bhadala appear infrequently in primary and secondary source material relating to Kachchh and are not mentioned at all in the three encyclopaedic treatments of the Muslim communities of Gujarat (Engineer 1989; GBP 1899; Misra 1964). The existing references to them are far from flattering (Gupta 1969). I did, however, find a reference to them in one of the nineteenth-century colonial gazetteers. It stated the Bhadala were strict about observing religious practices (GBP 1884). I photocopied the pages and took them to the shipyards, thinking my Bhadal friends might be interested. They all told me in no uncertain terms that the reference could not have been to them because at that time they lived in Mandvi (in an area still known as 'Bhadala Pod' despite the Hindu-controlled municipality's attempts at renaming it), not in Salaya where the reference located them. The entry for them in the *People of India* series says that Salaya was given to them on a free lease for a century by the King (presumably either Pragmal 1698–1715 or Pragmal II 1860–1876), although I have not heard this story from them, but it is quite common for people to claim their own ancestors were granted land in the past but have subsequently been illegally dispossessed. The majority of Bhadala men, the elderly included, have little more of substance to say about the 'past' than repeat what they have heard the 'official' sources state: that they came from Sind; they had been sailors on the vessels of wealthy merchants; and had helped the British in the construction of the port of Mombasa. The oldest Bhadala men, now well into their seventies, had served as sailors on the ships of other mercantile Muslims in the 1940s. These ship owners mostly left the industry after India's independence in 1947. The Bhadala continued to run their own small vessels between India and East Africa throughout the 1950s and 1960s, scraping by from trading earthenware and food stuffs with Gujaratis along the African coast. In the 1970s, a small number of Bhadala men fortuitously prospered by trading between the Emirates and India as Dubai developed as a free port. Throughout the 1980s, they increased the size of the ships, which in some cases became fleets, and with their new-found wealth they consumed lavishly and invested in the mosques and other symbols of piety scattered throughout their settlement.

Conclusion

What people say about things is more often than not the same as what I can read in old books. Of course, this may simply mean the author of the book was an astute observer and managed to accurately convey the eternal truth of what they saw and heard. As we have seen, however, the ancient references are vague and as improbable as the events they describe; the colonial references are acerbic and written with one eye on the policies of the Empire; the Gujarati materials tend to be more intimate and revealing, yet they are eulogistic and self-serving and often written in the impregnable prose of nationalism. The narratives of the lives and adventures of the merchants have been rewritten in a nationalist genre. Today, in Mandvi, interpretations of the endeavours of the nineteenth century saturate most nostalgic representations of the past and the mercantile demigods who made fortunes in the ports of the Indian Ocean stand as contemporary role models, as paragons of Kachchhi virtue, as shrewd, intelligent men, ruthless, but kind-hearted and philanthropic. These selective accounts unsurprisingly exclude failure, bankruptcy and loss and never refer to the fact that John Speke, for example, observed that the Indian traders in Zanzibar lived in 'utter banishment' (1864: 169) or that Richard Burton (1872) heard tell of an Indian merchant on the island so affected by elephantiasis that his scrotum had enlarged to a circumference of forty-one inches. Making the past is an art form with substantive provisions; it is an art at which many Kachchhis excel. Chinese whispers, fusions of sources, contexts and purposes come together in self-aggrandisement. The past, then, is no small matter and punches were thrown at the 2004 meeting of the Kachchhi History Society over a trifling difference of opinion. The myth makers hold their own interests to be those of Kachchh and many are well connected to the organisations of Hindu nationalism. The Bhadala's absence from this dominant representation of the past is not an omission but one of the points that drives its formation. Their absence from the well-rehearsed accounts of the past, replete with their regal, nationalistic and elite biases, reflects their subaltern position as Muslims and the related hostility they face for having usurped the traditions of seafaring. Their exclusion from the standard narrative also stands as a powerful metaphor for their current levels of political engagement in Gujarat, but I will come to that in Chapter 4.

Scrutinising the standard narratives with facts and evidence from other domains (archive material, neglected sections of the gazetteer literature and contemporary ethnographic observations) allows us to imagine what might have been going on behind the façade of the narrative; however, I have done so in this chapter not simply to present and question the hegemony of the standard narratives or to provide the reader with some general background material about the history and geography of Kachchh, but to ask what empirical social truths the standard narratives themselves are constructed from. The results of this investigation are not alternative dates, places or heroes; rather, I have identified three syndromes within the treatment of the past (and present), which we might term, after Appadurai (1981), its 'substantive provisions' or concrete measures. Aside from the role of texts and the mores of culture that primarily concern Appadurai, I have also sought out the structuring structures of the past or what Sahlins calls the 'structures of significance' (1985: 8). In the Kachchh case these are, first, the tendency to see local society and, indeed, the past, through the prism of larger standard narratives of nationalism, terrorism and so forth. This is also seen throughout the study in the way the Bhadala and other Muslims transpose the heroes and villains in the history of Islam on to the local population (Chapters 2 and 3) and in the way conflicts over a particular temple site are understood (Chapter 4). The second syndrome, as seen in the story of the Jakhs, is the ability to transform foreign invaders into sources of domestic prestige. This pattern is clearly seen in the logic and structures of Muslim hierarchy (Chapter 3) as well as in the deification of saints and other foreigners to have visited Kachchh (Chapter 5). Finally, as seen in the story of Ramsinh, there is the matter of the return of the traveller with foreign wealth (the topic of Chapter 5). Together, these provisions are not simply abstract ideas from which narratives are constructed but reflect *the* fundamental processes on which Kachchhi society and its relationship to other societies are based. It seems to me each syndrome suggests a common humanity and applies equally to all regardless of religion.

The next chapter takes us from this rather lofty discussion straight into the estuarine mud to look at the transmission of knowledge in the shipyards.

2

SHIPYARD
APPRENTICESHIP AND
THE TRANSMISSION OF
KNOWLEDGE

The scale of and activity in the dozen or so shipyards dotted along the banks of the estuary between Mandvi and Salaya cannot fail to impress anyone visiting for the first time. Close up, the activity in these yards initially grates on the senses; they are noisy, smelly and visually chaotic places. The air is full with the sounds of hammers on iron and wood and with the mixed odours of mud, sawdust and chemicals stewing over open fires. Men shout strange things at one another as they clamber over and around ships with fantastic speed and agility. The yards produce ocean-going vessels of considerable draft from thousands of pieces of timber without the use of plans, technical drawings or sophisticated machinery. Apprentices are drawn into the workforce and learn, through participant observation and other less attractive procedures, the techniques of shipbuilding and the sociality of shipping. Eventually, for them, the experience of sensory chaos ceases to be salient, as neophytes become familiar with the techniques, technology and processes of production and gradually tame their new environment.

Like others (notably Coy 1989; Pálsson 1994), I have been struck by the parallels between anthropological fieldwork and apprenticeship. In part this was because my own arrival in the yards coincided with that of two other new recruits; in this chapter the material is arranged around their experiences because these experiences also broadly represent those of many other young men. There is an excellent ethnographic literature on skill, apprenticeship and the broader implications of apprenticeship for social theory (notably, Bloch 1998; Bourdieu 1977; Herzfeld 2004; Hutchins 1996; Ingold 2000; Jenkins 1994; Keller and Keller 1996; Lave 1984, 1988a, 1988b; Lave and Wenger 1991; Marchand 2001; Messick 1993; Starrett 1995). These studies often have very different epistemological starting points; generally, however, they show the following. First, that great feats of computational imagination, mastery and ingenuity exist outside formal education; second, that knowledge is not simply possessed by a homunculus or even by the 'mind' of the learner; finally, they also show that apprenticeship is related to the reproduction of the social order, a fact that often rightly links this literature to studies of organisations, identity and work (see Kondo 1990).

I recognise much of the ethnography in these studies in the ways my informants learn and do not learn through apprenticeship. However, at some point my data appear to part from some of the broader theoretical claims of this literature. This separation is not because I present startling facts that challenge conventional wisdoms or theories of mind; nor do I discuss bizarre and hitherto unknown ideas or even suggest that the existing literature is incorrect; rather, it seems to me that discord arises primarily because of the perspective I have taken on the data, a corollary of which is that my aim and objectives differ from those that motivate much of the literature on apprenticeship.

My ethnography suggests an indigenous theory of practice, which, once outlined, means it is practically impossible to return meaningfully to much of the existing general theory as it stands. I shall discuss what I mean more fully, and some of the theoretical implications of this problem, in the final sections of the chapter, but first to my approach and to the shipyards.

The structures of shipyard apprenticeship

As I discussed in the Introduction to the study (pp. 5, 7 and 8), apprenticeship in this case is the period apprentices spend in shipyards before they become sailors – the moment at which they are held to have served their time on land and another stage of learning begins at sea. During this time their bodies and minds are disciplined to perform certain skills within a clearly defined hierarchy. They are also inculcated with a set of dispositions towards tradition, religion and politics that reproduces dominant patterns of capital and creates a dependent constituency for the masters (the Bhadala ship owners). After Maurice Bloch and Jonathan Parry's (1995) model of exchange relations, I suggest that apprenticeship relations are the short-term cycles of exchange that underpin the longer-term exchanges concerned with the reproduction of the social and cosmic orders. Again, here I should reiterate that power and wealth are imperfect in their methods and their aims are challenged from time to time. There are, of course, failure, disobedience and insubordination within the relationships of apprenticeship on the part of the apprentice; likewise, the masters, on occasion, are prone to put favouritism and generosity before profit; they are also liable to crush those they take a dislike to rather than nurture them with a long-term gain in mind.

I approach apprenticeship as a social and collective activity that is inevitably and significantly riddled with all the inequalities and contradictions of societies and their collective endeavours. I draw upon the sociology of Maurice Halbwachs and his studies of collective memory in order to clarify my approach and outline the spirit in which the ethnography is presented in this chapter. Halbwachs (1980, 1992) illustrated that collective memory is not natural, nor is it part of a mystical group mind but is always partial and socially constructed. By this he meant that individuals carry collective memories; there are as many collective memories as there are social groups; and memories of the same fact can thus be placed in different social frameworks because individuals are part of more than one group (see Connerton 1995: 36–40; Coser 1992). More importantly, however, for the purposes of this chapter, Halbwachs also saw that memories are brought together as forms of association only by the various ways in which people can also become associated (1992: 53). Individual memory is therefore part of collective memory because we cannot think about it without the use of other thoughts that have come from the social milieu. In this way, the framework of collective memory binds our most intimate of remembrances to one another.

To my mind, Halbwachs' treatment of collective memory and the practices of knowledge and violence in shipyards are of a remarkably similar order; some recent literature has arguably closed the gap altogether by stressing the corporeal nature of knowledge and experience (Connerton 2004; Jenkins 1994). Following Halbwachs, therefore, I suggest that apprenticeship is best examined as a confluence of ideas and people in particularly structured ways; in this case in the formation of a crew. I also suggest that apprenticeship is a way of taking apart particularly structured relationships between people and ideas and refashioning them in other particularly structured ways. Both kinds of structure, however, although often subversive in relation to the wider social milieu, cannot exist in isolation from that milieu and are thus governed by similar or similarly challenged norms of personhood, morality and so forth. In sum, there are continuities and discontinuities between the experiences of apprentices as they move into and out of the shipyards.

The drama of apprenticeship lies not only in the fact that the apprentice leaves his familiars for the unknown of the shipyards, but also in the numerous subtle challenges that are made to his ideas about mundane things, such as bodies, hierarchy and respect, and what he chooses to do with the ensuing conflicts of interest. The violence contained by these processes reverberates between the apprentice and his familiars and between the masters and apprentices within the shipping group. However, it would be incorrect to think that this violence is framed in any straightforward sense by the idea of learning a craft. Masters organise apprenticeships in order to profit from the ships their recruits build and, later, crew and maintain. Likewise, the physical and social skills apprentices acquire in shipyards (learning how to build ships) are necessary means to other ends. Therefore, teaching and learning are not the ultimate goals of either master or apprentice. Masters have little or no interest in perpetuating craft traditions for their own sake other than for the reproduction of capital interests; conversely, apprentices are dreaming of the high seas and the shopping malls of the Emirates while they labour. So it is that, while both master and apprentice are engaged with methods of accumulating wealth and improving their standing, their methods and thus their intentions are asymmetrical from the outset.

What is going on in shipyard apprenticeship?

Salem was greeted with indifference when he first arrived for work in one of the shipyards. For the first few days, he stoked the fire and made tea. In the second week, he passed hammers, nails and chalks to the foreman. One afternoon, during his third week, as work on the vessel came to a halt for tea, the foreman suggested to him that they forgo their break and finish fixing a particularly troublesome plank on the stern. By this time, the other labourers had downed tools and were reclining in the bilge watching the pair at work high above them. There was a marked air of expectation, as if something unpleasant was about to happen. After a few minutes, their conversations tailed off, heads turned and faint smiles were exchanged. Salem was happily working away watching and learning from the foreman's lead, unaware that he, too, now had an attentive audience. The foreman turned to him and asked him to pass a *chappal*. Salem was confused and assumed he had misheard because in the Kachchhi language a *chappal* is a slipper or flip-flop and he could not see how footwear of any kind would aid their current task. Feigning irritation at his charge's inaction, the foreman again shouted for a *chappal*, this time in more urgent tones. Salem, barefooted, bent down and attempted to remove the foreman's flip-flop. The foreman kicked out at him, Salem was knocked off the scaffold and fell at least two metres into the bilge, landing in a confused tangle of limbs on a pile of timber.

His undignified arrival in lower sections of the ship was greeted with raucous laughter and a volley of expletives attesting to his stupidity. Astonishingly, and more by luck than design, other than a few cuts and scrapes he was not seriously injured. Before Salem had a chance to regain his breath and to lift his face to reveal his confused and tearful eyes, the foreman had climbed down into the bilge, heedless of Salem's condition, to receive his congratulations for such a perfectly staged humiliation. Salem, rather like apprentices on building sites in England, had been asked to fetch the equivalent of a left-handed hammer. As he was later told, in the argot of the seafarers a *chappal* is a small wooden wedge used to position planks – not a slipper or flip-flop.

This incident was obviously humiliating for Salem but there is more to it than as yet meets the eye and I shall return to it again later.

The division of labour is remarkably similar within all shipyards and is reproduced among the crews when the ships are at sea. Those who work for them are from a large number of different ethnic and caste groups. The forty to fifty men employed to build a ship are, however, primarily divided into five horizontal ranked grades, split vertically between carpenters (*suthar*) and labourers (*mahjor*). The carpenters are predominantly Hindu seasonal migrants from Andhra Pradesh, while the labourers, the primary focus of this article, are local Sunni Muslims. Roles are specifically distributed among men both horizontally and vertically. The vertical distribution of labour is divided into different categories of work, so that all those within the category of 'labourer' are also ranked quite clearly in relation to one another. Vertically there are also hierarchically ordered command structures, with labourers ranking above carpenters on the basis of ethnicity rather than skill. The horizontal axis intersects the vertical at various levels of labour and carpentry, and parallel tasks are allotted to different groups of men within either category. In a rather literal sense, the social framework needed to run and crew a ship is constructed along with the vessel itself.

Lowest in rank among the labourers is the *petoriya* (assistant, galley hand), who maintains the fire, serves bitter black tea every few hours, runs general errands and serves as the butt for most practical jokes. The bulk of the men working in shipyards are known as *khalaasi* (labourers and sailors). The word *khalaasi* is reported to come from the tradition of paying sailors in grain and a lump sum known as *khalaas* for the season's work. Responsible for the manual labour in shipyards, they drag and stack wood and move raw materials with pulleys, ropes and scaffolding. They also learn how to bend and manipulate materials and how to secure materials by drilling, bolting and caulking. The *sarang* (foreman) mediates conflicts and organises the division of labour among the *khalaasis*. Typically, the *sarang* is experienced in shipyards and also has some seasons of sailing experience. He is also responsible for the elementary informal instruction of apprentices in ship design and the technologies of production. Of highest rank are *nakhuvas* (captains) and just below them *malams* (navigators). Both are recruited to a particular vessel long before it is afloat to supervise construction and to impress their authority upon the future crew. The *seth* (ship owner, lit. master or owner) occupies a position of unquestioned authority over the ranks previously described.

Workers in the shipyards are thus organised by a social hierarchy in which the Bhadala ship owners are lords and masters. The caste and ethnic identities of shipyard workers are often retained as forms of address but the positions of status to which they refer are firmly subordinate to the organisation of labour. Salem's fall from grace was encouraged by a man whom Salem himself knew to be of lowly repute at home in Mandvi and who would not have dared to publicly trick him in a more familiar environment for fear of a legitimate reprisal or the imposition of social sanctions. Suddenly, Salem had no recourse to familiar principles of respect and justice that his high status in his neighbourhood had accorded him since he was a boy. He considered revenge outside the yard but was advised against this course of action because it would jeopardise his career prospects.

The promising allure of the future binds shipyard workers to their labour and, perhaps, makes the humiliation they endure less painful. For most, the ideal is to become a sailor, to experience life in the Emirates and to make friends and influence people back in Kachchh through petty trade in luxury goods. Others aspire to jump ship after a few seasons, as Rasheed had done, in order to take work in the Emirates or on supply vessels servicing the oil industry. Salem had these things in mind in the days after the material and symbolic certainties that had carried him thus far were violently pulled from beneath his feet. That moment revealed a great many things that he was yet to become through apprenticeship. He did not of course realise it at the time, but he did in years to come, long after his parents and neighbours became aware of the fact he was no longer who he once was. At that time, the most effective way of ensuring his safety, dignity and general acceptance was to make sure that he revealed nothing for his colleagues to pick upon or, in other words, to make sure that he 'fitted in'. He went about his new duties with diligence and, only two months after he started work, he laughed as heartily as the others when another new recruit attempted to pass the foreman his slipper.

Shipbuilding involves an assembly of irregularly shaped parts in particular structural relationships. The keel, prow, stern, bulwarks, garboards, gunwales, stringers, transoms, strakes, balusters and so on are formed from either gnarl and crook timbers or seasoned and milled hardwood. These parts are variously bracketed or joined using hooked scarfs, mortises and tenons, and tapered scarfs and butts.

If, however, we regard a ship as a human project, rather than as a collection of physical objects, we can see that such a project is, above anything else, a social activity requiring intention, planning and organisation. It also follows that building a ship means a variety of things for those involved depending on their allotted tasks and position within the command hierarchy as outlined above. In fact, building a ship, for particular individuals, may involve little more than carrying timber back and forth or managing account books. It also follows that the majority of work in shipyards is routine, repetitive and somewhat tedious. For apprentices, tedium comes from the fact that at first they have very little to do and later because they get to perform the same task over and over again, in effect learning many skills for the first time and then relearning them to the point of habitude through repetition.

Paul Connerton has suggested that habits are forms of knowledge and remembering through which the body 'understands' (1995: 95). It also seems to me that habits are more than repetitious technical abilities: they are affective dispositions that develop elective affinities between the interests of apprentices and their masters, which give meaning outside the realm of the task itself. Dale Eickelman (1978) has illustrated, in relation to prayer and mnemonic learning, how repetition itself contributes to the creation of such elective affinities. Thus by bringing these ideas together we can see that 'habitual' work practices and 'learning' skills are not abstract signs, but carry with them moral and political sway.

In the following sections I have separated the description of the acquisition of technical abilities from the description of the affective nature of these dispositions, although in reality they are connected in myriad ways, including time, place, activity and social hierarchy.

Sukhet was one of five new apprentices taken on for the construction of the *Al Ibrahim*. When he started work in the yard, construction was already well under way, the keel and the garboard planks were in place and a team of around thirty men had been assembled. For Sukhet, and the many like him, building a ship involves a range of skills, tasks and organisational strategies under the instruction of superiors. At first, he was given little responsibility and was told what, when and how to do things. As the construction of the ship progressed, so did Sukhet's ability to predict what, when and how things should be done. When instructions were given to him they became increasingly less specific and only implicitly incorporated the what, when and how of the task.

When apprentice sailors arrive for work for the first time in shipyards they literally look awkward. They may know some of the other labourers but are unfamiliar with the language, hierarchy and use of space in the shipyards. They do not know where anything is kept and do not know what most of the things they cannot find are called, as the language of shipbuilding requires a specialised vocabulary. As neophytes, they move cautiously, unsure of the appropriate distances to allow between themselves and the other men in the yard. As the weeks pass, they get a feel for the environment and how to move and behave and, in time, the vocabulary, working rhythms and forms of deference literally become second nature.

In the initial months, Sukhet moved wood from its delivery point to various stacking and distribution points. He learned how to lift, drop and manoeuvre sections of timber, either alone or in a team. Lifting and moving wood is heavy work that requires organisation, technique and skill; brute strength is not enough. The handcart drivers who bring the wood from timber mills are experts in handling wood; some of them have missing fingers and toes attesting to the fact that they have painfully learned how to do so. Sukhet began to understand that moving heavy objects through confined spaces requires a consideration of the movements of other men and practices that make the task easier. He learned and sometimes forgot the names of various kinds of timber and parts of the ship. As he moved wood around for more experienced labourers he also began to appreciate the order in which pieces of wood were required and where they fitted into the overall design of the ship. He also grasped how to use pulleys, ropes and block and tackle as he and other labourers lifted timbers into the hull. He was shouted at, punched and called a series of derogatory names, which mostly connected him to the alleged immorality of his mother and sisters. He grazed his toes and got deep splinters in his palms and under his nails; he also snagged his clothes on pieces of protruding wood.

After a few months, Sukhet was told to assist a more experienced labourer in repositioning a section of scaffolding that ran around the outside of the ship. He began to learn that the key scaffolding is run up around the stem and the sternpost and this determines the height and orientation of the remaining walkways and uprights. Scaffolding is not permanent and is constantly adjusted as different layers of planking are measured, positioned, nailed, and then removed and repositioned. Scaffolding is made from waste wood and is fastened with rope. There is no homogeneity in the materials, yet there has to be homogeneity in the final product as walkways have to be level and stable.

Sukhet quickly saw that making good scaffolding is a complex task that requires an appreciation of the space, an anticipation of future work on the ship and a grasp of the tolerance of the materials. Experienced scaffolders assess the rate of work on the hull and predict at what level the platforms will be positioned for the next stage in the work. The positioning of platforms also requires that evaluations be made about the highest and lowest points on the hull a man can work on from a platform of a given height. This allows the platform to be aligned for the work that is to be undertaken next. Scaffolding also requires a feel for the kinds of gaps to leave between levels to allow them to be easily traversed. A gap too great or small means that the scaffold is difficult to climb around and thus movement is cumbersome and time consuming. By learning to scaffold, Sukhet became familiar with different types of wood and their tolerances; he used rope, anticipated the work rate of others and began to learn how to work high above the ground.

A year or so into the construction of the *Al Ibrahim*, Sukhet was told by the foreman to drill holes in planks to temporarily secure them to the frames. He demonstrated to Sukhet how to work the drill, and marked each hole for the apprentice. Tentative at first, but having seen the drill operated hundreds of times before, Sukhet started moving the bow at right angles to the main shaft of the drill to make the bit rotate. He quickly mastered the fact that varying densities of wood require that varying amounts of pressure be applied to the chest plate, but never so much that the string ineffectually slips around the central cylinder. After two days, the foreman stopped marking the holes for the apprentice, who was now able to drill through the plank and a few centimetres into the frame without supervision.

Sukhet also removed the temporary fastenings that held the planks in place and helped reposition them further down the hull, before finally caulking and countersinking a securing nail. He worked for around a month with a caulking iron as a member of a team filling the spaces between the planks on the hull with strands of raw cotton treated with lime. As he performed these tasks the vessel took shape around him.

When Sukhet first started work he spent a lot of time lounging around. When he was expected to perform a task he was given clear and constant instruction. Gradually, such specific instruction desisted as he learned how to evaluate the priority of a task and to act appropriately in relation to the task depending on what other men were doing in the yard at the time. It took more than two years to build the *Al Ibrahim*. Sukhet had been nervous, frail and quietly spoken when he started his apprenticeship; after eighteen months he had become a senior labourer, with considerable responsibility. His body had changed; his hands, feet and knees had become hard and callused from contact with splinters, ropes, wood and tools. His skin had darkened in the sun, he swore like a sailor, and his muscles had strengthened through repetitive heavy work. He had learned to move around the ship, to climb carrying heavy loads, and the many possible pathways from one section of the ship to another. When the ship was commissioned for service he was among four other labourers who were selected to join the crew.

The stages of apprenticeship described here, from Salem's humiliation to Sukhet's promotion to the rank of seagoing sailor, typically last two or three years and are potentially the start of a long relationship with the vessel. Those fortunate enough, as both Salem and Sukhet were, to be selected to crew the ship on which they have laboured will have learned the ship's constituent parts and stages of construction and will have begun to appreciate the overall integrity of the vessel. In addition, they will know what it means to behave appropriately within the hierarchies of status and power among the crew and how to act in relation to commands as well as to the actions of others. These apprenticeships are informal and non-contractual but what is learned is revealed in an accumulative order as young men move upwards within the hierarchy. There are no diplomas or certificates and no more formal instruction than I have described for Sukhet's case. However, the successful apprenticeship is acknowledged by the master presenting the apprentice with a seafarers' identity card. This document is issued by the government but the apprentice is ineligible for such a permit without the patronage of a master. Inscribed in this card is a legal entitlement to go to sea but its real value is that it symbolically represents the mastery of a broad range of social and technical skills, including a basic understanding of the constituent sections of the vessel and competence with ropes, scaffolding and hoists that is necessary to crew, repair and load and unload the vessel.

In the following section I turn to the affective nature of these habitual dispositions which, for the apprentice, also begin to provide meaning outside the performance of shipbuilding.

What else is going on in shipyard apprenticeship?

At first, when I asked informants directly about shipbuilding they, like many other artisans in the literature, had very little to say about skill or the human aspects of shipbuilding. Instead, they listed components and the sequence in which they were assembled. Such narratives, similar to those I discussed in the previous chapter, are mostly devoid of context; they leave out the obvious and the taken for granted passes without saying. In their telling, the complexities of shipbuilding become a linear discourse and thus a different beast to the practices themselves (after Bloch 1991: 186). Such narratives also desire to explain and eradicate conflict, they freeze the picture and engage with the expectations of the enquirer and lend themselves too easily to re-description (after Jenkins 1994).

I was very often told that there was no point in studying shipbuilding because it was *sahelu kam* (easy work) or *sahelu gnan* (easy knowledge). At first, I thought my informants meant that there was nothing remarkable about it (and in this regard they were undoubtedly correct) and that it was a deskilled part of a low-status craft tradition within the low-status shipping industry. Later, I began to understand that what they meant by 'easy knowledge' was precisely the conceptions of skill and technique I was initially interested in. It was 'easy' because it came through non-reflexive practice and repetition. It was not 'difficult' like schooling or technical training because there were no complicated manuals of regulations or numbers to read and there was no pride or status to be had from its practice. Scaffolding, moving materials, drilling and nailing were explained to me as forms of 'easy knowledge', mastered by participation in the activity of shipbuilding through repetition, observation and humiliation, framed within the hierarchy of the crew and idioms of respect and patronage.

'Easy work' is not only defined in relation to formal education, of which the intimidating spectres of both the government and literacy are part. 'Easy work' is also given character in the shipyards in its symbiotic relationship to the 'brain work' or 'the work of the mind' of the merchant-cum-ship owner. This obviously reflects a widely held belief that working with the mind to deduce meaning from religious texts or profits from account books is of higher value than manual labour. The 'work of the mind' is said to be superior, and more corporeally sophisticated, than the easy work of physical labour, although both are importantly associated with the body.

It is perhaps worth pointing out that 'work' is only some of what happens in shipyards. Men talk, gossip, conspire, laugh, joke and engage in group conversations that sometimes last for weeks; conversely, at times, they are also subject to violence, humiliation and sexual predation – all of which are integral to learning the ropes and eventually finding their sea legs. Their conversations were often about film stars, prostitutes, motorbikes, cricket, fighting and the like. Most of these exchanges were light-hearted and frivolous. On an almost daily basis, however, at some point the conversation would become serious as they turned to moral questions and to topics such as the significance of genealogy for living persons, what hierarchy in Muslim society is based on, what correct religious practice is and what it is that allows some men to accrue money more readily than others.

It is through listening to and participating in these conversations and others outside the yards that it became clear to me that apprentices actually had very clear ideas about what learning entailed, where ability came from and what the broader implications of their activities would be. Simply asking them about shipbuilding made no sense and rightly provoked nonsensical answers that focused, for example, on the structural relationship between the keel and the prow. This was partly, of course, because my questions were initially framed inappropriately but, more importantly, we simply did not share an understanding of what shipbuilding was or what its aims and objectives were.

I was quickly disabused of any notion I might have taken into my relationships with apprentices that shipbuilding had a bearing on the ethics of noble labour or, indeed, on the romantic notion of a craft tradition. It took me longer, however, to see that shipbuilding and the mastery of its techniques was not the sole, or even principal, aim of anyone in the yards. From the apprentice's perspective the primary motivation to work and learn successfully is so that he will not have to work or learn in the shipyards any more. Furthermore, although shipbuilding was in part about creating loyalties and transferring skills through master–apprentice and peer–peer relationships, these connections were forged from considerable social violence. Patterns of class, ethnicity and status were refashioned through apprenticeship and the tensions this created constantly came to the fore both inside and outside shipyards. Underlying these tensions were conflicting conceptions of the bio-moral person that placed the violence of apprenticeship on a much larger stage than that of local patterns of status competition. It was possible to deduce, and later to elucidate from informants and friends, that what they were about was actually very well elaborated in their thoughts, even if this primarily meant drawing on other realms of knowledge.

I will return to the conceptions of sociality and skill acquisition held among my informants below after presenting some of the things apprentices are told and discuss in the shipyards.

Language in and around shipyards

Language, illocution and perlocution are intimately related to the acquisition and transmission of the 'easy knowledge'. Language and the gestures of language are readily accessible channels through which friendship and camaraderie are communicated in shipyards; they are also an integral part of the way in which ideas about legitimate religious practice are expressed and propagated. The majority of people in Mandvi are, at the very least, competent in Kachchhi and Gujarati; many others speak Hindi, English, Arabic, Swahili and a number of other foreign tongues. Throughout Kachchh there are considerable differences in the pronunciation of the language and, while it is difficult for a Gujarati speaker to follow Kachchhi, the variant spoken by Mandvi's Muslim seafarers is widely understood in the ports of the western seaboard of India and beyond. This dialect is sometimes called *dariyani bhasha* (language of the sea) or *vahaanvattani bhasha* (language of sailors).[1] It is a masculine language, developed to convey specialised technical information about ships, places, people and trade. The technologies of shipbuilding are articulated with a large and precise vocabulary. The grammar of this argot is the same as Kachchhi, but pronunciation and meaning vary considerably. As has been shown, in Kachchhi a *chappal* is a slipper, while in the speech style of the shipyards it is a wedge. There are many equivalent examples, and distinct technical words, for example, for the first fifteen planks of a hull, and an array of different terms for rope, for wood grain, meteorological and wave patterns, commerce and navigation.

Among the Bhadala, such language draws heavily on religious idioms, a fact also reflected in the names of ships, their decoration and the green (the colour associated with Islam in India) ensigns that flutter along with the Indian national flag from their bows. The names of ships are derived from Arabic and Urdu such as *Al Barakat* (wealth and abundance), *Azadi* (freedom), *Mahmudi* (goodness), *Naseri* (help) and *Salamati* (safety). Prefixed with 'MSV' (Motor Sailing Vessel) and suffixed by 'MV' (Mandvi), such names, although of religious significance, also suggest prosperity and safety. The languages of prayer, greeting and law are also derived primarily from Arabic. On the radio channels reserved for the country craft, *salaam alaikum* (peace be upon you) starts, and *kudha hafiz* (god's faith) ends, most conversations, rather than the international standards of 'do you read me?' and 'out' used on open frequencies. Most apprentices speak Kachchhi as their first language and have to make a concentrated effort to learn the specialised language of shipping and the standard terms for prayer and ritual. In time, the combination of language codes engenders local commonality between the seafarers, affords them a degree of privacy and discretion in the presence of non-seafarers, but also provides a set of religious terms in standard Arabic, to replace local terms apprentices have usually grown up with.

As Salem's fall into the bilge illustrates, the daily grind in the shipyards can be brutal and humiliating and often little mercy is shown towards the weak and vulnerable. Not all make the grade; some are bullied into other occupations, others are sacked for theft or laziness. This process falls somewhere between the selection of the fittest and the selection of the culpable. However, conversational exchanges in the shipyards are not all about inducing terror and refining the internal hierarchy. Often other kinds of jokes and parodies are carried on the breeze between the yards. The rules of address and the rights to speech mirror the grades of hierarchy that dictate labour on a ship. Generally, silence is proffered up the hierarchy; demands and commands rain downwards. So it is that unless asked to contribute to a debate, those lower placed in the hierarchy do a lot more listening than they do talking. Jokes and jocular behaviour in shipyards are another mechanism through which divergent understandings of the world are brought gradually into line with the dominant paradigm. As David Parkin has elegantly put this for other contexts:

> The jester does more than reinforce social hierarchy by reminding its incumbents of the values that put them there. Under the cover of his licence to abuse, he can also slip new cards into the pack and slightly change the rules of the game.
>
> (1980: 57)

The jocular language of the shipyards also typically degrades, humiliates and questions the intelligence and moral character of 'others'.

Informally, the Bhadala reveal their worldview to apprentices through ideologically nuanced utterances. Jokes, stories and parodies about Hindus are frequently told. A typical example, which circulated for a few months in mid-1998, is a joke about Hindu religious integrity. A Hindu man wants to discover 'truth'. He thus consults holy men (renouncers) and journeys to visit a series of them, each more powerful and less concerned with apparel. The holy men offer their own interpretations of 'truth', but the man is unsatisfied. He searches for the holiest of all men – who is totally naked! While the finale may lack the expected punch, the joke degrades Hindu 'truth' in a number of ways: the man has to consult other mortals to discover the truth, the truth he is given varies and is inconsistent, and the ultimate harbinger of truth is naked. While it is obvious that in a monotheistic tradition the anthropomorphic manifestation of truth might be subject to ridicule, the real element of mirth here is that the holiest man is naked and the joke, therefore, is more about sociology than theology. Even men labouring under a hot sun in shipyards dress modestly in *shirtpant* (typically, tailored nylon trousers and shirts); nakedness is immodest and improper. More importantly, nakedness is the most powerful sign of insanity; thus, the joke tells that the Hindu version of truth comes from the insane. The insane do not know how to behave; they are dirty and asocial beings who live by their own rules.

Similar jocular interventions are evident in the commentaries ship owners provide on the stream of Hindus and Jains who pass through and around the river estuary during the average working day. Often such commentaries show a clear understanding of Hindu religious thought and an implicit antidote to be found in Muslim religious practice. Mohamed, a swarthy and heavily scarred Bhadala man, was the unofficial champion of this kind of satire. His three decades of life had left their mark and he looked at least fifteen years older than he actually was. When he was not in Dubai or Bombay managing his family's commercial affairs and fleet, he spent a few hours every day in his shipyard overseeing the renovation work on one of his brother's ships. His workforce regarded him with both awe and trepidation. He had to do little more than stare intently at a miscreant and the offender would scamper away to busy himself. He did not suffer foolery lightly and had very clear ideas about what foolery was. His tongue, wit and, occasionally, his fist were brutal. The workers in the yard, somewhat sycophantically, often howled with laughter at the things he said but all were constantly in fear that they would be the butt of his next outburst.

He would offer sage advice to his workforce: 'Do not piss towards the sun because you will get a headache', 'Do not piss towards the moon it is disrespectful to Islam'. He would also comment on the wealth of other activities, aside from shipbuilding, that took place in the estuary on the average day. By doing so he was also taking his apprentices behind the standard narratives of action and religion. On a daily basis, Hindus from Mandvi and further afield come to the estuary to serve animals, to dispose of dangerous offerings made to angry gods and goddesses and to worship other deities associated with the sea. The spoils of these offerings attract the attention of hungry birds. This prompted Mohamed to say to his workers on more than one occasion: 'You see that woman? The one feeding the birds! She thinks her dead husband is a crow, but she cannot recognise him and feeds them all.' He was suggesting that in death the woman's husband had been reincarnated as a crow, but the woman was of such a moral character that she could not recognise him. By feeding them all she was promiscuously giving her produce to others. On another occasion, this time commenting on polytheism, he said: 'That man loves dogs. He feeds them well. They think that dogs are gods – what kind of people are they that see their gods running around in packs?' Hindus also give ritual items (mostly obsolete coinage) up to the sea in the hope of greater returns. Such regular offerings prompted the comment: 'These people come down to the river to throw their money away. You [the yard's workforce] can pick it out of the mud on your way home.' Related to this was the fate of the other ritual items (rice, incense and flowers) that wash into the shipyards. Apprentices incinerate this, often with discernable caution if not to say fear, along with other flotsam. Commenting on the rubbish-strewn tide line Mohamed said: 'They come over here and throw rubbish in our place showing that they have no respect for us.' Such comments contain a clear sense of injustice: Hindus who have no idea about truth or religious propriety manage to be politically dominant and have no respect for the enlightened Muslims who want to be left to their own business.

Daud had spent two seasons as captain of a ship before his father decided he should be sent to university in Bombay. There he had studied commerce and had become involved in petty crime. He was as rebellious as he was intelligent and, afraid he would end up in serious trouble either with the law or with organised crime, his father brought him back to Salaya to oversee the work on a new ship. Now in his early forties, he had a reputation for sensitivity and diplomacy and for looking after his workforce. He lent them money, financed weddings and often got involved in resolving disputes within their families. In the run-up to the 1998 state-level elections many senior Bhadala men publicly supported the incumbent BJP candidate because he had promised them funds for improving the water supply to their village. Despite the promise of benefits for the community the decision was not met with resounding approval by all. Daud was sitting with a group of labourers having tea in the hot afternoon sun when one of them suggested the BJP had worked hard for Kachchh and would be returned to power. Daud agreed, they had done well and performed their job as politicians by lining their own pockets. He, too, thought they would be returned to power. He was clearly irritated by the suggestion that a vote for the BJP was a good thing either for Kachchh or for Muslims. Standing up and taking an authoritative posture he told my microphone and the twenty or so men gathered around him:

> Listen, he [the local BJP candidate] has bought our vote. We agreed to that this time because those people in power in Mandvi would never give us water without a more powerful man to tell them what to do. He promises to give us something and we all run after him trying to become his friend. We do not see through him, we are blind. These people call our country secular, to them secularism means Hinduism. If we send our children to school here they learn that Hindu gods invented aeroplanes, Hanuman built a bridge

linking India with Sri Lanka and that the only thing Muslims contributed to this country was the destruction of temples. What kind of secularism is that? They are biased. I am all for secular education in schools, if I want my children to learn the Quran I will arrange for them to have a tutor at home. What will they do next? They want us out of this country. They will try to force us out. Where shall we go then? This is our home.

Litanies such as these are constant and create a derisory picture of the governance and Hindu ritual practice and the perceived superstition on which such action is based. The commentaries are mocking and sentient and are enmeshed in a more powerful linguistic commentary on Islamic practice and reform. Through linguistic commentaries on the actions of people in the landscape, ship owners and others well positioned within the hierarchy present a model of the world that is both amusing and persuasive to apprentices. This model is not based on abstract speculation, but on what can be seen and heard while men are labouring to build ships. Through these processes real and symbolic boundaries are constructed that were perhaps not present in the life of the apprentice before he came to work in the shipyards – or at least not as clearly demarcated or as elaborate.

If conversation in shipyards is mostly derisory towards Hindus, then, in the setting of the mosque or formal religious discourse, the target changes and it is the corruption of other Muslims that receives attention. Such meetings are normally held at Mukhdummi Sha, the protective saint whose mausoleum stands at the entrance to Salaya. This complex was rebuilt by the Bhadala in the 1980s and they sponsor the meetings and sometimes provide light refreshments for the congregation. The gatherings are addressed by religious scholars (often from Rajasthan) and apprentices are strongly encouraged to attend. I also attended quite a number of these meetings with Mohamed, Daud and groups of workers from their yards. The orators offer commentaries on passages from the Quran and outline what they consider to be *sunnah*: the actions of the Prophet as documented over time that the layman should aspire to reproduce. In the daily grind of the shipyards it is frequently asserted that 'it is *sunnah* to do x or y', to perform certain actions in everyday life, which pertain to both the sacred and the profane. Thus, it is *sunnah* to perform one's ablutions in a certain manner, to perform rituals at given junctures, to behave in a given way in a particular context and so forth. At the Mukhdummi Sha meetings, however, the transmission of these ideas is perhaps the primary motivation for the gathering and thus what the speaker has to say is held in greater regard.

At one of the first such meetings I attended, the speaker said that:

the reason for our poverty and the fact we are now second-class citizens in a land we once ruled is because we have forgotten how

Islam was at the time of our glorious Prophet. We have fallen on the wrong side of falsehood.

He asked the congregation if Muslims read the epic of the Prophet's birth or offered sweets to the dead in the early years of Islam. Did Muslims mechanically recite the Quran, trying to sound like Arabs without understanding the words in those days? Did Muslims collect votives, amulets and charms up in their hands like jewels from a chest? Did Muslims tie pieces of cloth to trees or garland tombs of the dead and promise sacrifice for atonement?

Most other speakers I heard were not as forthright with their vision and seldom did they hark back to a golden era of Islam at the time of the Prophet. They generally rested content with stressing the importance of pure-minded prayer and the centrality of the Friday Mosque to the social life of the religious community. Although the speakers would occasionally turn to Europe or America for examples of decadence and corruption, for the most part they used a very local geography to make their rhetorical comparisons. One speaker pointed out that there was no Friday mosque in Mandvi, despite a sizeable Muslim population, because the Muslims there had become divided on the basis of community and tended to go to their own mosques. This, he said, was not how Islam instructed people to live; mosques were supposed to be free for all Muslims and in prayer everyone was equal and together. At this point, it is worth recalling that the majority of shipyard labourers are from Mandvi and are shepherded by their employers to hear speakers critical of their own society.

In the language of these meetings Saiyeds (putative descendants of the Prophet) were often portrayed as 'magic men', 'Muslim Brahmins' and as relics of former times; although I should say here that many of the speakers were Saiyed in name and their criticisms were implicitly aimed more at the practices and other-worldly claims of other Saiyeds rather than at the legitimacy of the category. Therefore, it is Saiyeds as mystics rather than as scholars who trouble the Bhadala and this distinction should be kept in mind in this and following chapters. It was Saiyeds as scholars who told the shipyard workers assembled at Mukhdummi Sha that splashes of cow's urine on the clothes of one on the way to prayer is the worst possible pollutant for Muslim ritual purity and anyone so affected should return home to change their clothes before proceeding to the mosque. This example is clearly politically expedient in a society dominated by Hindus for whom the cow is revered. Apprentices talked about it long after the event and I commonly saw those who had been present at this meeting steer a very wide birth of the rear end of any cow they chanced upon in the streets. Other topics I heard included the prohibition of music and drumming at religious occasions, proper dress and hygiene and how horses should not be used in marriage processions.

Outside India, Moharam is a Shia event marking the martyrdom of Hussein, the third Imam. In India, the event is widely observed by Sunnis. Generally, among elite Sunni communities throughout western India there is hostility towards the lavish public displays of commemoration. Despite opposition to such public performance it remains the most popular of Muslim festivals. Thousands of people come from the surrounding villages to Mandvi to watch the musical processions and follow the dancers through the streets. The first days of the lunar month of Moharam are reserved for mourning the death of the Imam Hussein on the battlefields of Kabala. During these days, the buildings (*imambara*) that house the *tazias* (the mock shrines of the martyrs) are opened and decorated. In the following days, *tazias* are decorated with bright paper, plastic ornaments, electric lights and loudspeakers. There are three main *tazias* representing Ali and his sons, Hussan and Hussein, and numerous smaller structures.

The days that are thought to have special significance during this period vary considerably, with each mosque in Mandvi having a slightly different set of observances distinguishing it from other mosques. However, regardless of whether the first twelve or thirteen days of the month are reserved for austerities, the Muslims who participate in the festival come together on the tenth day on the Mandvi bank of the estuary. Then the *tazias* are paraded round the town, surrounded by flagellants performing a slow rhythmical dance to the accompaniment of drums and to cries of '*ya Ali, ya Ali, Shah Hussan, Shah Hussein*' (friend Ali, friend Ali, King Hussan, King Hussein). Towards dusk, amid large crowds, the different processions congregate at the river. Before each *tazia* there is a flurry of activity as men and women jostle for the chance to break a coconut and to offer a wish or a prayer as the *tazias* become conduits for individual desire. As night falls the *tazias* are carried into the centre of the estuary and as the tide turns they are swiftly rotated three times in alternate directions to enthusiastic cheers from the crowd. Very few Bhadala men participate in the procession (I return to comment on recent changes to this in Chapter 4) and, in what struck me as a highly symbolic act, they gathered in silence on the Salaya side of the riverbank to watch the fun and games from a respectful distance.

Unlike Mohamed and Daud, Rafiq had not received an expensive formal education. Now in his late thirties for the last ten years he had run one of his father's ships between Dubai and Somalia. Showing its age, the vessel had been brought back to Mandvi for a lengthy overhaul. He was a simple and honest man who worked alongside his crew on the repairs. One day, in the weeks leading up to Moharam, Rafiq told his men during a tea break that: 'During Moharam we should pray at the mosque and be sad in remembering the martyrdom of Hussein. It is not a time to play, flirt and dance in the street.' The following day, at a meeting at Mukhdummi Sha, the speaker of the day told of how the assassins of Ali and his sons marched triumphantly back to their city, mockingly shouting the names of the martyrs whose heads they had mounted on poles. The speaker told his audience that the Moharam processions held in Mandvi had turned tragedy and the commemoration of defeat into a time of celebration. He went on to describe how the standards (bearing hands and other symbols of the martyrdom) carried before the *tazias* are also inadvertently commemorating the victory of the enemy – not the sadness of martyrdom. He said the Moharam processions had been 'borrowed' from Hinduism and forcefully put forth a case explaining why these activities should be abandoned in the name of progress. His was a heterodox interpretation of events, but it left a lasting impression on the congregation and, whatever the historical contingencies of the event, it was deliberately portrayed as having its roots in the Hindu ritual tradition. The speaker effectively conflated Muslim defeat and Hindu ritual traditions. By presenting his case in this way, many of those present made their way home in the knowledge that the historical tragedies of the Muslim tradition were in some way connected to the existence of Hinduism.

At these meetings much of what apprentices hear takes as a negative example the practices of their own communities and neighbourhoods. They hear of what makes 'good practice', which is significantly wrapped in a particular way of conceiving time and space. The terms 'traditional', 'modern' and 'syncretic', as problematic as they are in anthropological discussion, are notions that shipyard workers hear at these meetings to describe social transformation and the visions of Salaya's ship owners. 'Tradition', sometimes glossed with the phrase 'the teeth of a donkey', refers to the order of hierarchy and religious practice that they perceive as characterising the social life of Mandvi. It is opposed by the 'modern', metaphorically described as 'the teeth of a comb', which is the social ordering of Salaya, ships, commodities and what are construed as new forms of Islam. The irregularity and heterogeneity of one half of the metaphor contrasts with the uniformity and homogeneity of the other. While 'syncretic', translated loosely from the Gujarati word *ugulumbugulum*, meaning 'all mixed up', refers to a distant past before the Bhadala became Muslim and lived as Hindus or at least lived elsewhere in some undefined religious condition.

'Modernisation', of a sort, is at the centre of the Bhadala's attempt to reform local Muslim society, and in some ways also stands as a source of legitimisation. In the language of the meetings held at Mukhdummi Sha the 'impure' are described as such not because of ignoble descent or dirty occupations, but because they are afflicted with Hinduism. It is only 'impure' people who are troubled by ghosts, fall victim to the 'evil eye' and patronise intermediaries that provide them with access to Allah. These things are associated with Mandvi and the 'syncretic' past. The 'pure' religious ideals and practices of the reformers invoke the mosque and the Quran. This invocation not only details correct action before Allah, but also describes the way in which apprentices can escape the perilous and precarious accretions of Hinduism. The reformers acknowledge the existence of Hindu cosmology in order to posit it as antithetical to the Islam that they promote. Hinduism and Islam are presented to neophytes in a graded and hierarchical relationship. Hinduism is corrupt, polytheistic, idolatrous and impure, and is paralleled among Mandvi's Muslims by a hierarchy premised on the axiomatic blood of the Saiyed.

In this sense, Hinduism and 'traditional' Islam are seen as engaging with very real human and metaphysical realities. They are not seen as being based on hollow illusory principles. Hindu deities and Muslim saints are seen as existing and as engaging with forces and channels of power in worldly and non-worldly forms. However, they are lesser forces than Allah (and the ways of relating to Allah through prayer, mosque building and sponsoring religious speakers), elevated as transcendental by the Bhadala's patronage. The kinds of religious practices advocated by the Bhadala offer something of a fragile path through the perilous realms of corrupt and demoniac beliefs. For example, one of the Mukhdummi Sha meetings was held on the subject of ghosts, magic and jinn. At this meeting the congregation learned that it was only the impure who saw ghosts and who could be afflicted with negative magic forces. Those most prone to being haunted were, of course, Hindus, followed by 'traditional' Muslims. The message was that ghosts, both benign and malicious, were out there, but they could be avoided through maintaining pure ritual practices. In this sense, in life, Islam is seen as having something of a salvationary potential against the feckless and immanent temptations of lesser gods and spirits. The examples given at this meeting concerned purifying ablutions after contact with defiling substances, such as urine and the products of sexual intercourse. Unless these substances are removed correctly they attract ghosts and other negative forces. At another level, the practice of regular prayer and reading from the Quran was presented as a routine that prevents individuals from improper speculation and from wandering into the realms of lesser powers and demons.

While Muslims wary of the potency of Hinduism, albeit as an impoverished system of belief, may sound parochial and far removed from the zealous puritanism the reader may have had in mind, these narratives and the concomitant patterns of status are also wrapped in a familiar and pervasive meta-narrative derived from the traditions of Islam. As is common elsewhere, the example of life offered by the Prophet is the ideal model for social action and his character is the basis for individual behaviour or *adab*. The Bhadala structure (whether consciously or unconsciously, I remain somewhat uncertain) their narratives of trade, pilgrimage and self-transformation in the idioms of the Prophet's life and his centrality to Muslim traditions most obviously in the terms of haj and hijra. In a sense, they use the examples of the Prophet as a template that both orders their experiences and creates connections between that experience and the Prophet himself.

Many of the senior Bhadala men have been on haj a number of times and would often talk about the experience with the apprentices in their yards. A few of them mentioned to me that haj was the departure point for their own attempts at improving the practices and deeds of Muslims in Kachchh. The obligation of haj is beyond the wherewithal of a great number of Muslims, including most sailors on the Bhadala's fleet. In many parts of the world this has given rise to more affordable local alternatives to which numerous visits may be considered broadly equivalent to haj. As Eickelman suggests this implies an 'integrated vision among believers of "local" religious practices with those of the "central" rituals such as the pilgrimage' (1981: 222). Among my informants there was a clear sense that those without the means to journey to Saudi Arabia could visit select local shrines to fulfil their obligation but the number of visits necessary was never exactly specified to me. The landscape of Kachchh is littered with the shrines of Muslim saints and, as I have shown, their custodians, Saiyeds, receive short shrift at the Mukhdummi Sha meetings. I discuss the reasons for this antipathy at length in the following chapter; however, the Bhadala do not oppose the efficacy of all shrines and actually foster the reputation and image of a select few.

Amid the vast connected network of shrines in India is a complex layering of order premised on the distribution of power and status between various shrines, within which are equally complex hierarchies formed between devotees, disciples and the entombed and their custodians. The Bhadala have separated what they consider to be the wheat from the chaff and have nurtured Mukhdummi Sha as the village saint, Haji Pir in the north-west of Kachchh as the District's saint, and Haji Ali in Bombay as having a galactic power over western India. Travel to these shrines at the annual *urs* (foundation day of the shrine or the birthday of the saint) or at other times when auspiciousness is called for is seen as a pilgrimage of a lesser order replicating the central traditions of homage and devotion seen in the haj.

There is also a converse trend in operation that suggests an inequality between central and local rituals. The haj, and the title 'haji' bestowed upon those making the journey, are clear markers of religious and social differentiation between ship owners and their sailors, between those senior Bhadala men who have never made the journey and those that have, and between those men who have made the journey once and those who have made it more than once. Thus, in certain contexts at least in Salaya, the greater the number of times one has been on haj the greater one's status. The specialist haj travel agents in Bombay sell three or four different priced packages reflecting the comfort and comprehensiveness of the tour.

I sometimes found the sense of implicit competition in Salaya over how much people had paid for their tours rather unbecoming of men in their fifties. For them, the haj gave their bodies opportunity to absorb the sanctity of the pilgrimage sites, to give them more status upon their return home and, at a more profane level, the haj was a form of conspicuous consumption that presented an opportunity of displaying wealth and piety simultaneously.

Apprentices are generally less inclined to see status competition between their masters than they are to see status as unequally distributed through the working hierarchy. For apprentices, the master reflects the upward-spiralling idea that, the more wealth you create, the more you are able to invest in haj, the greater your blessings and reputation for sanctity and wisdom, and, thus, the greater your potential for generating wealth. The voyages of the sailing season (to and from the Gulf States) are also importantly constructed as pilgrimages of a lesser order. Sailors are seen as communing with the sacred populations and atmospheres of the Gulf. This notion obviously relies on a rather vague conception of geography and the location of the sacred sites of Islam, given that sailors mostly spend time in Dubai Creek, but as I discuss further in Chapter 5 'the Gulf', as it is known in the local idiom, is a concept imbued with moral overtones and with the weight of history. Depending somewhat on context, this reflects the way in which the region is imagined by those who have never seen it, a generality in which sailors are complicit when they are at home. Importantly, 'the Gulf' region (not explicitly Saudi Arabia) is also held to be the cradle of Islam, the home of Arabs and the location of the life of Mohammed and his successors. The area is seen as radiating power and as carrying the sacred marks of religious triumph and defeat.

Noormohamed was born in 1956 into a Bhadala family who worked as crew on the ships of wealthier Bhadala families. In his late teens he served in the engine room of a tanker owned by an international petrol company, but he hankered after a life in Kachchh rather than one imprisoned on a tanker by the docks of Rotterdam and Swansea. He returned home to look for work. In the early 1980s, the country craft on which he was then captain was intercepted by a government patrol vessel as it approached Bombay. In port, customs officers found a large quantity of expensive watches concealed beneath the decks in a consignment of dates. Noormohamed took responsibility for the illegal cargo and was jailed for tax evasion and smuggling. When he was released a few years later, the owners of the impounded vessel presented him with a small ship as an expression of their obligation to the loyalty he had shown. The ship was a wreck waiting to happen but it served three seasons at sea, long enough to generate sufficient revenue, along with his savings, to buy another ageing vessel. Noormohamed was eventually forced to place this latest vessel on the dry dock to refit and enlarge it.

It was while this work was under way that I got to know him and he talked of the temporal and spatial conditions of the Bhadala in the terms of hijra. I should mention that Noormohamed was the only Bhadala man to discuss the relationship between Mandvi and Salaya explicitly in these terms, but when I tried out the theory on others they were generally in broad agreement that it was correct. Hijra literally means to 'abandon', 'to break ties with someone' (Masud 1990: 30), but it also relates to a particular form of migration. Primarily, it refers to the Prophet's flight from Mecca to Medina in AD 622. Those who accompanied the Prophet left behind their property and broke their ties with all Muslims and non-Muslims remaining in Mecca (ibid.: 31). This migration is understood as the obligation to move from *dar al-kafir* (also *dar al-harb*, the lands of people who refuse to submit to Allah, non-Muslim lands) to establish *dar al-islam* (Muslim lands, lands of submission). Hijra is thus a spiritual migration, a transition from accommodating authority to resisting it because of a growing realisation of its illegitimacy.

Noormohamed's family had moved from Mandvi to Salaya in 1954, two years before his birth, and he explicitly characterised this move as a passage from *dar al-kafir* to *dar al-Islam*: a spiritual move towards wealth and legitimacy and as a rejection of the dominant social order in Mandvi. Like the majority of Muslims in Gujarat, in principle the Bhadala follow the Hanafi legal school, although they do not often talk about this. Generally, they prefer to simply call themselves 'Sunnis', and by doing so they deny the doctrinal relativity of orthodoxy. However, the fact that they are associated with the Hanafi school has a number of implications for the creation of *dar al-islam* and its relationship to *dar al-kafir*. This tradition stresses the importance of the territory colonised by hijras and the total severance of property relations between *dar al-kafir* (Mandvi) and *dar al-islam* (Salaya). Thus, territory and the maintenance of boundaries are vital in Hanafi conceptions of identity and in the execution of law because a Muslim, who does not migrate from *dar al-kafir*, although a Muslim, is to be governed by the rules of *dar al-kafir*. This is why Hanafis allow transactions in *dar al-kafir* that are not allowed in *dar al-islam* (Masud 1990: 39).

In a very tangible way, Salaya is regarded by both those who live there and those who live away from it as a different kind of place to Mandvi. In Salaya, there are fewer restrictions placed upon the sale and consumption of meat products (stopping short of beef), Friday and religious holidays are observed, the construction of mosques and religious monuments is not strictly subject to the planning laws of the non-believers and the call to prayer is not subject to the same restriction. Understanding the relationship between Mandvi and Salaya in terms of hijra is especially potent as a metaphor of social and religious reform because the migration is replicated by apprentices who originate in *dar al-kafir* but go to work in *dar al-islam*.

In a sense, they are gradually drawn into *dar al-islam* as they are encouraged to attend congregations at Mukhdummi Sha and, eventually, the village's mosques for prayer.

Haj and hijra are both defining realities and metaphors in the lives, practices and rhetoric of the ship owners and their crews. The hijra is an idiom of temporal and social differentiation, a fact reflected in the way religious discourse in Salaya dismisses the practices of those in Mandvi. The haj and the lesser pilgrimages of the shipping season ensure a circulation of people, goods and information between distant ports and the homeland and create complex patterns of status differentiation among seafarers and between seafarers and landlubbers. Hijra is a form of movement derived from the life of the Prophet, as migration from the land of the non-believers to form *dar al-islam*. And, as Barbara Metcalf suggests, the haj allows the pilgrim to 'hone himself to the prophetic model, the person of the Prophet Muhammad, in whose footsteps on this occasion he can literally walk' (1990: 100–101). The haj and the shipping routes enliven the invisible sacred lines that Muslims create towards the land of the Prophet through religious and domestic architecture, prayer and bodily practices.

Having outlined some of the practical skills and affective dispositions apprentices acquire and are subject to in and around the shipyards, I now wish to take the reader to the point I identified earlier where my material parts company with much of the existing literature.

Knowledge and the body

The theories of learning and knowledge I have in mind focus on everyday activity and its constitution in relations between the social system and individual experience. Clearly, my material complements much of the ethnography presented in this literature and shows some of the complexities of learning tasks in a social environment. However, when this literature turns to make broader claims based on its ethnography I find that either I have to leave my informants behind in order to follow the debates or, alternatively, I have to dismiss their knowledge as relative when held up against the claims for universality embodied by much of the literature. What I am interested in here is my informants' understanding of learning and the broader patterns of knowledge and society they draw upon to reach such understanding.

In various ways, the published theories explore the differences between knowledge and narrative and the observable actions these things are supposed to represent. The authors have rightly identified a 'gap' between the two realms and have tried to articulate what happens in it. In other words, they have attempted to identify the psychological or corporeal processes that connect learning activities to the words used to describe it.

Occupying a central place in much of this literature is Pierre Bourdieu's (1977) seminal illustration of how, through learning to be social, habitual dispositions emerge to reflect the acceptance of dominant patterns of ideology, social hierarchy and structure. In order to show this, Bourdieu attempted to create the language and a conceptual space in which the ritual either/or choice between objectivism (read modes of production) and subjectivism (read aspects of practical mastery) could be avoided. His aim, as is well known, was to make possible both an objectively intelligible practice and also an objectively enchanted experience of that practice.

It is never really clear what an objective account of the mode of production would look like given the variety of subjective positions within it or, as in my case, a more general but mutual misunderstanding between the 'objective anthropologist' and the 'indigenous informant' about what is actually being produced.

Those following Bourdieu seemed to have moved further away from his ideal and have increasingly turned the explanations of their ethnographic materials into theories that draw on Western philosophy. They attempt to collapse the problematic dualisms within it that mask the truth, driven largely by the deconstructive paradigm of the 1980s and 1990s in which dualisms were largely seen as theoretical problems. In a well-known series of publications, Jean Lave, for example, has attempted to develop a theoretical paradigm that 'encompasses mind and lived-in world' (1993: 7). For her, any conceptual notion that ratifies the dichotomy between 'mind' and 'body', or 'learning' and 'not learning', is an obstacle in the way of such theory.

My problem with this position is not simply that it differs from the ideas of my informants, who stress that learning is dependent on an ideological division of the person into different constituent parts and that what I think of as learning is, from their perspective, not learning. Indeed, from the perspective of the practice theorist or the developmental psychologist, shipbuilders are probably doing what practice theorists or developmental psychologists think and theorise they are doing. However, my approach is to pursue what my informants, themselves, think they are doing and to compare these ideas with their activities in the wider world. This literally seems to me to be a matter of emphasis rather than critique.

Trevor Marchand's (2001) interpretation of what happens in the 'gap' begins to suggest a way out of the problem I have just discussed. He shows how structured knowledge is inculcated through apprenticeship among minaret builders in Yemen. He suggests that knowledge is not simply 'embodied' and can take many forms depending on the context, task and intention. He also observes similarities between craft apprenticeship and formal religious paths of Sufi learning. The religious path is as follows: *islam* (submission, the embodiment of practice), *iman* (cultivating religious faith, understanding) and *ishan* (intentionality guided by cultivated spiritual faith). I suggest that this is not merely an interesting parallel but that for shipbuilders this path, and the corporeal transformations it evokes, are the fundamentals of their indigenous theory of practice in which the affective nature of habitual dispositions is related to the transformation of bio-moral substances.

Shipyard apprenticeship and the wider world

As Salem was kicked into the bilge, his fall represented something more than simple humiliation. I have already suggested that hierarchy in the shipyards challenges, and to some extent subverts, common patterns of hierarchy outside the shipyards. Inside and outside the shipyards footwear is generally regarded as defiling and polluting, a condition attributed both to the filth of the streets and to the position of the feet at the lowest part of the body. As Salem bowed to touch the feet of the foreman he was acting out his own lowly position in a new hierarchy as well as his lack of knowledge of the language and technology of shipbuilding. Salem was shown simply and effectively that he had much to learn.

In what follows, I briefly set out some of the principles of social hierarchy operating outside the shipyards (in advance of a lengthier discussion in the following chapter) in order to highlight the contrast they absorb with the professional graded ranks inside the shipyards.

Outside the shipyards, 'easy' work of labour and the work of the mind also finds expression in a hierarchical division between types of knowledge, such that *ilm* refers to religious and other scientific knowledge that can be known by the book and cerebral studies; and *maarifa* refers to personal knowledge gained from experience and non-religious knowledge such as craft skills. My informants in the shipyards did not use these terms with me at first but many later agreed, as I sought further clarification, that the terms referred to the same thing, albeit in a more 'proper' (read genteel) form. This division of types of knowledge, in turn, reflects the class division I discussed previously (pp. 31–32) between merchants (now to include scholars and saints) and labourers (now to include slaves, sailors and artisans). Littoral society in Gujarat is primarily composed of these two classes, which encompass the other classificatory distinctions of sect, ethnicity and to some extent 'race'. This division is reflected in distinct residential patterns, as well as in differences between the dominant forms of caste organisation present in each class category. The result is a society broadly composed of mutually dependent yet socially distinct patrons and clients.

Like Rasheed and many of the other apprentices, Salem hails from a well-placed mercantile caste whose family had fallen on hard times. From his family's perspective sailing was a dirty and unfitting profession for people of their standing; less I think because of the type of work than the fact it involved working for the Bhadala ship owners. The oldest Bhadala men, now well into their seventies, had served as sailors on the ships of other mercantile Muslims in the 1940s, including vessels owned by Salem's ancestors. These ship owners mostly left the industry after India's Independence in 1947. The Bhadala continued to run their own small vessels between India and East Africa throughout the 1950s and 1960s, scraping by from trading earthenware and food stuffs with Gujaratis along the African coast. In the 1970s, a small number of Bhadala men fortuitously prospered by trading between the Emirates and India as Dubai developed as a free port. Throughout the 1980s, they increased the size of the ships, which in some cases became fleets, and with their new-found wealth they consumed lavishly and invested in the mosques and other symbols of piety scattered throughout their settlement.

Their success, however, has not met with a generally accepted rise in their status and, as is the fate of many nouveau riche, in the eyes of many Muslims they remain uncultivated and of low status. I now turn to the question of why their undeniable success has not lessened their reputation as halfwits.

Mckim Marriott and a number of others writing after him on corporality and society in South Asia (Marriott 1976; Marriott and Inden 1977; McGilvray 1982) have suggested that actions, such as profession and speech, and intangible influences, such as perception, desire and posture, embody and convey essential qualities or 'substance-codes', which act against each other to continually transform the (in)dividual and, in a more general sense, the caste body. From this perspective, all combinations of substances and codes make up a continuous and graded series of beings ranging from the divine through the human to the immoral and the inanimate. Similarly, for many of my informants, the Muslim body is the conjunction of 'reproduction' (as physiology) and 'morality' (as part of the physiological condition) in particular 'bio-moral' combinations. Here, too, there is a tension between what is thought to be given by descent and parentage and what are understood as the possibilities for corporeal transformation through certain kinds of actions in life.

As I discussed above (pp. 75 and 78) in relation to haj and other kinds of pilgrimage the moral persons of seafarers can be transformed through their associations with particular places and their ability to absorb either positive or negative aspects of their history and sociality – especially those places that have a significant role in their interpretations of Muslim social history (also Simpson 2003). In a more specific sense, this model of code and substance has a genealogical inflection. Substance is provided by inherited blood, which provides propensity for certain kinds of action; action modifies substance within the limits of the dictates of that substance. The mechanisms of this relationship are explained in an explicitly Islamic idiom. People are formed from a soul (*ruh*) of two hierarchically ordered elements: a lower level (*nafs*), dictates desires, potential for violence and other base instincts, and a higher level (*aql*) determines intellectual, spiritual and moral faculties. Together, various combinations of these levels act against each other to form human mind and body actions. More generally, the distribution of these elements determines the attributes of the caste body and of the distribution of castes in a loosely ranked hierarchy within the encompassing division between merchants and labourers.

Broadly speaking, high-ranking mercantile Muslims are seen as having a greater proportion of *aql* and a propensity towards *ilm* as discrimination, discernment, commerce and the Prophetic ideal, which outside the shipyards finds ultimate expression in *barakat* (spiritual efficacy and abundance) of local saints, a matter to which I return below. Conversely, those who are *nafs* heavy, so to speak, are seen as having a propensity towards *maarifa* and base appetites, personal indulgence and physical labour. Those with the highest concentrations of *nafs* are considered to be 'hot', while those laden with *aql* are considered to be 'cool'. Purity of the soul is thought to be guaranteed by generations of endogamous marriages, preserving the qualities of putative ancestors of repute. Conversely, exogamy of varying degrees is seen as enlivening the base elements of the soul. In short, the Bhadala do not fare well in this hierarchy and are seen as among the most corporeally corrupt and thus hot-headed of people. I return to this matter in the following chapter.

Parry has suggested that underlying Marriot's representation of the person is a Marxian ideology in the classic sense because it actually sustains and reinforces the static ideology of caste as a symbolic elaboration of the louring disorder which creates and sustains the world of order and regulation (1994: 114–115). This is arguably also the case for the way in which I have represented the Muslim body. Therefore, as Parry also suggests, vigilance is required to uphold the purity of the body and the larger bodies of caste and kin; the best way to ensure this is through the maintenance of tried and tested patterns of hierarchical caste interactions in order to postpone chaos and disintegration.

Given this characterisation of bodies as forms of ideology, it becomes reasonable to ask: how can a sailor be meritoriously transformed through his association with particular places, such as the sites of pilgrimage if this model also explains caste hierarchy as a distribution of different sets of people with a given nature? How can hot-headed sailors make fortunes from mercantile endeavour, which, within the terms of the model, is impossible if not to say an abomination? I tend not to see these questions as responses to existential contradictions but as *the* challenges apprentices are forced to face in the setting of the highly unequal power relations that form the backdrop to the minutiae of their labour.

Inside the shipyards, clearly, as the Bhadala transformed from humble sailors to wealthy merchants, the idea that propensities towards action in the world were fixed at birth could not be used by them with any credibility to explain their evident success. Today, they quite simply tell their apprentices that if they work hard and discipline themselves through their craft and routines of prayer then they, too, stand a chance of becoming ship owners – however improbable this promise might actually be. This does not simply present the apprentice with the choice of belief in either things being given at birth or things being alterable in life; rather, the two sets of concepts dichotomise his body and give the apprentice licence to act in different ways, for argument's sake, inside and outside the shipyard – although it is never as simple as that because the important questions of belief, loyalty, ambition and material needs tend to blur the distinction.

Such conflicting conceptions of individual propensity and potentiality are not simply matters of philosophical curiosity or corporal confusion; the conflict resonates with the competing concerns of traditionalist and reformist Islam in South Asia generally and in Kachchh in particular. Outside the shipyards, the apical social figures are the saints (Saiyeds), descendants of the Prophet. Their miraculous powers are given by their condition at birth determined by their genealogy. They are the measure against which the corporeal natures of others are ranked. In many cases, Saiyeds act as intermediaries between man and Allah and between man and the blessings of their own deceased ancestors. This role has long been the target of reformers in South Asia who stress the direct nature of the relationship between man and Allah over the corrupt nature of intermediaries.

The Saiyed is thus the most visible mark of a hierarchy in which the Bhadala have little chance of mobility. Therefore, inside the shipyards, where the Bhadala is master, the Saiyed is not given a place. The Saiyeds who function as intermediaries, to whom many apprentices and their families are inextricably bound, are simply dismissed as fraudsters. The Bhadala have drawn upon the idioms of reform as a persuasive way of denying the dominant conditions of corporeality within that hierarchy and as a way of creating alternative patterns of status through the redefinition of legitimate religious practice. Put in rather stark terms, apprentices are drawn largely from a social world that is ordered around the symbolic gravity and ritual practices of the saints towards a world in which the Bhadala master pays their wages, holds their future in his hands, built the mosque where the apprentice is encouraged to pray, and who tells his workforce not to patronise the saints they have been devoted to since birth. There are as many uneasy resolutions to this tug of loyalties as there are apprentices, but those who stay in the service of the Bhadala, especially after they have spent time in the ports of the Emirates and made money from private trade, tend to quietly (so as not to cause offence to their families) distance themselves from the intimacies of the cult of saints (so as not to cause offence to their new masters).

The affective dispositions of the apprentice's labour thus have many varied social implications that also have life outside the shipyards. Conversely, the affective dispositions the apprentice has previously learned in other contexts also play a role in his expectations of what will occur in the shipyards. This point returns us to the parallel outlined by Marchand (2001) between craft apprenticeship and structured paths of Sufi learning. This path places the initiand (in the Gujarat case known as a *murid*) under the tutelage of a Saiyed who ideally guides the student through the stages of *islam* (submission, the embodiment of practice), *iman* (cultivating religious faith, understanding) and *ishan* (intentionality guided by cultivated spiritual faith). The relationship between master and novice is structured around conceptions of learning in which the internal self is transformed through external actions. The principal idiom of personal transformation is that of habit (*adat*) through which the constituent parts of the soul, as outlined above, are transformed. Upon pledging loyalty (*baia*) the novice enters a dual process of scrutinising his faults (and attempting to remove them) and his virtues (and attempting to improve on them). The student internalises the image of perfection represented by his master through recitation, prayer and study. Metcalf has also observed a similar parallel between craft and religious learning. She writes: 'whether one is learning a craft, or poetry and language, or music, or moral and spiritual qualities, the process of outer practice, the creation of habit, and finally a realisation of that process in one's being is precisely the same' (1984: 11). It strikes me, however, that the analogy could be cast slightly differently and that this model of learning through unequal social relations, and the patterns of paternalism, respect and deference this entails, are seen in all aspects of Muslim society in western India and not just in spiritual and craft contexts, although they are perhaps most visible there.

There are five elaborate shrines in Mandvi with resident Saiyed custodians and numerous other less developed sites. Most families of the non-Bhadala workforce in the shipyards have some connection to at least one of these shrines. For many of the shipyard apprentices, their earliest experiences of formal education were in such shrines, where they may have attended Quran reading or literacy classes. While the rules for interaction between masters and students are most clearly defined between a Saiyed and his initiated *murids*, boys attending the shrines for classes or to play in the cool gardens are expected to respect the attendant Saiyeds in a similar fashion. The son of the last Saiyed to occupy the *gadi* (throne, seat of power) of one of these shrines outlined the rules they tried to impress upon their young charges. They had to address the master respectfully, to face him and not to expose the soles of their feet if seated before him. They were not to cast a shadow on his body or prayer mat. They were forbidden from using his utensils and his place of ablution. They were to be quiet and not speak with others in his presence, leave him without permission or contradict him in any way. The boys were also strongly encouraged to remain loyal to one particular shrine and not to visit others; they were also supposed to abandon any prayers or rituals they knew that were not approved parts of the ritual cycles of the shrine.

This model of learning and the associated forms of respect and obedience continues almost seamlessly into shipyard apprenticeship with all of these ideas finding expression in one form or another. There is, however, one fundamental difference, which again reflects the conflict between the idea that the limits to human action are given at birth and the idea that things are utterly alterable in life. The *murid* knows that he will never become a Saiyed due to his ignoble birth; the apprentice in the shipyard *knows* (because he is repeatedly told) that it is possible for him to become a ship owner.

As we have seen, the relationship between an apprentice and his master is a cumulative one that depends on the disparities between his behaviour and that expected of him by his master decreasing over time. The relationships that construct the shipping hierarchy may be structured by the agendas of those that control the capital, but they are also reinforced by the long-term ambitions of the apprentice. The transformation of apprentices, therefore, stems not only from competition among sailors for scarce positions within the crew, but is part and parcel of the expectations apprentices have before they arrive in shipyards.

Conclusion

Apprentices in shipyards learn how to move cross-members and erect scaffolding. While they are occupied in such activities they are subject to, and engage with, other ideas about the world. Gradually, the apprentice is transformed internally from novice to habitué as habit becomes habitude. Through this process they experience the dichotomisation of thought and practice in relation to established patterns of behaviour as Muslims. Their labour is premised on distinctions between essences. The soul is of two parts: one (*nafs*) is related more intimately to the body (*jism*) and the other to the higher levels of intellectual and moral faculties (*aql*) of the mind. The result is a closely related triad of body (incorporating mind as an aspect) and dialectical soul. Outside the yards, this model is heavily oriented towards a genealogical inflection: men are born to a limited range of things because of their ancestry. However, inside the shipyards, apprentices are literally told that the perfection of labour can allow them to become merchants as the possibilities for action are transformed over the course of a lifetime. In sum, apprentices learn to avoid the unpleasant consequences of not learning, to become different, wealthier kinds of people and to tread the delicate path of maturity, as they see it, where mastery of the salient physical world leads to mental alacrity, spiritual acumen and material bounty. To my mind, this is no less an ideology than that of the body with a genealogical inflection as represented by the Saiyed. The idea of the protean body binds apprentices to their labour and pitches the short-term cycles of exchange (apprenticeship) against the longer-term cycles of social reproduction and power (reformist stances against the prevailing orthodoxies).

The distinctions made here between 'merchants' and 'sailors' and 'soul' and 'body' are potent categories into which the world is divided. These dualisms are not natural facts and are clearly highly contested. However, the range of their possibilities is dictated by the historical conditions of trade and the division of labour within this trade. And, in this sense, apprenticeship and the indigenous theory of practice, which explains what happens in the gap between action and description, is the path along which apprentices come to understand power by ascribing its purpose to their most mundane activities while, importantly, being made aware of this fact in other contexts.

Apprentices from Mandvi find their conceptions of what constitutes 'being Muslim' and 'being in a hierarchy' at variance with the images projected by their new employers. They are encouraged to renounce their lackadaisical approach to prayer, their relationships with supernatural inter-mediaries and the use of ritualistic paraphernalia. They also learn that Hindus and Mandvi's Muslims are bound in a temporal and spatial model, in which their own families are only halfway along a trajectory of progressive evolution between Hindus at the base and the Bhadala at the local pinnacle. The rhetoric of their masters' reform isolates Hindus and other Muslims as subjects deserving of scrutiny and as objects around which reform is structured. The following two chapters explore in more detail why this should be so.

3

REFORM AND STATUS COMPETITION BETWEEN MUSLIMS

This chapter examines the substance and content of religious reform as an expression of status competition between Sunni Muslims. In the previous chapter, I discussed how the performances of ritual, festivity and prayer among Mandvi's Muslims were taken up during religious discourses in Salaya as illustrations of corrupt forms of religious practice. In particular, some Saiyeds (putative descendants of the Prophet) were singled out as professional magic men, as repositories of archaic superstitions, beggars and as 'Muslim Brahmans'. Religious reform is often defined as much by what it opposes as by what it represents and, without sparing the blushes of their workforce, the Bhadala accuse those occupying high-status positions in Mandvi of decadence, and by doing so create a mark against which to position their own suitable standards of behaviour (*adab*) and interpretation of the *sunnah*. Although the language of antipathy towards Saiyeds might appear to be a simple quarrel over definitions of legitimate religious practice, as I suggested in the previous chapter, underlying this is an implicit attack on the traditional conceptions of the body, as a conjunction of reproduction, morality and genealogical inflection, which traditionally sustained a hierarchy that continues to subjugate the Bhadala. By dismissing a society that subordinates them as heretical and corrupt they are attempting to overturn the social order and to lead their crews into less treacherous waters, where they will take a firm grasp on the helm, as it were, and claim their rightful place at the captain's table.

Mandvi's Muslims claim to be descendants of mercenaries, slaves, traders, saints and warriors, including the armies of Alexander the Great. As with the Hindu population, there are no claims of autochthony. Their origins, in a broad westerly sweep, range from mainland Gujarat, Rajasthan, Uttar Pradesh, Punjab and Sind, to Afghanistan, Uzbekistan, Iran, 'Arabia' and 'Africa'. Somewhat ideally, and most apparent in the standard narratives about identity, social differentiation in Mandvi is traced to the putative geographical origin of the putative primogenitor of a particular lineage or marriage group. Not all places around the Indian Ocean have produced equal kinds of people and some places have produced better people than others. However, once a place has produced a particular kind of person, the qualities they embody are mobile and can be carried to other places and passed to future generations. The population is ordered on the basis of movement and exchange across the Indian Ocean and on how different geographical areas with different kinds of history are associated with the emergence of particular kinds of transportable human quiddities, or essences, which are susceptible to transformation through particular kinds of marriage practices. This is similar to what William Shepard (1987) has termed 'historical connectedness' – a genealogical reflex that is ideally represented by an unbroken chain of people (*isnad*) to later generations to the Prophet and his companions. The higher levels of the hierarchy in Mandvi claim such historical connections, and the degrees of distance from this ideal order the whole encompassing hierarchy. Overall, sacred connections (blood as substance and geographical association) and the 'pedigree' of lineages are the resources of social order. The Bhadala fall short in terms of both connections and lineages and thus occupy lowly status positions.

To put the basis of this hierarchy in the bluntest possible terms, those placed well within the hierarchy regard those in the lower orders quite literally as mongrels. I was often surprised and shocked to hear my friends in Salaya described in such terms in Mandvi. People in the town would tell me with utmost confidence how those in Salaya were 'ignorant blacks' and 'vulgar monsters' whose 'bodies had taken over their minds'. Others similarly regarded in the terms of the hierarchy who are unhappy with their lot may covet the connections claimed by the elite and the ideal of a coherent and unbroken lineage in a broader sense. However, in the short term at least, appropriating or inventing suitable traditions is not effective as a vehicle of social mobility. The Bhadala have utilised another method, which both questions the basis of hierarchy from the outside and plants voices of dissent within. The first half of the chapter describes the hierarchy, its nobles and mongrels; the second the structures of antipathy and method used by the Bhadala.

Muslims in Indian society

Anthropological literature on Muslims has tended to explain social and religious hierarchies either as a form of parochialism or as a result of the corrosive influence of other religious or folk beliefs. However, it no longer seems tenable to dismiss 'Muslims' in Gujarat as ignorant of the basic tenets of their faith (as in Pocock 1972: 44), when they define themselves as Muslims and, importantly in the contemporary political climate, are defined as such by Hindus, government surveys and rioting mobs. If the view is taken that there can be a consistently pragmatic relationship between textual theocracy and social action, then hierarchical social organisation among

Muslims may appear to contradict the basic tenets of the faith. The ethnographic evidence, however, supports the common sense view that interpretations of texts vary from place to place and that the interpretive process and its implications for social action can also take many forms (Das 1984). In order to escape the tension between the dictates of authoritative text and actual practices, this chapter focuses on Muslim social organisation 'as it is not as it should be', to use Francis Robinson's (1983: 155) apt phrase.

Many scholars of Muslim societies in South Asia have noted differentiated, loosely ranked and named social groups that display a tendency for endogamous marriage. Such findings inevitably provoked the following questions. Do Muslims have hierarchical caste systems? If so, how are they organised? The debates were most clearly led by Louis Dumont (1980), Fredrik Barth (1960) and Imtiaz Ahmad (1978) and focused on the relationship between Muslim and Hindu forms of hierarchy (and also Lindholm 1986; Vatuk 1996; Werbner 1989). Consequently, contributions were mainly concerned with commentary on the 'theory of caste', and, in the process, the ethnography seems to have been drained of its 'local colour' (also an apt phrase), becoming mere grist for theoretical mills. Writing on Gujarat in the 1960s, Satish Misra suggested the Muslim system developed in a 'symbiotic relationship' with the Hindu caste system and thus had become part of the whole (1964: 132) and 'no distinction as such is felt to exist between the Hindu and the Muslim configurations for both are capable of being described with the same word [*nyat*]' (1964: 139). In contrast, Mattison Mines (1975) claims Muslim social hierarchy in Tamil Nadu is not comparable to the Hindu caste structure because ranking occurs predominantly at the level of the individual (in terms of age, wealth and religiosity) and not at a wider social level. Others have argued that Muslims are socially ranked, but that ranking is not based on an overall logic comparable to that underlying Hindu caste systems because there is a lack of 'integrative ideology' (read purity and pollution) to account for ontological differences between men (Barnett *et al.* 1976); rather, they suggest, Muslims have 'fluid systems of stratification' based upon male occupation, residential locality, women's rituals and the occupation of in-marrying women's brothers and fathers. Furthermore, they argue that Islam (by which they appear to mean texts) proclaims the equality of all men before Allah, admitting neither hereditary privileges nor professional intermediaries. Evidence of such equality, they suggest, can be seen in joint prayers, intermarriage and commensual relations between groups. And, as Muslims do not separate status from power as Dumont's (1980) *Homo hierarchicus* does, social mobility, as a form of class mobility, is possible regardless of social position at birth.

Is it really the case that individual ranking takes precedence over aggregate ranks and that there is no conception of purity and pollution in Muslim communities? In parts of Calcutta, for example, it has been reported that Muslims emphasise purity of descent, evident in the use of terms such as *sudh* (pure) and *birre* (impure, mixed descent) to refer to the condition of a group's descent and its hierarchical position within society (Siddiqui 1978: 258). Therefore, it seems safe to assume, here at least, that prioritising purity of descent presupposes that a violation of governing lineage principles results in accumulative 'impurity'. Similarly, Muslims in Ranchi are reported to hold that inter-ethnic marriages result in impure offspring (Ali 1978: 26). From this example, we can further assume that mixing 'ethnic' identity in marriage results in the degradation of the progeny's blood. Additionally, Muslims of Old Delhi are organised into *biraderis* ('one body') and are socially governed by principles of purity of blood and bone in terms of descent, which in turn determines *adat* (habit, behaviour, custom) as occupation and character (Goodfriend 1983: 121–122). In this case, purity of blood and descent is viewed as the basis for particular kinds of behaviour. A further example from Tamil Nadu indicates that more general traits and dispositions are also transmitted through blood. Tamil Nawwayats desire to marry among themselves in order to 'maintain the blood' and to 'preserve the pedigree'. Blood transmits 'qualities': morality, ability and physical traits, which can be lost or diluted through admixture (Vatuk 1996: 245). While suggesting the qualities ascribed to particular kinds of blood are important idioms for understanding descent, these examples also cast some doubt over the idea that social mobility occurs at the level of the individual, and that social equality is unambiguous at birth and that intermarriage between Muslims is a reflection of such equality.

A second theme in the literature on Indian Muslims addresses social differentiation based on claims to 'foreign' and 'indigenous' origins (or more-or-less so) and a division between those who came to India as Muslims and those who converted to Islam *in situ*. In many studies these divisions are loosely described and it is noted that those claiming foreign origins are of high status, those who claim to be from the lands immediately to the west of the Indus are of medium to high status, and those who claim indigenous origins are of middle to low status (see, for example, Goodfriend 1983). These facts are seldom elaborated and are commonly explained by the distinction between *ashrafs* (nobles, Saiyeds, Shaikhs, Mughals and Pathans in Assayag (2004: 43) and Metcalf (2005: 239)) and *ajhlaf* (commoners); or, alternatively, these distinctions are simply passed off as fanciful. Of the studies mentioned above, only Misra placed any emphasis on the concept of 'race' as an organising principle. He claimed, however, that it has lost its potency as the defining feature of social hierarchy in Gujarat (but see below). This, he explained, was because the growth of 'caste-like' organisations led to the development of inward oriented ceremonial tendencies within particular communities (Misra 1964:

138). Thus, the autonomy of the 'caste-like groupings' excludes the possibility of coherent hierarchical exchange relationships and, in the non-ceremonial sphere, wealth and economic standing play a crucial role.

While the examples discussed above clearly suggest that pure-blooded and mixed-blood populations are ranked, we are not as yet given a clear understanding of which qualities and descent lines may rank above others or why it is desirable that these descent lines should be maintained in a pure condition. In an eloquent essay, Bernard Lewis (1971) sketches a history of dominant Muslim (Arab) attitudes towards race and colour. He argues that there is no sense of discrimination on the basis of race evident in the Quran, and the Hadiths prohibiting Arabs from marrying blacks and some others were written much later in a different political and economic climate. Yet, there is clearly a racial hierarchy at work in Islam as a world religion and Lewis sets about describing its emergence. He outlines two general points of historical note that I submit to ethnographic scrutiny in what follows. First, in the early years of Islam, 'Arab' and 'Muslim' were synonymous, or at least all Muslims were Arabs. As Islam spread after the death of the Prophet, new converts emerged who became Muslim but were not Arab. Not always, but very often, these new converts were conquered and among them the Arabs retained a position of privilege. Second, in time and through slavery, judicial distinctions between different kinds of people emerged and black skin became equated primarily with servitude after the possession of white slaves in Arab lands declined. In the early Islamic period, Arabs looked down on the sons of slave mothers whether they were white or black, as the stigma was attached to the status and not to the race of the mother. Over the course of the following centuries, a distinctive colour prejudice emerged and the association of blackness with slavery and whiteness with freedom and nobility became common.

Thus, there is a historical separation of Arab from non-Arab, of Muslim from non-Muslim and of freeman from slave (also see Ahmad 1978: 14–15). Lewis also suggests that the stigma attached to being a non-Muslim or a slave is erased after three generations from conversion or freedom. However, there is, of course, no possibility that a non-Arab will become an Arab after three generations, unless they move to a place where they are unknown and once there claim to be so. Lewis points out that the manumitted slave of a non-Arab owner is not the equal of the manumitted slave-girl of an Arab owner (1971: 91). The fundamental distinction between Arab and non-Arab is further complicated by the 'miscegenation' of Arab Muslims and their non-Arab concubines. A pure-blooded Arab, whether a freeman or not, remains superior to slaves or freemen of non-Arab fathers, a distinction that can be made all the more obvious by skin colour. This suggests that an integrative ideology perhaps developed around the history of economic and material domination that Lewis documents, because in what ways is an impoverished Arab superior to a successful and wealthy freeman of mixed descent?

In Hanafi law the concept of *kifaa* refers to the equality of birth and social status in marriage. Suitable partners (and their families) thus should ideally share Islam, free status, financial compatibility, complementary reputations for rectitude and piety, occupations and comparable lineages. As we have seen, in the same legal tradition 'freedom' and 'Islam' can be obtained in a general population after three generations and wealth and reputation are transient matters of social contingency. The relationship between descent and status, however, is another matter because descent is less malleable and suggests an essential component of status with a greater temporal fixity. Misra noted that the doctrine of *kifaa* 'buttressed the strong family system and race-consciousness in Gujarat' (1964: 131), suggesting that 'race' was a key marker of descent. The ethnography of the following section firmly supports this now rather aged claim but, more importantly for the general argument of the study, shows that contrary to Barnett and his colleagues (1976) there can be a clear separation of status and power among Muslims based on hereditary privileges in a broad sense. I suggest Muslim society in Mandvi (and again I stress this is most clearly so in the standard narratives on identity and social difference to which I return in the middle sections of this chapter) is ordered by legacies of race, colour, conversion and, above all, descent. Despite considerable variance in the form of castes as well as in the methods of their systems of classification, 'Arabs' are ranked in relation to one another in ways that differ slightly from the general population of 'non-Arabs' but, nevertheless, non-Arab, part-Arab, mixed and slavish descent groups are also ranked in relation to one another. The data are not genotypic; rather, what I am presenting here is the sociology of claims to particular kinds of ancestors and origins.

Historical connectedness and *jamat*

Commerce, Partition and the allure of the metropolis have undoubtedly reduced the significance of the Muslim population in Kachchh since the early nineteenth century when MacMurdo (1820a: 233) wrote that they formed half of the population. Today, I estimate in the absence of concrete data that between a quarter and a third of Mandvi's population are Muslims. In the town the term *jati* is commonly used to describe social division; it corresponds to the taxonomic metaphor of 'family' or 'kind'. The term is often translated as 'caste' (Misra 1964: 139) but is more accurately thought of as 'type' and has a remarkably broad range of applications, from 'black' to 'white', 'Indian' to 'African' and 'Muslim' to 'Hindu'. Muslims commonly use *jati* (type, caste) as a classificatory term both as a descriptive adjective for the social and physical qualities of a caste and as a noun connoting a specific section of the population. In neither case is it used as mere stereotype, but as reflecting a corporeal and spiritual condition. Muslims also use the term *jamat* to describe different levels of inclusion and exclusion. This term can be used to refer to different levels of social segmentation such as occupational groups, castes or, indeed, the global reach of Muslim societies. However, the term is also the name given to Muslim caste-like organisations, in the sense of bodies of hereditary or elected representatives who manage internal disputes, funds, charitable work and, in many cases, communal buildings and institutions.

There are three dominant kinds of social organisation among Muslims in the town. The higher-ranking Muslims tend to have little in the way of formal organisational structures. These groups tend to be in competition with each other to provide spiritual or judicial services to the lower ranks and as a way of maintaining their allure, reputation and clientele, and tend to treat their caste fellows as rivals rather than as part of a potential community. Competition notwithstanding, they intermarry and, on occasion, coalesce around particular political or material issues. The second type I choose to call 'proprietary *jamats*'. These are corporate groups that maintain collective identities, such as names, place of origin and customs. Some are well organised and have communal institutions and elaborate community codes. The third type is the 'non-proprietary *jamat*' (the inferior kind), which are of 'mixed blood' and are composed of groups of diverse origins subsumed by a corporate *jamat*. The groups within non-proprietary *jamats* retain different symbolic identities, again in the form of names, places of origin and customs.

All three types vary considerably in their composition and may be variously composed of people who share the same traditional occupation, current occupation, ethnicity and regional origin, or of those who respect the authority of a particular shrine or framework for social administration and jurisprudence. Sometimes some of these conditions coincide. The membership is generally determined by birth. In life, an individual may reflect the identity of their *jamat* through the distinctive use of language, dress, diet, ritual spaces and particular kinship terminology and practices. At the proprietary level they are often represented by social institutions, which may include mosques, schools and meeting halls. Although most *jamats* are ideally endogamous, the ideals of endogamy vary considerably between them. A *jamat* can function as a marriage circle; however, given the widespread preference for patrilateral parallel cousin marriage, a *jamat* can also be an association of lineages with each being for the most part endogamous. Inter-*jamat* and polygamous marriages are rare. Members of particular *jamats* tend to live in clusters around their communal institutions or in specific areas of the town. Upon death, the body is buried in a *jamat*-specific cemetery or in a *jamat*-specific section of a general Sunni cemetery.

All *jamats* are comprised of a number of patrilineal descent groups (sing. *atak*, also *nasb* or *biraderi*) named after apical ancestors or particular places of origin. If a *jamat* is of a proprietary type then the lineages within it will ideally be fragments of a maximal lineage, claiming descent from a particular descendant of the original figure. When lineages divide, it is normal for a segment to adopt the name of the apical living male figure. However, it is common to hear the explanation: 'although we are called *this* we are really *that*'; the 'that' claim invariably creates an association with the maximal lineage. Some lineages can trace common descent in Mandvi and among closely related populations in Bombay or overseas. The more expansive lineages may have many distant representatives that share names, and possibly affinity, but who are unable to trace common descent ties. If the *jamat* is of the non-proprietary type then such relationships are not necessarily present and it is common for lineages within a non-proprietary *jamat* to have entirely different ancestors and, indeed, different origin myths. Within *jamats* the ordering of lineages reflects the logic of *jamat* hierarchy outlined below. However, in the case of proprietary *jamats* the differences between the highest ranking and lowest ranking lineages are small compared with the overall range of the *jamat* hierarchy. In the case of the non-proprietary *jamats*, this range tends to be greater than among the proprietary *jamats*. In both cases, however, lineages within particular *jamats* are ranked in relation to lineages of other *jamats* only in relation to the relative position of their *jamat* and not the relative status of a particular lineage.

I cannot pretend that the following classification includes or accurately describes the social positions of all Muslims in the town because there are also migrant professionals, bureaucrats and artisans from other parts of India, the ostracised and those who may belong to pan-Kachchh, pan-Gujarat or pan-India associations that have no formal representation in Mandvi. However, Muslims in Mandvi can rank these *jamats* with reasonable consistency (for parallels see Jain 1978; Siddiqui 1978). There are eight high-ranking groups with no formal *jamat* organisations, fifteen *jamats* formed as proprietary *jamats* of varying size and degree of organisation, and three low-ranking non-proprietary *jamat* groups. The highest ranking *jamats* claim foreign origins but do not have formal *jamat*-type community organisations. Saiyeds hold the apical position on the basis of the claim that they are descendants of the Prophet through Fatima (the Prophet's daughter) and Ali (the Prophet's first cousin). The dominant Saiyed lineages trace this descent back through the well-known sixteenth-century preacher Jalaludin Surkh Bukhari and the twelfth-century preacher and mystic Abdul Qadir Jilani of Baghdad. They are followed by *jamats* known as Quresh and Ansar, the putative descendants of the companions of the Prophet. Below them are two *jamats* of broadly equivalent rank, Arab and Sheikh, who, as their names suggest, also claim historical connections to the birthplace of Islam. The next layer is of three *jamats* claiming noble origins derived from positions of high rank in the Mogul administration or within the ruling dynasties of Sind: Baluchi, Mogul and Munshi. Below these groups, unless otherwise stated, all groups claim to originate from Sind and are indigenous converts to Islam. The upper-middle section of the hierarchy is occupied by the proprietary *jamat*-type commercial *jamats*, Memon and Khatri, and Pathan who claim to have come as warriors and traders from the North of Pakistan and Afghanistan. The middle and middle-to-lower sections of the hierarchy are dominated by proprietary *jamats* of artisans and agriculturalists, the aristocracy of labour: Kumbhar (potters), Lohar (metalworkers), Agriya (agriculturalists from northern India), Dhobi (washermen), Ghanchi ('oil pressers' from 'Gujarat'), Hazam (barbers) and Jat (agriculturalists). The lower section of the hierarchy is also comprised of proprietary *jamats* with clear organisational structures but no obvious communal institutions. Generally, their names suggest relationships to various rulers of Sind; namely, Mir, Miyana, Sangar, Sama and Sumara. Below them are three non-proprietary *jamats*: Bakali, Bhadala and Laskri. At the bottom of the heap are Siddi (Basu 1993, 1998), descendants of black Africans; among them is a division between those who were brought from south-east Africa as slaves in the eighteenth and nineteenth centuries and those who claim to have come from Abyssinia as mercenaries for the Rajput kingdoms of western India.

This hierarchy is a division of labour with, in descending order, ritual specialists, theologians, merchants, administrators, warriors, craftsmen, agriculturalists and labourers ranking over slave populations. However, this hierarchy also ranks putative regional origins with those from the Arabian Peninsula at the apex followed by those from Iran, Central Asia, South Asia and, finally, from Africa. I suggest this is a reflection, first, of the earlier discussion on the transformation of status to 'race' as a ranking principle and the primacy of the Arab peoples in the history of Islam and, second, of a sense of historical connectedness to the era of the Quran and its personalities who were named by Allah. Those claiming Arab descent are ranked in relation to one another and the general population of non-Arabs; non-Arab, part Arab, mixed and slavish descent groups are also ranked in relation to one another. Social order in the town reflects in many ways the social hierarchy of Islam as a world religion with race, history, nobility and slaves all playing their part. Over the centuries littoral society welcomed and bade farewell to visitors; the legacy is a highly mixed population within which such order found a happy home. Perceptions of the past, place and segmentary genealogy provide a measure against which the realities of descent can be measured and graded.

Substance, purity and pollution

There is a broad consensus among my informants that Muslim conceptions of purity (*pak*) and impurity (*napak*) are of two orders. One form of impurity is transient, derived from bodily processes (urination, menstruation, birth and death), that can be removed by acts of purification (also Barth 1960: 139). Generally, bodily products originating above the neck are regarded as pure, while those from below the neck such as urine, sexual fluids and growing pubic hair are seen as impure. These sources of impurity relate to the outside of a person, to the hygiene and the tangible ritual and social purity of a body. The second order of impurity is more fundamental and relates to blood, as substance, and the bio-moral combinations it sustains. Blood can, therefore, be pure and impure as well as the array of conditions in between the two extremes, which broadly reflects the distribution of *jamats* through the hierarchy.

The purity of blood is measured against the example of the Prophet, considered the most perfect of all created beings. Although Saiyeds are never seen as the equal of the Prophet, they are only second best and their blood and corresponding potential for learning, knowledge, discernment and *adab* (as *they* define it) are held in the highest esteem. Conversely, at the other end of the spectrum, impurity is generated through the progeny of mixed marriages across the broad range of possibilities subsumed under the term *jati*. 'Miscegenation' is thus a violation of the segmentary principles that maintain order and is seen in a negative light to a greater or lesser degree at every level of social segmentation. *Jati*, as I have suggested, is a broad taxonomic classificatory system in which the *jamats* and lineages are of the same but lesser categorical order. The lowest ranking non-African Muslims are the non-proprietary *jamats* of which the Bhadala are one of three. These are comprised of lineages claiming several different geographic, racial and ethnic origins that have united under the banner of a single *jamat*. Among the Bhadala, for example, there are intermarrying lineages with names that link them to modern Turkmenistan, Afghanistan, Pakistan, other parts of India and Africa. Similarly, the 'Laskri (soldier, in the sense of lascar) *Jamat*', for example, is an amalgamation of three Sindi *jamats* whose numbers were depleted with overseas migration and with the departure of many Muslims for Sind at the time of Partition. The *jamat* is comprised of eight distinct Sindi Rajput descent groups, a number of the thirty-six Suma descent lines found in Mandvi, and Turks (those claiming to originate from Turkmenistan), Pathans, Kachchhi Qureshis and Kachchhi Sheikhs. In some regards the Laskri *Jamat* represents the entire hierarchy within the boundaries of a single *jamat*. The latter two groups carry the appellation 'Kachchhi' as they claim prestigious and pious origins, but the claims are treated with suspicion (see below). Both Bhadala and Laskri *jamats*, however, in the terms of the dominant logic hierarchy, are an organised form of miscegenation, which violates the ideal and natural boundaries of a group of people in the same descent line.

Many of the names I have given as *jamat* names are also found as lineage names within other *jamats*. For example, there are four groups of Pathans in Mandvi: the high-ranking proprietary 'Pathan *Jamat*', two high-ranking lineages in the low-ranking, non-proprietary Bhadala and Laskri *jamats*; and a lowly group of only a few families who did not claim allegiance to any of the above. As Pathans, they are linked by shared ideas of a common past that saw them migrate from the north-west of the sub-continent into Kachchh as warriors and traders. However, they are hierarchically ordered in such a way that economic circumstances and their position within the social hierarchy do not equate. Within the proprietary *jamat* of Pathans there are a series of endogamous lineages, which, at the highest level of segmentation, claim a common ancestor, place of origin and origin myths. These Pathans are of the highest rank because their essence is regarded quite literally as being closest to the 'original'. Today, they are endogamous, reflecting the ideal that *jamat* boundaries are, ideally, inviolate. Within the low-ranking, non-proprietary *jamats*, such as the 'Laskri *Jamat*' and the 'Bhadala *Jamat*', there are endogamous and exogamous lineages claiming diverse ethnic and regional backgrounds, which are accompanied by different origin myths, dress and ritual customs. Although both *jamats* are endogamous, they are regarded as modern institutional forms that have little relation to the origin or character of their members. Within these *jamats* blood is 'mixed', which is said to have a destructive effect on both their moral character and their propensity towards discerning social action. Lowest in rank are the Pathans who marry according to their own preference, situation and circumstance. In addition to having rank relative to one another, Pathans are ranked against the other *jamats* by the same principles. As I discussed earlier, the ideal is that members of different *jamats* do not intermarry; the greater ideal is that members of different lineages do not intermarry. The more these principles are violated the less status the offenders are accorded. I never heard any dissension towards the idea that these four groups were 'actually' Pathan. Clearly, if all are accepted as being Pathan, that is as having had a particular kind of essence in the past, their relative rank reflects how concentrated or how dilute that essence is today. There are no social connections between the four groups; no uniting sense of 'Pathan' identity or any attempt to explore similarly held genealogical connections or origin myths. Thus, the strong identity of Pathan has paled in relation to the measure of local social status based on the historically contingent relationships between lineage and *jamat*.

In Chapter 1, I outlined the principal imaginative frameworks through which the past and social changes in littoral society are understood. The first of these is to see local society and, indeed, the past, through the prism of larger standard narratives, the second is the ability to transform foreign invaders into sources of domestic prestige. While I feel it hardly necessary to point out the relevance of the second syndrome for this discussion, it should perhaps be spelled out that, in relation to the former, local hierarchy is understood first and foremost in relation to Muslim social history and those named by God in the Quran and, second, in the terms of spatial and temporal distance from this ideal. It is, however, hard to see just how this hierarchy has retained its form and power given that it relies so heavily on the idioms of descent and purity in a population that is so fundamentally mixed. It is tempting to simply argue that those who control capital resources, and have had prolonged exposure to literary forms of representation, are in a better position to manufacture the purity of their origins than those at the lower end of the scale – because here again it is primarily colonial sources that are reanimated in support of particular claims. However, there is more to it than that, and in the short term at least there is little chance of mobility within the hierarchy; moreover, challenges made against it do not rely on occupational change nor, perhaps surprisingly, solely on changing claims to religious piety (cf. Mines 1975). Rather, some explanation for the entrenched nature of the ideas on which this hierarchy is based can be gathered from the ways in which Sunni Muslims in Mandvi discuss the effects that mixing blood has upon bodies, souls and moral dispositions.

Here, the model of the Muslim body as outlined in Chapter 2 also plays a role in the explanation. People are of body (*jism*) and soul (*ruh*) conjoined at the heart. The two orders of the soul are in a hierarchical relationship, with the lower level (*nafs*) dictating an individual's base instincts and the higher level (*aql*) providing intellectual and moral faculties. Together, these two levels act against each other to form human mind and body actions (habit to ideal habitus or *adat* to *adab*). I have described how, in the shipyards, the Bhadala stress that individual transformation is possible over the course of a lifetime through discipline. In this hierarchy the rules of the game are not so generous and, on the whole, propensities are seen as being given at birth and the nature of the substance that created life. Material conditions aside, potters are potters, merchants are merchants and saints are saints because they were born that way, it is their nature. It is the higher-ranking Muslims who are associated with *aql* and the qualities of discernment and decorum and who thus have the potential for both commerce and religious learning. At the other end of the spectrum the low-ranking Muslim is associated with *nafs* and thus with base appetites. When people of different type and substance marry and reproduce it is only the base aspects that are enhanced in offspring and not the higher orders of intellect.

Thus far I have characterised this ranking as being premised on the very general idea that those from the lands to the north of the Indian Ocean are superior to those of the south, and those from lands nearer to the Arabian Peninsula are superior to those from further away, with the exception of Africans who are inferior to all, including those of mixed blood in the non-proprietary *jamats*. This hierarchy clearly also has racial connotations.

Race in the South Asian context refers to stereotypical skin colour and concomitant inherent, heritable, persistent or predictive characteristics of individuals (Robb 1995: 1). 'Miscegenation', of a kind, concentrates the base elements of the soul, and, not so metaphorically, skin colour is also seen as reflecting the character of the 'mind' or at least its potential effect over the body. In this view, emphasis is again placed upon the ways in which 'reproduction', as a form of physiology and morality, as part of the physiological condition, conjoin in particular 'bio-moral' combinations to make *jamats*, measured at the ideal level against the Prophet and more immediately against the Saiyeds. A proprietary *jamat* from this perspective shares unique biological and moral substances, potentially intensified or at least not diluted through endogamy. Thus 'pure' blood as substance from generations of endogamous marriage reproduces cool, controlled and calculating spiritual and business-like minds, which is reflected in the whitish complexion of the skin. Conversely, 'mixed blood', and thus the non-proprietary *jamats*, produce volatile people, whose tumultuous nature is also reflected in dark skin pigmentation. The corporeal division is entirely compatible with the model of transient and corporeal purity and impurity outlined above, which distinguishes between bodily substances from above and below the neck. Those who work with the mind (merchants or religious scholars) are purer than those who work with their bodies (slaves, labourers or sailors).

The movement of *jamats*

Although my informants did not express the idea, it appears that in this hierarchy status is much easier to let slip than it is to gain. The natural tendency is for downwards movement, given the vulnerability of lineages to fragmentation and schism and the impossibility of inventing a plausible and noble genealogy overnight. Furthermore, and more fundamentally, it is as if *aql* were a strictly limited good – endlessly diminished by admixture with little chance of replenishment. Most of my informants were doubtful that *aql* of a lineage could be enhanced even through the generations of reciprocal patrilateral parallel cousin marriage, which would at best prevent the further deterioration of the soul. In this rather bleak picture of the future of human potentiality, the base elements of the soul will grow increasingly dominant. Unchecked, the darker, more brutish, side of human nature will force aside discernment and scholarship, hence, it seems to me, the distribution of negative rewards for those in contravention of the ideals and the general preoccupation with elaborating institutional frameworks to postpone the inevitable decline into corporeal chaos. Given the gravity of the potential catastrophe, there are surprisingly few avenues for upwards mobility.

Each *jamat* is associated with a series of standard narratives (commonly called origin myths in the literature) which describe very particular ethno-historical origins. These narratives typically connect members of the *jamat* to particular places around the Indian Ocean and implicate them in the rise and fall of various epochs and dynasties. *Jamat* myths of origin, however, are strange sociological objects. They are strategies for legitimising and sanctioning social order and hierarchy and creating connections between the present and the historical past. They are, as I have also mentioned for standard myths about the more general past, adaptable, transformative, eclectic and seamlessly incorporate fact, fiction, text and tradition; yet, they also appear as, and are constructed as, static forms of socially differentiating truth. Origin myths reveal what kinds of claims are important, how authenticity is structured and cadenced in language and time, how the salience of claims changes in time and how claims of one group relate to those of others. However, claims of a particular group do not exist in isolation from received conceptions of history, political expediency or related claims of neighbours and highly regarded patrons. These kinds of origin charters are ultimately legitimised by textual evidence (also Appadurai 1981) and the greater the continuity over time that the reference can be found and the greater the antiquity of the original text the more prestigious and effective the claim. In this case, the most prestigious textual source is clearly the Quran but it is equally possible that authority granted to such myths is derived from profane sources such as newspapers, *jamat* journals and books.

As we have seen, the apical sections of the hierarchy claim descent from the Prophet and it is against his image that the rest of humanity is ordered and to him they turn to establish connections through myth. Most *jamats* contain men generally considered 'experts' on their myths and history. It was mostly through such individuals that I came by the myths of origin. According to one such man, Kadir, a retired government revenue officer, the Qureshi Jamat are Allah's chosen people. He directed me to a verse of the Quran (106, *Al-Quraish*), which he said meant they were to be shown special privileges and respect by the rest of the Muslim population, a claim imbued with considerable weight if you consider the Quran to be the unblemished words of Allah. He told me the Quresh are descendants of Nadr ibn Kananah in the line of Ishmael, himself a descendant of Abraham (with Hagar), Noah and Adam. Mohammed himself was son of Abdullah in this noble line. He said his ancestors had been the first to submit to Mohammed's message and had fled from Mecca to Medina with him to live under the protection of the Ansar. From this time, as companions of the Prophet, the Quresh and Ansar (see also *Al-Taubah* 9: 100.1; 9: 117.1; 9: 117.2.) had occupied positions of status, their blood pure and blessed.

While this story appears simple enough, its success is in its ingenious selectivity and the capacity of the story to outdo any rival claims to Qureshi descent that might appear in the town. The words 'Quresh' and 'unbeliever' are frequently used interchangeably in different English translations of the Quran (compare, for example, *al-Anfal* (8: 19.1.) of Pickthall (1930) with that of Yusuf Ali (1934)). It is however clear that the Quresh enjoyed special honour among the 'tribes' of Arabia and controlled the Kaaba and the associated ritual practices. When Mohammed began to speak against their gods, they persecuted and ridiculed him and his followers. He was ostracised and exchange relations with him were suspended. This sanction was committed to writing and the document was placed in the precincts of the Kaaba. According to one translator of the Quran, Mohammed and his followers spent three years shut up in his stronghold, leaving only at the time of pilgrimage (Pickthall 1930: xiii). The ban was eventually lifted in response to petitions from a section of Qureshis sympathetic to Mohammed. The document was removed from the Kaaba for reconsideration only for it to be found that it had been eaten by white ants, leaving only the words 'In thy name oh Allah' (ibid.). Mohammed departed Mecca to seek refuge in Yathrib (later known as Medina) with the Ansar. They pledged to defend Mohammed from aggressors and, in the ensuing years, entered a series of battles with the Quresh before the Meccans ceded to Mohammed. Simply, Kadir's claim to be descended from the original Quresh converts is the most prestigious one available. Their early submission to Islam confirms their enduring wisdom; it gives them a strong sense of historical connectedness to the narratives and blessings of the Quran; they are absolved of responsibility for conflicts between the Quresh and Mohammed; and the story distinguishes them from other less reputable sections of the Qureshi population.

Those seeking to improve their lot might tinker with their myths to demonstrate nobler descent, a process Jackie Assayag labels with the neologism 'Ashrafization' (2004: 42). In Mandvi, it is an open secret that some claims to descent are fabricated, especially in the mid-to-lower orders of the hierarchy. Whenever I discussed false myths with others, I was frequently surprised by the response. Unsurprisingly, some simply dismissed the offenders as fraudsters and scoundrels; however, others, notably those well placed in the hierarchy such as Kadir, tended to meet my questions with a calm but conspiratorial smile. At first, I took this peculiar but common response to be a polite acknowledgement of my progress along the path of understanding the complexities of the social organisation of Muslims in Kachchh. Later, I considered the possibility that the smile was a mask for nagging doubts about the credibility of their own claims to status. Now, as I explain below, I favour a more generous explanation in which the smile reflects both a sense of self-recognition and paternalistic recognition of the faith of the lowly.

Many of the *jamat* myths of those less favoured in the hierarchy, such as the Kumbhars (potters), include general claims for Qureshi descent. Others, such as the Sumaras, are more specific, claiming to be the descendants of the Bani Tamim lineage of the Quresh. Such claims reflect aspiration and are commonly supported by spurious cross references from colonial accounts of tribes and races in antiquity. In contrast to the myths of Kumbhars and Sumaras, Kachchhi Qureshis (distinct from Qureshis as part of a non-proprietary *jamat*) claim their ancestors petitioned for Mohammed's freedom and that they had secretly taken meat to his compound during his ostracism in Mecca. The logic of this myth is the same as Kadir's and steers the difficult path through the stories of the Quran in order to claim descent from an unnamed section of the Qureshi population who assisted rather than hindered the Prophet. In this case, however, it is widely held that this story is an attempt at strengthening the Qureshi aspect of their identity as Kachchhi Qureshis. My informants produced two explanations for the improbable name of this sub-caste. First, they were Sindi Muslims who had come to Kachchh and shown remarkable piety and were thus honoured with the name Quresh. Second, they invented a claim for Qureshi descent, this was rejected and they became known as Kachchhi Quresh. In this sense, 'Kachchhi' is an endearing term for 'counterfeit' or 'home grown' in the same way that locally produced carbonated fruit drinks are called 'Kachchhi Coca Cola'.

Locally, these claims amount to very little and others summarily reject their authenticity with a smile. The logic for rejecting them is simple: noble descent fosters spirituality, wisdom and even wealth; such claims are clearly erroneous because these people are dirty, ignorant labourers. Behind the smile of men such as Kadir there may have been a sense of satisfaction that I had begun to understand the significance of his status and the fact that others coveted his *jamat*'s prestige. In a sense, however, the obvious fabrication and mimicry of myths among those of low status does little more than confirm to those higher up that those beneath them are ignorant and do not know the value of truth.

Why then, if inventing myths is a largely unsuccessful strategy for social mobility, should anyone bother to invent them? In response to this question Kadir's smile also reveals a form of collusion between low and high *jamats* against a legacy of Hinduism. The low *jamats* are understood to be indigenous converts to Islam and the transformation of myths is seen as a part of the gradual realisation of this process. The high *jamats* tolerate the low *jamats* tinkering with myths because in the process they eradicate elements of Hindu mythology and strengthen their identity as Muslims in terms that reinforce the status of the high *jamats*. I am sure that creating rules for this game is a part of the game itself, and generally my informants have cynical if not to say hard-nosed attitudes when explaining the motivations of others; however, criticism of this hierarchy tends to be atypically mute and claims for higher status are generally carried out in the spirit of the existing hierarchy. Evident patterns of social mobility and competition occur only within the three qualitatively different sections of the hierarchy: the putative descendants of the Prophet and his companions, the proprietary *jamats* and the non-proprietary *jamats*. Within the lower two sections, mobility in either direction is possible within the limits of the upper boundaries of each section and in the higher section mobility is possible within its lower limits. The strategies used include occupational change and displays of wealth and piety through inflationary practices such as *purdah* (the increased seclusion of women in architecture and clothing), levels of *mahr* (payments given to incoming wives at marriage) or the adoption of Urdu as the *jamat* language. Given such a situation, it seems reasonable to suggest for this case that Muslim social hierarchy cannot, as Misra (1964) suggested, be seen as a part of the Hindu caste system because the idioms of hierarchy differ so markedly – nor, as Barnett *et al*. (1976) claim, can it be seen as lacking an integrative ideology other than power equalling status. The driving force behind the Bhadala's attacks on other Muslims is the fact that in this order of things power does not signify status; they have a lot of the former but precious little of the latter.

Denouncing the divine body

The selective antipathy shown by the Bhadala towards Saiyeds and Mandvi's Muslims suggests an alternative strategy for social mobility that denies the authenticity and morality of the prevailing social hierarchy. Connections through geography, substance and lineage, the traditional markers of hierarchical order, legitimate the ordering of men against the ideal of the Prophet. In the order of society I have described in this chapter, humans are fundamentally unequal at birth, conditions that variously determine their potential in life. At the apex of this hierarchy is a class ascribed with special powers that mark them off from lesser mortals. Rhetorically, the Bhadala oppose such ontological inequality, a position relatively straightforward to legitimise and substantiate given the well-known rhetoric of the equality of men before Allah derived from formal reformist traditions in India and elsewhere (see van der Veer 1992). Challenging ontological differentiation and the gradations of status that arise from it leaves the way open for an attack on social hierarchies and special powers.

Saiyeds are revered and often venerated because they are putitative descendants of the Prophet Mohammed. They are seen to have a share in his substance and the inherent and immutable qualities it gives rise to (see Werbner and Basu 1998). The grace and potency of their genealogy yields *barakat* (commonly elsewhere *baraka*), the blessing, holiness and spiritual power inherent in a saint (Metcalf 1984: 373), which distinguishes them from normal men. The status of a Saiyed lies in being able to present a cogent claim for prestigious historical connections and manifesting it through a charisma (*barakat*) routinised or at least suggested by genealogy. The shrines (*durgahs*) of Saiyeds proliferate in both urban and rural

Kachchh. The simple ones are the marked graves of lesser saints, which may in time be developed should the site acquire an efficacious reputation. The elaborate shrines stand either for single powerful saints particularly favoured by the vassals or for a saint and successive generations of his descendants. In the latter case, the site may contain many hundreds of tombs and grand mausoleums if the cult has met with success. As sites of popular devotion, these shrines are generally peaceful, fragrant and meditative places with graceful architecture and abundant shade. Devotees see them as charisma-rich locations because the sanctity of the entombed can be channelled into the world of the living to cure disease, enhance life and to solve disputes. In these locations miracles occur as the boundaries between the living and the dead and the sacred and the profane dissolve. Boons are granted, individual desires fulfilled and protection is sought against the perilous realms of spirits, witchcraft, bad health and infertility. In many shrines there are also living Saiyeds, specialists in controlling flows of charisma through meditation and proscribed rituals. They live amid the graves of their ancestors, earning an income from managing the charisma of the dead and administering the often considerable estates in their charge. Personality cults often develop around these living figures. Such cults might be unstructured constituencies dependent on a master for decisive intercession on legal, spiritual and moral questions, or highly organised hierarchical movements offering instruction in spiritual matters.

Most, but not all, Saiyeds, their personality cults and followers are dismissed in Salaya. They are commonly accused of swindling, of trickery and of passing off ignorant advice to those so blinded by devotion that they cannot see the falsehoods they are being fed and are paying for. On the whole, however, the senior men in shipyards behave with decorum, politeness and gentility to strangers and unknown visitors who might pass by. One day, however, Mohamed and I had gone to Mandvi to obtain customs clearance for his vessel. After the paperwork was complete we stood on the docks, looking towards Salaya, conversing with a group of men engaged in re-rigging a vessel. Along came a man dressed from head to toe in green silk. He smelt strongly of perfumed oil and carried with him a number of peacock feathers and a bundle of charms. He looked like a rogue but his words were considered and his tone contemplative. He said he was a Saiyed from Rajasthan who was making a tour of the holy places of Gujarat. He flattered Mohamed, waved the feathers in the general direction of his head and asked for alms. Mohamed received the blessing and passed the man a ten rupee note. The man did not leave as expected, however, and attempted to initiate a conversation, perhaps believing he had stumbled across a potential patron. To everyone's surprise, especially that of the Saiyed, Mohamed told him in no uncertain terms to get lost. The man was clearly shocked and as he regained his composure he informed Mohamed that this was no way to treat an elder, a man of religion and a traveller in a strange land. Mohamed replied by saying that waving feathers around was no sign of religion, that the man was certainly old but not his superior and if the man was hungry he should go to eat in a lodge like everyone else. This highly unusual and confrontational exchange provoked audible giggles from the men on the ship and this spurred Mohamed on: 'I have been on haj [he had not]. My family has built mosques and given generously to orphanages. What are your qualifications?' There was a moment of silence before the man replied: 'Well Haji, I may be a poor man but I at least know how to behave.' He turned his back and walked away.

As we made the journey back to Salaya, Mohamed said he was sick of undeserving beggars asking him for money in the name of religion. I did not know whether to believe him or not but he said that some Saiyeds begged by telephone. I asked him why he had taken the man's blessing and paid for the service. He said:

> That fellow on the docks, who was he? I have no idea! You have no idea! He may have been the son of an oil presser from Uttar Pradesh who has moved over here and started to claim he is a *bawa* [Saiyed] but he might not have been. You have to be careful. These people have powers whether we like it or not. I took his blessing before insulting him just to be on the safe side.

In Salaya it is common to hear the suggestion that the Saiyeds' descent is fabricated or that they trace ancestry though female blood lines. Both cases are seen as evidence of the morally corrupt nature of Saiyeds and rather inevitably lead to the accusation that most Saiyeds are of mixed blood – rather like the Bhadala's is commonly assumed to be. On the face of it, the hostility the Bhadala display towards Mandvi's Saiyeds is because spiritual intermediaries are a corruption of the religious practices of Muslims. However, as I discussed in the previous chapter (p. 75), the picture is not quite that clear-cut because the Bhadala not only patronise and visit a number of local and extra-local shrines, they also see a wide variety of religious practices other than their own as efficacious. What separates good from bad practice and power is whether something can be considered *sunnah*, the path given by Allah through the example of the Prophet for Muslims to lead good lives. In order to understand the criteria for rejecting the authority of some Saiyeds, aside from the sheer convenience of it, it is also necessary to consider the different types of prayer, supplication and invocation available to practising Muslims. David Parkin describes four kinds of prayer, which he calls reciprocal, non-reciprocal, indirect and reflexive (2000: 5–8). Reciprocal prayer occurs when a devotee speaks to Allah and receives a reply in the form of a boon, vision or calming sensation, commonly known as *dua* (supplication). Non-reciprocal prayer such as *salat* (or *salah*, the invocation of Allah five times daily) and

shahada (declaration of faith) are offered to confirm belief in the existence of Allah and to confirm an individual's loyalty, but they are offered
without the expectation of return. The silence that meets these prayers
does not, however, necessarily preclude the worshipper from receiving
an intercession or grace. The indirect forms of prayer such as *tawasul* are
intercessionary prayers where:

> the worshipper may communicate indirectly to Allah through
> a human intermediary, whose prayers are answered directly by
> Allah (or other powers) by virtue of his being a vehicle of divine
> grace (*baraka*), itself a property of his descent from the Prophet
> Mohammed.
>
> (Parkin 2000: 7)

The reflexive kind of prayer is *zikra* (or *dhikra*), remembrance for the sake
of Allah.

The boundaries between these divisions, especially between the first and
third categories (indirect and reciprocal forms of prayer), are highly
conflated in the cults surrounding local shrines in Kachchh. The kinds of
prayer offered in shrines, a few of which also contain small mosques,
include *salat*, *shahada* and *zikra*. However, the type of prayers does not
always reveal its purpose and even non-reciprocal prayers can be performed
as the supplicant seeks a boon or intercession. Robinson (1983: 188) has
described a significant difference between the worship of a saint and the
worship of Allah in a saint's presence. However, this distinction is insuffi-
cient to fully appreciate the logic of the Bhadala's antipathy towards some
Saiyeds and it is necessary to refine this distinction further. Broadly, there
are six kinds of intermediary roles performed by Saiyeds both alive and
dead. First, a living Saiyed may act as a conduit for the worship or appease-
ment of a deity without human form. For example, particular local deities
associated with fertility, rainfall and procreation can be induced to action
through the mediation of a Saiyed. Second, a Saiyed can mediate essences
between the living and the dead. For example, at the time of death, food
offerings (*vondh*) are presented to Saiyeds and those who conduct funerary
rites in order to provide sustenance to the deceased during their journey
to heaven. Similar offerings are also given on death anniversaries and in a
number of houses I am familiar with food is sent to Saiyeds at every meal
time for the sustenance of the deceased in heaven. Third, a living Saiyed
may himself be worshipped as a deity or as an aspect of Allah when the
boundaries between intercessionary powers and the source of power dissolve. Fourth, a living Saiyed may mediate communication and *barakat*
between supplicant and saint through their divine historical connection.
Fifth, a deceased Saiyed may be called upon directly by a devotee to inter-
vene in some worldly matter. Such dialogues with the deceased indicate

that after death their powers continue to radiate into the human world and that they continue to have influence among the living. Finally, Allah may be worshipped directly in the presence of either a living Saiyed or a deceased Saiyed of fame, ensuring that the prayer is more efficacious.

The reformist line on the position of saints in Islam, offered by the Ahl-e-Hadith movement and others in western India, is that humans are ontologically equal in their potentials, no human is naturally closer to God or more adept at spiritual mastery by virtue of birth and, therefore, Saiyeds and all that is associated with them are corruptions and obstacles in the way of man's rightfully direct relationship with Allah. This kind of sentiment is audible among the Bhadala but not evident in practice. In the meetings at Mukhdummi Sha (itself a mausoleum) and frequently during informal conversations in the shipyards, the first four kinds of intermediary role are described as corrupt because they wrongly attribute Saiyeds with both the power of intercession in worldly matters and the ability to conduce direct (in the sense of indirect prayers) communication with Allah. The attitudes and practices among the Bhadala towards my fifth category of intermediary activity are somewhat ambiguous because, on the one hand, they will happily denounce the practice of offering reciprocal and indirect forms of prayer to deceased Saiyeds, but with equal ease offer such prayers in times of sudden need. For example, on quite a few occasions, especially during bad weather, men would bolt from the cabins in the shipyards that housed the ship-to-shore radio receivers, jump on a motorbike and ride the seven kilometres to Tamachi Pir in the sand dunes to the west of Mandvi to request the saint grant the safety of their ships and relatives out at sea. Furthermore, they would openly offer reciprocal and indirect forms of prayer at the village, district and regional level shrines (mentioned in the previous chapter) that they deemed to be legitimate.

Offering non-reciprocal prayers to Allah in the presence of a deceased saint, regardless of the weather conditions, is broadly accepted and also practised on excursions to local and supra-local shrines on the condition that the dead are judged on merit rather than on their condition at birth. This obviously begs the question as to why saintly presence is desirable at all if no human being is more proximate to Allah than any other. However, while practices and rhetoric do not exactly match either in relation to Muslim social hierarchy or in terms of saint worship, the Bhadala have consistently rejected all local Saiyed cults and the efficacy of all local shrines of the traditional order. I never saw a Bhadala man visit a shrine in Mandvi and in this sense they literally treat Muslims in Mandvi as if they live by the rules of *dar al-kafir*.

The saints of the traditional social order have been dismissed by the newly rich only to be selectively reinvented. Reinvention, as we have seen, involves reordering the hierarchy of shrines and placing the centres of spiritual power far from the reach of those in Mandvi. The Bhadala have also taken to patronising an individual Saiyed (as a scholar rather than as a mystic) to the exclusion of all others. On occasion this man appears as their religious leader and speaks frequently at Mukhdummi Sha, but in the process his identity as a Saiyed has become obscure. He is not associated with a shrine or with a particular sacred place and, more importantly, he is not from Mandvi but from the hinterlands and thus remains separate from local status politics. Stripped of his charisma, he has essentially become the servant of a newly defined purism.

Conclusion

The traditional body of the Saiyed is the nexus of charisma and status and the confluence of reproduction, morality and genealogical inflection against which all other men are ordered. The Bhadala are implicitly denouncing the traditional image of the perfection offered by the Saiyed body. They proffer it is an illusion and a corruption designed to maintain the status quo, to divide men and separate them from Allah. They hope that when this object of order is safely undermined they will be in a position to impose their own order on the structures of disarray that remain. Apprenticeship is the means by which these ideas are transmitted and the process presents a series of challenges to the apprentice's understandings of hierarchy and his place in the wider world. The apprentice often starts with an image of hierarchy constructed against the perfection of the Saiyed's blood as substance. He is gradually disabused of this schema through his labour and the sedimentation of affective dispositions that persuade him of the existence of an individual work ethic in which men are equal at birth, make their fortunes in life and have the luxury of a direct relationship with God. In this vision, all men are equal in their potentials; therefore, there is no ontological hierarchy at birth and, in turn, there is no social hierarchy other than status being derived from power. This challenge is presented in the reassuring terms of religious reform and not those of social revolution. However, it should also be obvious that the apprentice's old ideas are not simply replaced with new ones and that the two necessarily compete and cause conflict in the wider world and variously come to the fore in different contexts. The apprentice is dichotomised and eventually contains within his potential courses of action local forms of both Ernest Gellner's (1969) 'high' and 'low' and Parkin's (2000) 'monist' and 'dualist' dual syndromes. I have drawn this opposition in stark terms and it is perhaps never this clear-cut because reformist discourse finds expression in Mandvi (albeit far less audible and far less well funded) just as the Bhadala's chosen saints retain power in Salaya. Furthermore, in recent years the Saiyeds of Mandvi and other nearby towns have held meetings to determine strategies that will allow them to win back their popularity; in some cases I am familiar with they have banned coconuts and other ritual paraphernalia from their premises and erected signs using Gujarati script for Arabic words in order to give their precincts more gravity.

There are also some quite clear continuities between the two systems in terms of language and patterns of individual behaviour in unequal encounters, which suggest that what the Bhadala are about is not quite a revolution but more of a reinterpretation of the tradition. Additionally, the patterns of hierarchy, respect and deference described in the previous chapter within *pir–murid* relationships strongly resemble the patterns of hierarchy and bodily performance in shipyards between Bhadala masters and their apprentices. In both cases, those at the apex of the hierarchy are held in utter regard by their subordinates. In the shrine, turning to other saints is described as compromising the potency of the *murid*'s own master. Furthermore, initiates are encouraged to follow the ritual practices dictated by their master to the exclusion of all others. Similarly, the relationship between a sailor and his employer is also a cumulative one that depends on the disparities between their religious observances decreasing over time. Apprentices are expected to be loyal to the interests of one master and not to entertain demands of others for personal gain. The neophyte is also encouraged to forsake previous religious practices in favour of those encouraged by their new masters, especially the patronage of most saints. However, there is an important difference that reiterates the general argument of this chapter in slightly different terms. In the shipyards, the apprentice is explicitly told that, should he work hard, mastery of the salient physical world leads to mental alacrity, spiritual acumen and material bounty. In the previous chapter (pp. 84–85) I described how Saiyeds may take on *murids* (aspirants or novices) and how this relationship is structured by conceptions of learning in which the internal self is transformed though external actions. However, importantly, the degree of transformation is always limited by the facts of corporeal hierarchy described in the first half of this chapter. This relationship is based on the *certainty* that the non-Saiyed apprentice, no matter how adept, mentally agile and sound of heart he proves to be, will never become a Saiyed by virtue of his ignoble birth, nor will he ever ascertain the same condition as his master because of the limited potentiality of his body.

4

HINDU NATIONALISM
AND THE
MUSLIM RESPONSE

Hinduism has often been described as a related assortment of many faiths, traditions and sects, rather than an integrated religion. The secular traditions of government, which emerged in India after Independence, consciously legislated to protect other religious traditions in the country. Such diversity, on both counts, is disputed by the leaders of the new political nationalism who present Hinduism as a unified religion profoundly rooted in Indian soil, and the other religious traditions as unwanted foreign influences. Thus 'Hindutva' or 'Hinduness' has come to stand for the equation of Hinduism with nation and national identity as a way of seeing the world based upon doctrines supposedly derived from ancient Hindu thought. Nationalistic Hindu political groups have been attempting to redraw the country's history by inscribing their polity on the landscape of the continent. In their vision, India is the Hindu motherland, weakened by waves of hostile Muslim infiltration, consequently conquered by the British, and torn apart at the time of Partition in 1947.

Part of this nationalistic project, described by Barbara Miller (1991) and Sheldon Pollock (1993), is to bring to the fore Hindu religious epics, such as the Mahabharata and the Ramayana, as forms of history and morality as well as to invoke a sense of nostalgic loss. Of the two texts, the Ramayana has come to play an important role in the political imagination of Hindu Gujarat. It is a short tale of loyalty, adventure, morality and idealism in which Ram (an incarnation of Vishnu) is sent to restore order and rule in the world after it is threatened by Ravana, an evil ascetic of nearly invincible qualities. Public representations of morality loosely based on the Ramayana have become more prominent in recent decades as political tools that reinforce the twin themes of xenophobia, against Ravana, and 'rulership', ideally represented by Ram. The text provides simple and powerful imaginative instruments, whereby, on the one hand, a divine political order can be conceptualised, narrated and historically grounded, and, on the other, a fully demonised 'other' can be categorised, counter-posed and condemned (Pollock 1993: 264). Life is being given to these texts as rivers, mountains and whole regions are being inscribed with the sacred past. Lying behind the gaudy colours of the new cartography are battles and defeats at the hands of the 'invading' Muslims. The achievements and grandeur of Hindu civilisation are viewed as having fallen at foreign hands. The ruins and archaeological traces in the countryside of Gujarat are being reinvented as evidence of the former grandeur of Hindu India, which fell to the wrongdoings and injustices of Muslims. Reconstruction after the powerful earthquake of 2001 hastened the process and old villages were given new names, which were often drawn directly from the epics (Simpson 2004). As the landscape has been reanimated with temples dedicated to the heroes of these texts, the history of religious contest and dispute is also being redrawn in order that the nationalists might reclaim the past and the land.

India's most publicised political episodes have revolved around conflicts between Hindus and Muslims over contested religious sites at the country's centres of pilgrimage and popular devotion (see van der Veer 1994). The most important of these conflicts is the series of agitations that has focused on the sacred Hindu temple town of Ayodhya in Uttar Pradesh. Since the early 1990s, large numbers of people have died all over India in clashes led by self-styled servants of the Hindu deity Ram, known as *kar sevaks*, who pledged themselves to reclaim the Babri Masjid (Barbar's Mosque). Their leaders declared their intention to reclaim the site, demolish the mosque and construct a new Hindu temple on the spot because, at some disputed point in the past, it is held that Muslim conquerors built the mosque on the birthplace of Lord Ram.

Although the Babri Masjid is a long way from the southern shores of Kachchh, the dispute and the twin themes of xenophobia and rulership are not. In this chapter, I explore two local incidents of violent confrontation between Hindus and Muslims and the patterns of polarisation associated with them. The first confrontation occurred between the Bhadala and Hindus (specifically with men from the caste known as Kharva) in the 1980s, the effects of which are traced through the changing practices associated with Nava Naroj, the festival marking the start of the sailing season. The second confrontation was sparked by the rise of political Hindu nationalism in Gujarat, which culminated in widespread religious violence during 2002. The first incident was local in its effects; by way of contrast, however, as a result of the second example tens of thousands of people were displaced, vast regions of the state were placed under curfew and high-level commissions were formed to investigate what happened. The violence and the events preceding it have been extensively documented and it is not my intention here to recount the chronology of events or to conduct a forensic examination of their causal relationships (for that see Engineer 2003; Sondhi and Mukarji 2002; Varadarajan 2002). Most mainstream liberal commentaries have expressed their outrage against the fact that the actions of the 'state' were not in accordance with the Constitution and that the 'state' displayed a weak commitment to values of substantive justice – ultimately expressed as governmental lawlessness. By way of contrast, for many of my Muslim informants it came as little surprise that the 'state' was either supine or complicit in the violence; I will return to this matter later.

In my view, however, the examples of violence discussed in this chapter suggest that neither political nationalism nor the rise of violence against Muslims in Gujarat can be simply explained away as an elite conspiracy or as an expression of alienation of the poor from a rapidly expanding economy (see Breman 2004). In the first instance, violence erupted at the confluence of divergent fortunes, the Bhadala prospering through trade while their former Hindu rivals were forced into the fragmented market for international labour. In the latter case, the rise of Hindu nationalism in Gujarat, I suggest a central factor behind the violence of March 2002 was competition between urban and rural Hindu elites for both control of the ruling party and for the reins of power in the longer term. These examples also highlight two of many possible Muslim responses to aggression. In the first case, the Bhadala were prompted to refashion the class inequalities that placed them in a position of conflict in the first place, by creating new economic dependants (men such as Rasheed and the hundreds of other apprentices in their shipyards) to cushion them against future violence. In the second case, there was clearly not much they could do other than actively seek strategic alliances with other Muslims (including those they had vocally opposed just a few years before), in an attempt to foster a sense of unity to withstand the insults of a society caught in the spell of a Hindu nationalist government. Together, these examples show the following. First, how Muslims have been ushered into positions of social and economic independence and self-reliance and marginalised from the democratic process. Second, how through its very actions the state enlivens its own central legitimising and foundational myth, which is that Muslims are uninterested in participating in the democratic processes of modern India.

The god that disappeared

The Naroj (Persian, sea-day) calendar is divided into 365 sequentially numbered days, roughly equivalent to a solar year. The first day of the year is known as Nava (new) Naroj. The festivities of this day in August mark the symbolic end of the monsoon and the ritualised commencement of a new sailing season. In practice, however, ships would not put to sea until October when the frequent squalls and unsettled weather brought about by the receding monsoon have died away. In the past, this system of reck-oning marked the beginning of a new accounting year that was also used in those ports outside India where Gujarati merchants were present in large numbers. The origin of this system is unknown to me (the Zoroastrian calendar also commences on a day known as Naroj) but its use serves as a standard method of marking the passing of time across the Indian Ocean and, importantly, compensates for slippages between the ritual lunar calen-dars of seafarers and the seasonal events of the solar cycle. The calendar used by Sunni Muslims is based on lunar cycles and divides the year into twelve months, each of twenty-nine or thirty days in duration. No system of intercalation is used so that it is shorter than the Naroj cycle by around eleven days. It follows that in the Sunni Muslim calendar months are not related to seasons and over a thirty-three-year cycle lunar months take a complete turn to fall during the same solar season. Similarly, the Hindu calendar (Vikram Savant) is designed around a geocentric universe and thus uses synodical lunar months of between twenty-nine and thirty days' dura-tion. Because it is between ten and eleven days shorter than a solar year, festivals that fall on a particular day of Naroj may not do so the next year despite the fact that the calendar is repeatedly realigned with the changing of the seasons by the insertion of half months. In both cases, the calendars cannot simply be adapted to mark the seasonal junctures of the sailing season. While the Naroj calendar serves this relatively straightforward purpose, it also has the somewhat unusual consequence of creating a ritual juncture equally important to both Hindus and Muslims.

Throughout the nineteenth century, numerous travellers and colonial officials wrote of their delight at witnessing the festivities of Nava Naroj (for example, Postans 1839; GBP 1901, Vol. IX, Part I). The nineteenth-century accounts state that seafaring natives, both Hindus and Muslims, broke coconuts into the waves of the Ocean as a form of prayer in order to secure their safety and profit in the coming months. The god they flocked to the shore to venerate was the amorphous figure of Dariyapir, Lord of the Ocean. Today, the festival remains one of the most significant in the ritual year but Dariyapir has, quite literally, disappeared. Many of my informants told me that, in the past, when the Bhadala lived in Mandvi, Hindu and Muslim sailors used to jointly celebrate Nava Naroj at the god's abode between the town and the beachhead. Now on this site, the compound walls of a new Hindu temple, dedicated to the Sanskritised deity Dariyalal, rise from the earth on the edge of an ancient Muslim cemetery. The graves outside the walls are well maintained and regularly cleared of encroaching sand. The identities of the entombed are not certain, yet they have recently been resurrected and attributed with the miraculous powers of saints. The spent shells of coconuts litter the ground and each grave is shrouded in Muslim-green cloth. The site is contested and plays a central role in the rehearsal and reiteration of communalised Hindu and Muslim identities. Taking the example of Dariyapir's disappearance, the following sections of the chapter explore the changing ways in which this festival is marked and the myths that have enveloped the polarisation of Hindus and Muslims over time.

In Salaya, in 1998, Nava Naroj fell on a Friday and after the lunchtime prayers many of the congregation wandered down to the beach for an additional prayer to mark the occasion. They gathered in two circles on the sand, one comprised of ship owners and the other of crew. The *moulana* of one of the village's mosques led the recitation of *zikra* (remembrance of Allah) to the accompaniment of gulls mewing and tumbling over the breaking waves. After the earnest recitation had come to a close, there were a few moments of silence before the men stood. Some bowed to offer additional private prayers in the direction of Mecca, but most started to wander slowly back into the village. The event was careful and measured; those present were mostly known to me as the men most vociferous in their attacks against elaborate rituals. It is patently obviously that not all of the Bhadala men share exactly the same views on religious practice or the society in which they live. While there is no need to dwell on these differences at length, there is one important schism between them that came to the fore most visibly on the occasion of Nava Naroj. The *jamat* is broadly divided into two groups of lineages. One faction controls the village's communal buildings, the other the local shipping association and most of the mosque committees. The faction controlling the shipping association is politically dominant, despite the fact that the leader (known as 'Patel') of the *jamat* belongs to the other faction. This inequality is best explained by looking at who each faction employs as crew on their fleets. The subordinate group's fleet is predominantly, but not exclusively, crewed by men who are kin of the patriarch. The dominant group, in contrast, predominantly employ non-Bhadala men from Mandvi who provide them with a much larger political constituency of dependants and a wider spread of influence; they also seem to run their ships more profitably.

It was mostly, but not exclusively, men from the dominant group who went down to the sea to perform *zikra*. On their return to the village they passed men from the subordinate group who had organised their own celebrations. These men had cut back the dry foliage from around the neglected structure of a shrine and had painted the name of the entombed saint 'Apu Pir' on its low perimeter walls. Around the structure, ice cream and sherbet vendors had gathered, along with a few small, hand-operated fairground rides. The shrine had been decorated with brightly coloured cloths and the smoke of incense filled the air. The men were smashing coconuts on the tomb and as the coconut milk splashed on to the concrete they offered prayers to the saint. As the group of men who had been down

to the seashore to perform *zikra* passed the shrine they made a few dis-
paraging remarks in hushed voices about 'playing' (also van der Veer 1992)
around the shrine and how it was unsuitable for Muslims to be praying
using coconuts; despite these remarks, they greeted the other men with
civility.

Throughout these performances occasional shrill cries of delight and the
sound of drumming could be heard on the breeze from Mandvi. For the
Kharvas, Nava Naroj is a day of abandonment, culminating with a wild
musical procession from the Dariyalal temple to that of Ram in the heart
of their neighbourhood. The rituals performed pay homage to Dariyalal,
but more importantly Nava Naroj (and the preceding day *gofol*) is reserved
for venerating heroic ancestors and telling stories of heroism.

The voracious logic of caste myths

The Dariyalal Temple lies at the heart of the ritual life of the Kharvas.
Construction started on the structure two decades ago as a material expression of their attempt at upwards mobility by Sanskritising their traditions,
a process in which they appropriated and elaborated strands of the
mythology of their former mercantile patrons, mainly followers of elite
sects with the cult of Vishnu at their core. The new temple also banished
Dariyapir from the local Hindu pantheon. Claiming the site as their own,
they have erased the suffix *pir* (commonly used to denote Muslim saints)
and added *lal* (a high status Sanskritised term of respect). However, the
change from Dariyapir to Dariyalal involves more than a change of name
because – in an attempt to obliterate traces of Muslim influence (or at least
evidence of a shared tradition) – the new deity has been given a form, flattered with new mythology and installed amid an elaborate arrangement of
suitable symbols and traditions. The god has not simply been purged of his
association with Muslims and what might be thought of as 'syncretic' traditions; he has been comprehensively reinvented as the defender of Hinduism
against Muslim predation.

The temple structure is small, square and domed. Inside is an icon of
the bearded deity sitting, resplendently, upon a fish. He is brightly illumin-
ated and surrounded by silver windmills, symbols of the wind and of the
wind farm on Mandvi's beach. At his feet stands a series of stone horses
daubed with saffron paint. The walls are papered with pictures, photographs
and newspaper clippings attesting to the magnificence of Kharva traditions
and seafaring prowess – of the kind described in Chapter 1. Outside, within
the walls of the compound, are a collection of hero stones and a stone
tortoise. The following sections explore the symbolism of the artefacts in
the temple as idealised expressions of caste identity and some of the sociological conditions that have contributed to the formation of this identity.

The word Kharva perhaps comes from the Sanskrit *kh* from *kharash* (salty) and *war* from *vat* (road or way). A gazetteer attributes the etymology to 'ksháraváhas' (salt carriers) from which 'Khar'rva' is derived (GBP 1901, Vol. IX, Part I: 520). Kharvas live in most ports of Saurashtra and Kachchh; together, these settlements form the 'Bar Gam Samaj' (a society of twelve villages).[1] This pan-peninsular organisation has its own legal code and semi-autonomous court, which has sat regularly since the 1860s. Colloquially, Kharvas are called *malam* (from the verb 'to know', in this case navigation) or, more poetically, *dariya chhoru* (sons of the sea). They form Mandvi's largest single caste, perhaps representing as much as one twelfth of the town's population, and live on the southern fringes in the areas adjacent to where the Bhadala used to live. Their history and traditions are those of the sea, as are their names, deities and festivals, and, like sailors in many parts of the world, they are generally regarded as troublesome, dangerous and unruly. In a rather exacting parallel to the image of hierarchy in Sunni Muslim society described in the previous chapter, the Kharvas are also seen as unruly and of low status because of their mixed descent. In this case, however, their genealogical claims link them to the ancient Rajput lines of *suriya* (sun), the related *ragu* (fire) segment and *chandra* (moon); evidence for which they suggest can be found in *shakha* (principal lineages), which carry high-status Rajput names such as Solanki, Zala, Jethva, Rathod and Jadeja.[2]

Simply put, the Kharva are sailors (in the sense of a structural class position) who no longer sail. Still, they refer to themselves as sailors and are referred to by others as such; they also build and worship in temples dedicated to the deities of the sea. In the past, their men worked as crew on the ships of Hindu merchants (Bhatiyas and Lohanas), and Kharvanis (Kharva women) served in mercantile houses. Such relationships continue today and in some cases can be traced back through seven named generations (of both client Kharvas and patron Bhatiyas or Lohanas) to the latter half of the nineteenth century. These genealogies also trace the success and failure of particular business enterprises in East Africa and macro population movements throughout the Indian Ocean. Kharvas continue to unify in speech (we, our), sometimes with notable pride, their own activities with those of their patrons. Today, many Kharva men work as drivers, machine operators and labourers for the long-established firms of Kachchhi Bhatiya and Lohana merchants in Oman. As the Hindu merchants gave up shipping during the late nineteenth and early twentieth centuries, finding it either unprofitable or unmanageable, the patron–client-type relationships forged through shipping were almost directly reproduced in other kinds of economic activity, most notably in shops and factories in Muscat.

Unsurprisingly, among the Kharvas there is a strong and generous sentimentality towards the past. Many Kharvas reinvigorate and re-imagine the past through their activities. There are model makers, amateur historians and linguists, journalists, short-story writers, biographers and artists all of whom depict small boats in big seas. Across the generations there is a shared preoccupation with ships, shipping, travel and the successes of their ancestors. They are busy painting the past in nostalgic colours; and, in an attempt to preserve some of the perceived or desired grandeur of what went before, they are constructing causal relationships between their ancestral past and themes derived from classical and nationalistic Hinduism.

It is striking that, although the majority of Kharva men work onshore in Oman in non-seasonal posts, a great many of them return to India by plane with the onset of the monsoon – just as they did in the past when the seas grew too rough for their vessels. I was curious as to the reasons behind this unusual and apparently extremely expensive pattern of migration. The explanation I heard most commonly from other Hindus was that they returned for the 'off season', rather than at any other time of the year, because that was when the Muslims (the Bhadala and their crews) came back to Kachchh. I also heard other explanations and Rasheed (the central character in my Introduction) once told me with some enthusiasm that the caste had a secret rule that if a man was away from home for more than a year then his wife could look for sexual gratification elsewhere. He always had one ear to the ground listening for the names of those who had not returned; it was, of course, a Kharva woman with whom Rasheed fell in love and it was Kharva men with whom Rasheed was constantly fighting. In contrast, Kharvas told me that temperatures reach unbearable degrees in Oman during those months and they thus sensibly appreciate the comparatively cool climes of Kachchh. I was also told that the cycle of returning with the monsoon was 'in their blood' as their ancestors had done so for hundreds of years; and, 'the off season is a time of community and marriage when we all came together with wealth and stories from outside'. The 'off season' (roughly from day 300 of the Naroj calendar up until the turn of the year) is, indeed, a period of intense community activity; most marriages among Kharvas take place then, the annual caste publication appears around Nava Naroj and tea shops and the bazaars are filled with returning migrant workers during this period. However, outside the intimacy of family and friendship of the returnees, the general perception is that Kharvas return home as defenders of the faith to prevent the Bhadala, or other Muslims for that matter, from freely marching upon the city walls.

This role has been symbolically elaborated by the Kharvas themselves; however, the material conditions that put them there, despite their attempts at upward mobility through Sanskritisation, are to be found in the cyclical reproduction of mercantile society and the class divisions on which it is constructed. The creation and degree of dependency described in the previous chapters among sailors and their Bhadala patrons is also representative of modern relationships between the Kharva migrants and their mercantile employers. The degree of dependency among Kharvas is reflected in the fact that they are commonly referred to as *laskhar* ('lascar'); a term that means seafarer but also has militaristic implications, as in army servant or artilleryman. Relations of inter-caste material dependency and inequality, symbolically elaborated with mythology and hierarchical conceptions of corporeality, produce Kharvas as the foot soldiers of the mercantile classes, fighting their street battles and aiding in disputes when more than honed negotiating skills are required. In the past, they claim to have protected cargoes on board ships and used weapons against the predations of pirates. These days, the kind of threat has changed and they are now vigilant against those perceived as challenging the interests of the Hindu nation. This is not, of course, to say that they simply obey their master's voice; rather, that theirs is a historically conditioned role, reproduced explicitly as a matter of *dharma* (religious duty, law and custom), embodied by the caste itself as a matter of pride and cunningly elaborated in the traditions of the new temple.

During the early periods of fieldwork on which this study is based, a violent clash between Bhadala and Kharva men, which had taken place in 1983, loomed large in all descriptions and explanations of social antagonism; largely, I think, because there were no other events to rival its rhetorical supremacy and because the violence vividly revealed to all how class and power operated in the town. In the late 1990s, it often felt as if history had collapsed into this moment and all events and actions were interpreted through its imprint. That, as we shall see later in this chapter, was all to change in 2002 when Hindu and Muslim polarity became a statewide issue and the symbolic potency of a local bout of violence was eclipsed. Paul Brass has written about the impossibility of constructing sequential narratives of the violence after the event because the accounts are subjective, the truths partial and the aims of those narrating events have changed given the violence itself (1997: 5–20). It is evident from the many conversations I had about this violence that state interventions, accusations of 'anti-nationalism', public protest and revenge had been integrated into narratives about the violence. I also heard rumours of forced conversions to Islam, abducted women and the plots hatched by underworld dons and foreign intelligence agencies. These narratives seem absolutely typical of the kind Brass (1997) and others have reported to be grafted on to grander narratives of communal violence. As these forms of narrative merge they necessarily change character and their status as evidence and artefacts alters. With this caution in mind, however, I think the following events probably did take place, although I cannot say with any certainty in what order they occurred.

By all accounts, two decades ago Salaya was infamous for smuggling. Its inhabitants had rapidly become wealthy and, according to people on both sides of the estuary, men from Salaya, often very well dressed, bejewelled and on new motorbikes, would come into Mandvi at night to sit with their friends to smoke cigarettes and to make eyes at passing Hindu women. This led to tensions, enlivened by the kinds of standard narratives of a Muslim conspiracy I discussed in the Introduction, and gangs of Kharva men roamed the town looking for lone Muslim men to harass. Relationships between Hindus and Muslims were more generally also tested because festivals had coincided that year (given the slippage outlined above between Hindu and Muslim calendars) and trouble had flared up in a number of places where Moharam processions had passed through squares in which Hindu festivities were taking place. At around the same time, the customs department decided to crack down on the Bhadala's activities and they raided Salaya. Exactly what they found is unclear. I was told by people in Mandvi that the officers uncovered mountains of gold, bails of dollars and a cache of hand grenades. It is certain, however, that a Bhadala man later died in police custody, after he had been paraded around Mandvi with a sign tied around his neck on which was written 'I am the dog of smugglers'. Bhadala men came over the river to protest outside the police station about his death. They were met by a large group of Kharva men, many of whom were armed with swords. In the violence that followed a number of people lost their lives, others were seriously wounded and the trouble spread to other areas of the town before the police imposed a curfew.

Violence in India often occurs along the lines of pre-existent patterns of social organisation and social institutions and, likewise, can be domesticated or tamed by such structures (Brass 1997; Tambiah 1996). The broad class division between merchants and sailors discussed in the Introduction (pp. 31–32) encompasses parallel hierarchies of Hindus and Muslims. In a sense, the violence was a logical extension of widely recognised notions of authority, prestige, duty, devotion and legitimacy that comprise conventional merchant–sailor relations for both Hindus and Muslims. Everyone in the town knows, and not as a mere stereotype, that sailors are subject to the political demands of high-status merchants and are prone to violence because of their uncultivated manners and 'natural' volatility. Sailors are the lascars for their supposedly genteel and aloof patrons, an inequality that previous chapters have spelled out for Muslim seafarers as being simultaneously reaffirmed by roughly parallel economic, symbolic and corporeal hierarchies. The ritual and moral ties between Hindu sailors and merchants are more elaborate and enduring than their Muslim counterparts, but they are essentially similar in their nature.

There was also a detectable air of pride, especially among upper caste mercantile Hindus, about the communal clashes of the 1980s: it was *their* violence, it reflected *their* problems and *they* had been victorious; just for once the communal spotlight was not only focused on the distant, anonymous, cities of eastern Gujarat or northern India. A Bhatiya man in his late twenties who had childhood memories of the events told me: 'It proved to the nation we were Indian.' 'What did?' I asked. He launched into a long and self-conscious explanation of his anxieties over nationality and identity. He was a Hindu but people commonly described him as a Sindhi. He felt Kachchhi but his caste (and his family in particular) was well known for their close and lucrative associations with Oman, an Emirate. His family returned to Kachchh from Sind at the time of Partition and he said that others had been suspicious of them, suggesting they were not really Indian. In his view, hostility towards Muslims, as problematic as it was given his history, was a sign of being *really* Indian. For him, the violence of the 1980s brought the Hindu mercantile communities of Kachchh from the margins of an imagined India to its core. I objected that he had not gone out on to the streets armed with swords so how could it reflect on him. 'That is true,' he said 'but it was *our* men who did, *our* Kharvas.'

This violence emerged as an almost inevitable consequence of shifts in patterns of long-standing social relationships and divisions. It provided a new set of conceptual resources, metaphors and rhetorical devices through which to describe hostile 'others'. It is surely not a coincidence that work started on the Dariyalal temple and new mosques in Salaya were erected shortly after this series of incidents; or, to put this in more careful terms given the lack of an exact chronology, the fact that new mosques and temples were in the pipeline speaks of an atmosphere in which violence was, perhaps, brewing.

Much of the mythology woven around the Kharva's temple and its artefacts is appropriated from the origin myths of one of their patron castes, the Lohanas, for whom Dariyalal is a central deity (*ishtdevta*). In Sind, Dariyalal (also Uderalal, Jhulelal) was associated with the waters of the Indus (see Aitken 1907: 165–166) but has been transformed, during his migration with the Lohanas, into a mercantile deity associated with the Indian Ocean. Dariyalal was born to Hindu devotees of Varun (a water god), during the reign of the Muslim king, Marakhshah, over the city of Nagar Thatta. The child grew up selling dhal to pilgrims along the banks of the Indus. It soon became clear that he was blessed with miraculous powers. Varun appeared before the child and took him down into the sea, returning him safely to shore with twice the amount of dhal. At about the same time, Marakhshah published an edict ordering the vassals to convert to Islam or face death. The terrified Hindus prayed to Varun hoping the god would be able to prove to the king the power of the Hindu religion. In answer to their prayers, Dariyalal appeared from the waves before the king's minister and asked him to cease his persecution. On hearing this, the king ordered the deity be brought before him, but Dariyalal could not be found. Later, he resurfaced in the water, from where he produced armed warriors on horseback who so terrorised the king that he stopped his campaign of forced religious conversion.

In this myth, commonly told by devotees at the temple and frequently to children on Nava Naroj, the power of the sea is harnessed to generate wealth in the form of trade goods, but, more significantly for the Kharvas, the power of the deity overcomes the predation and aggression of Muslims. The warriors conjured from the Indus are represented in the temple by the saffron horses standing before the deity. Like the mythical beasts they represent, these carvings are also said to have miraculously appeared on the coast. A lengthy and more fanciful version of these myths was published by the Lohana caste association in the 1940s (Maharaj and Dwivedi [Guj.] v.s. 2003: 88–105). It contains a significant elaboration that further emphasises key elements at work in the story. A merchant, a devotee of Dariyalal, came to Bakhar (an island in the Indus) by ship with his family. When the local Muslim ruler saw the beauty of the merchant's daughter he wanted to take her as his wife but the merchant refused. Subsequent threats by the ruler so troubled the merchant's family that they fasted and prayed to Dariyalal for help. The deity appeared to the girl in a dream and said that he would protect them by sending an earthquake to destroy the kingdom. In the destruction that followed, the Muslim's kingdom was left barren. The merchant and his family were unharmed and they set sail to pray and offer thanks to Dariyalal.

The origin myths of the Kharva's mercantile patrons, Lohanas and Bhatiyas, stress ancient victories against either proselytising or invading Muslims. In contrast, while the Kharvas have loosely adopted the tales of Dariyalal from the Lohanas, their origin myths suggest they were defeated and displaced by Muslims. Kharva's caste myths claim that their ancestors migrated from Rajasthan to Saurashtra in the thirteenth century in order to defend the important Shiva temple at Somnath in Saurashtra against the armies of the Muslim Ala-ud-din Khilji. Naran, a retired Kharva sailor, told the story of their defeat at Somnath in the following way:

> Somnath was the most beautiful and powerful temple in India. Hundreds of Brahmans performed rituals to the huge lingam. There was always singing and dancing. The temple had a vast wealth and was good to the people. Ala-ud-din Khilji came from the north to destroy it and to confiscate its riches. Our people were living in Rajasthan as kings and warriors. We Kharvas were a noble and courageous race. When we heard that Khilji was coming to Somnath we left our lands to fight him. We journeyed down through Rajasthan and into Saurashtra and met with the kings there. They greeted us and gave us their best horses. Some people believed that Shiva had invited Khilji to Somnath to revenge him. Many thousands of us died in the battle to save the temple. In the end it was destroyed and the lingam was ruined. After the battle we were left weak and starving and fled to hide along the coast.

In other accounts, Kharvas also claim to have fought Mohammed of Ghazni at the temple (see below); either way, they were left weakened and dispersed along the coast. However, rather than assuming that the merchants' victory and the sailors' defeat is simply a mythical elaboration of the hierarchical relationship between the two groups, I suggest that the sailors' narratives serve to create a sense of injustice and place them in an antagonistic position vis-à-vis Muslims. The structural oppositions in the Dariyalal myth (land and sea, land holding and commerce, and Hindus and Muslims) are made contemporaneous in their retelling as they rehearse and recreate contemporary social divisions. Such standard narratives may be archaic, and may or may not coincide with evidence from the archaeological record, but, I believe, they are not primarily told as sequential tales with a logical conclusion; rather, they stand for a set of structural power relations that are salient in the present. In fact, on a number of occasions, I was told in no uncertain terms that the Kharvas' attack on the Bhadala in the 1980s, armed with swords like the warriors of old, was revenge for their defeat at Somnath.

Before work on the Dariyalal temple began, the hero stones and tortoise lay forgotten in the sand dunes. They were uncovered by an archaeologist from Bombay and rapidly incorporated into the nascent traditions of the temple. While the tales surrounding these artefacts are clearly transformations of ancient themes, they have been given a heightened importance given the communalised identity-building projects prompted, perhaps, by violent events of two decades ago. The hero stones are unusual because they depict ships – unlike similar sacrificial stones in Kachchh that show either a raised hand for women or a mounted warrior for men. Today, the Kharva have grafted new meanings on to these stones, enabling them to stand for a host of courageous and exceptional ancestors who sacrificed their lives to the sea, such as the twenty or so men who lost their lives to Japanese submarines during the Second World War and Ramsinh Malam, the artisan-sailor discussed in Chapter 1 (pp. 41–42), who learned his crafty ways in Holland.

While many aspects of the temple are influenced by local competition with Muslims, the emerging traditions of the temple also draw upon the ideas and practices of elite Hindu sects of their mercantile patrons, reflecting the Kharva's attempt at improving their status position within Hindu society. The mercantile sects have incarnations of Vishnu at their core, and elaborate ritual practices and patterns of priestly hierarchy that make them quite distinct from other forms of popular Hinduism in the area. These movements, especially those dedicated to Lord Swaminarayan, have experienced tremendous growth in the last two decades as the small enclaves of elite followers have been swelled by the effects of mass proselytisation and the relaxation of caste restrictions relating to initiation. These movements, along with the Jainism, have left a clear imprint on popular Hindu religious thought and practice of all kinds. The values associated with them, such as vegetarianism and self-discipline (rejecting addictive substances, for example), are widely practised at all levels of Hindu society in Gujarat. The most common types of upward social mobility involve aspirants adopting values resembling those of these sects. At least one of these movements has been co-opted by a political party as a means of crystallising a mass Hindu following united around a common deity and set of ritual practices rather than relying on the more unpredictable route of caste loyalty for electoral gain. In the Kharva case, I only met a handful of people who had actually become initiated into one of these sects but the community generally was attempting to shed its reputation for drunkenness and its non-vegetarian diet.

The Dariyalal temple and its new traditions also mark a clear shift away from the older Shiva temples, such as the crumbling structure dedicated to Ratnakar Sagar (the sea as a mine of jewels). Lord Vishnu, the central deity of the Vaishnava sects, is popularly held to have ten incarnations, passing from lower forms of life to divinities in the guise of humans, such as Ram and Krishna. In the Dariyalal Temple, the deity is carried by the Vishnu's first incarnation, Matsya (a fish), who saved the Vedas from being consumed by demons in a terrible flood. However, perhaps the most contrived but most well-known piece of pantheonic symbolism in the temple relates to Vishnu's second incarnation (or third, depending on the tradition) as Kurma, the tortoise in the temple compound. After the great flood, the deities were weak, their powers lost in the ocean. Vishnu sprinkled the ocean with a variety of medicinal herbs, advising them to churn the mixture to create a regenerative elixir. They attempted to use Mount Mandara to stir the waters but were not strong enough so called on the help of demons. Even their united strength could not stop the mountain from sinking into the ocean bed. Vishnu came to their rescue in the form of a giant tortoise, Kurma, and bore the weight of the mountain upon his back to stir the ocean until treasures arose from the depths.

Thus, in the Dariyalal traditions there are two related aspects of Vishnu. First, the deity is the legitimate defender of the faith; in the case of Matsya and Kurma, Vishnu arrives on the earth when *adharma* (anti-religion) is strong or *dharma* (religion) is threatened. Second, as with the stories of Dariyalal, Vishnu as both Matsya and Kurma has the power to procure treasures from the sea. These aspects are combined in a claim made by the custodians of the temple who suggest the cartographical outline of Kachchh resembles Kurma, the tortoise: Rapar and Bhachau form the lowered head; Anjar, Mundra, Mandvi and Abhrasa form the spine of the shell; Nakhatrana and Lakhpat form the bottom of the shell; and Bhuj, and the northern regions, give the impression of a leg.

In this claim, they state, on one hand, that the land *is* the deity and therefore it is but to be expected that wealth has come to the people of the land from the sea. On the other, and here again the boundaries between the myths of Dariyalal (sea) and Vishnu (land) meld, the deity is the soil or, at least, as in the case of the merchant visiting Bakhar, the deity has power over the soil when Hinduism is threatened.

The symbolism within the temple reveals the atavism at the heart of the Kharva's nostalgia and the audible sense of injustice they feel towards the Bhadala, yet the business of seafaring continues to slip away from them. On Nava Naroj they offer vegetarian sacrifices to the deity and the ancestral stones and perform in story and song the kind of narratives I have discussed. Thus, for the Kharvas, Nava Naroj has become a way of looking into and retelling the past through the communalised lens of the present. They also claim that their social and geographic displacement was a result of defeat at the battle for Somnath. From the perspective of such *ex post facto* rationalisation, rather than recapitulating somewhat abstract nationalist discourse, they are rewriting and revenging their own displacement. In a sense, they have personalised the rhetoric now associated with mainstream political Hindu nationalism and have provided themselves with a powerful set of incentives through which to seek redress against the general evils perpetrated by Muslims in India and against the Muslim hijacks of the shipping industry. As putative descendants of Krishna and Ram through Kshatriya descent lines, the Kharvas have ritually constructed themselves as warrior-sailors – with traces of the deity in them and on whose land they also tread. They have created a powerful charter through which they appear to be the legitimate defenders of the land against Muslim invaders, defeated in the distant past at Somnath and vengeful in the present.

The changing performances of Nava Naroj are illustrative examples of divergent practices among Hindu and Muslim sailors. This divergence has been accompanied by the growth in the numbers and scope of the standard narratives of religious difference, which encourage and delineate distinctive identities, emphasise religion and homogenise, depersonalise and dehumanise rivals. One elderly Kharva man, Ramji, who passed two decades of his earlier life at sea, regularly called the Bhadala 'crows', black scavengers. The crows stole the food of the traditional merchants of Kachchh to whom he attributed the grace and beauty of flamingos. Once he described the violence of two decades ago as 'trussing the feet of the troublesome crow'. Other Kharva men would lament that Bhadala did not know how to 'plough the sea'. These men resented the fact that Bhadala ships were powered by engines and had sophisticated navigation equipment; they dismissed the shipbuilding industry in Salaya as shoddy and for short-term profit rather than for more discerning long-term investment; they also expressed hostility towards the methods and strategies they thought the Bhadala used in their business. They were nostalgic for sail and for the traditions of navigation that relied on the moon, wind and waves. They harked back to an era when ships were built to last and their mercantile patrons were successful. Their negative characterisation of 'modern' shipping is not simply the grumbling of elderly men unable, or unwilling, to accept and accommodate change. Their resentment and frustration are expressions of failure and, in my view, of their vulnerable positions within a fragmented market for international labour. The logic of their subordination, however, prevents them from seeking retribution against the high-caste patrons who have divided them and ensured they are on the front line of new communal conflicts.

Despite their laments, it cannot be the worst of times judging by the number of newly constructed houses in the Kharva's area of the town. Their labour in Oman is generally de-skilled and they have little collective power because they are divided between employers, industries and types of contract (or absence of a contract), but net gain from their labour is high when compared with the standard of wages in Mandvi. For individual men in the vulnerable world of international labour migration, continuity over the seasons and years is given largely by their enduring relationships with the descendants of those on whose ships they used to serve. Again, there are of course exceptions, where relationships have broken down, turned sour or become over-burdened by debt. Generally though, a good and mutually beneficial relationship with a merchant is held as the highest ideal and those Kharva men who had drifted outside the confines of such patron–client kinds of relationships to either work for employment agencies or, perhaps, start a small business of their own, were talked about by others as if they had betrayed caste traditions. In the previous chapter, I discussed how the institutionalised frameworks of caste and kin among Muslims were kinds of resistance, however futile, to inevitable corporeal chaos. The evidence suggests a similar preoccupation among many Hindus with the preservation of lineages, the integrity of caste boundaries and the fixed expectations and duties within certain kinds of relationships such as those between merchants and sailors. This is not merely to avoid the fundamental chaos of unregulated human nature but, in a rather more mundane sense, to preserve – in the face of rapid social change – the precarious positions of those who enjoyed privilege and status in the past. Those with most to lose are not the merchants, the five-star generals of the caste world, but the infantrymen who sustain themselves on temporary work permits and cycles of seasonal migration to non-seasonal employment.

In their standard narratives, describing the differences between Hindus and Muslims, Kharva men presented me with a wide variety of reasons as to why they mistrusted the Bhadala. For them, Muslims are seen as having been aggressive from the outset, arriving and spreading into Asia from Arabia through conquest and holy war; destroying temples and converting or dispersing the population as they did so. Also, in part because of their claims to foreign origins, Muslims are seen as undermining the stability of the country by supporting foreign powers or putting the interests of Islam before those of the country. The Kharva also talk about the Bhadala as if they are part of a homogeneous Muslim community (when they clearly know they are not) who are actively seeking political affiliation and financial support from the Middle East (which they are not). Such myths are conflated with the very real concerns over Kashmir, the status of Muslim personal law, the rivalry and skirmishes between Pakistan and India and the partitioning of the sub-continent into India and East and West Pakistan in 1947.

Many of Mandvi's Hindus have never been to Salaya despite its proximity. Thus, there is often a very significant gap, invigorated by rumour, between what people in Mandvi think of those in Salaya and the reality of their conditions. For example, I never, sadly, saw the blood sacrifices the villagers were supposed to perform or the widespread tendency for polygamy (I am aware of one such arrangement in the village) and I was never served the beef on which they were supposed to gorge. In Mandvi, people stared at me incredulously when I said I had friends in the village with degrees from universities in Bombay and Dubai. More generally, I have never personally heard of or seen Muslims in Kachchh actively supporting Pakistan in international cricket, as they are commonly rumoured to, and nor have I ever heard firecrackers going off in the street when Pakistan claim victory in border skirmishes in Kashmir or, for that matter, cricket. Some seafarers actually have good reason to dislike Pakistan, having been incarcerated for months at a time because they were Indian when their vessels were impounded by the Pakistani navy. At times, when relations between India and Pakistan have been good, many Muslims from Kachchh have made the long rail journey, via the border crossing in Punjab, to visit their many relatives in Karachi. Few I have spoken to about the experience have anything positive to say about the city or about Pakistan. Most found it, at least when compared to their beloved Kachchh, dirty, intimidating, aggressive and, as one informant put it, 'dominated by religion'. For a great many Muslims in Mandvi, one of the things they enjoy a great deal (and are made to appreciate much more by visiting Karachi) is living in a town where not all are their co-religionists and not all spaces and activities are controlled by elders or the watchful eyes of neighbours. Thus, they are at liberty to go to seasonal fairs or the beach and stroll around the lake on a Sunday evening. Outside their neighbourhoods and with their friends, life is not all about the mosque and prayer, although at a superficial glance it might appear so.

For Bhadala men things were rather different. Very few of them came over to Mandvi for anything other than shopping and business, let alone for recreational purposes; not only is the town loosely thought of as *dar al-kafir*, but some of the natives have proven to be distinctly hostile in the past. On the whole, the Bhadala stayed in their village, mindful of their behaviour, participating diligently in the displays of unity and submission such as Nava Naroj. Senior Bhadala men would organise football tournaments in the 'off season' to keep the younger men from trouble in Mandvi; at religious discourses in Mukhdummi Sha the congregation was told that running around the bazaar chasing hollow dreams was not only against the *sunnah*, it was a 'crime against the gift of life'. Most simply did not go into the town unless they had to and they had taken to football in order to differentiate themselves from a nation of cricketers; the sport also served to keep them away from the bright lights of the town's bazaars. Playing football for me in England was, in part, about the sociality of going to the pub afterwards. Since there are no pubs in Gujarat, and even if there were none of these men would be seen going in to one in full view of the village, after the game most men drifted off home or to the mosque. I learned this quite early on, when, after an hour of being fouled and cursed on the pitch by a man wearing a t-shirt saying 'Just do it International', I asked him if he wanted to have a fruit juice in town to cool off. He told me frankly that when he was young (perhaps twenty years ago) he used to go into Mandvi at night but had realised the error of his ways because, as he said, 'it is written in the Quran that idle pursuits such as gossiping and making eyes at women were against the spirit of Islam. Now in the evenings I read our Glorious Quran and have no need of such things.'

I was rather taken aback by the simplicity and apparent sincerity of this statement. Could it really be that this rough looking and talking sailor was as sincere in his practices as he claimed to be? As the months passed, I learned that Zoheb ('Just do It International') did what he said he did: he went home and read the Quran on his own for a couple of hours before taking his evening meal. It was not until much later, when I met Zoheb and others in Bombay that their standard narratives began to slip and I began to appreciate that what they did in the metropolis was another matter entirely (rather like a walk along the beach was for many of Mandvi's Muslims on a Sunday evening). The Bhadala men who manage shipping offices in Bombay or elsewhere may also be away for much of the year but they flit between Mandvi and their other interests as needs demand. In Bombay, they (including Zoheb) took me on excursions to seedy brothels, swanky bars near the fashionable Juhu Beach and to the apartments of those on the fringes of the film industry. The point here, of course, is not to suggest they are hypocrites or to imply that their religious personality is not important to them, but to highlight the fact that my friends and informants behave and dress quite differently in different places. When they are away from Salaya/Mandvi they generally spend time with peers, which perhaps gives them a greater freedom than when they return home and act out suitable roles before fathers, mothers, wives, children and the watchful, sometimes accusatory, eyes of elders and neighbours. However, this change of behaviour is also due to the conditions in Mandvi and Salaya and the forces at work within. The conservative, isolationist and religiously minded Bhadala is the one the Kharva sees as he looks out across the estuary and, to a significant extent, this is the pattern of Muslim behaviour that he as a Hindu has helped to create.

What the Bhadala did in response

The three metaphors Hindus use to represent the morality of the violence in Kachchh during the early 1980s are the perennial struggle of Hinduism against Islam, Lord Ram's defeat of Ravana and revenge for an ancient battle at Somnath. I heard no similar attempts to mythologise these events among Muslims. Mohamed once told me in his own inimitable style that 'shipping was a Hindu business. We took it from them. They wanted revenge, so called upon the government to come and punish us.' More generally, the Bhadala's response to these incidents also reveals a similar pragmatism. They retreated to their village and held their positions. Until the government recently started to build a new access road to the beach, there was a single cement road into Salaya. The old route dates from the late 1980s and is bordered by high walls on both sides and passes through a series of tight bottlenecks. The design of the road discourages outsiders from wandering into the village and clearly offers the inhabitants some defensive advantages over intruders. Traditionally, houses in Kachchh were built to be secure, often constructed around a courtyard with a single entrance. In Salaya, however, the level of security is noticeably higher. There are very few windows at street level and most houses have bars over their windows even on the second floor. Most compound walls are at least two metres high with equally impenetrable entrance gates. Some of the houses are rumoured to have secret subterranean rooms or extra compartments built in to enlarged wall cavities.

While fortification was one response to the violence, others turned to different strategies. Some went to stay, a few permanently, in Bombay and Jam Kambalyia in Saurashtra. Others sent their sons away to study in Christian boarding schools in Maharashtra and international schools in Dubai. Before this there was little tradition of formal education among the Bhadala. Expensive education in faraway schools was also a prestigious consumption good for some. The inadvertent consequence, however, of searching for such safe havens is that today there is a significant number of articulate men in their thirties who are well versed in the liberal arts, bible studies and the history of ancient Greece. They understand their rights and privileges and can read and reproduce the language of bureaucracy and government. At school in Maharashtra, they made enduring friendships with a fashionable and affluent set, some of whom are now on the fringes of the Bombay film industry. The experience of education also brought these men together in uneasy alliances, often to represent their illiterate and sometimes hot-headed fathers in business and politics in Salaya. It is this small group of men who have taken the lead in the village, are at the vanguard of social and religious reform and who have invested most in generating loyal constituencies in their fathers' names.

In relation to Nava Naroj, the sacrificial coconut, an archetypal Hindu offering, and Dariyapir have been abandoned in favour of an unmediated prayer to Allah on the waterfront. Nava Naroj has thus become a careful, albeit fragile, enactment of modernity as a reformed social and religious order. Although the performance of *zikra* reveals differences among them, it also unites the majority in a public and highly politicised ritual. *Zikra* is thus an explicit device of separation and a counter-enactment to the observances of Hindu sailors and other Muslims. In this sense, the different rituals of Nava Naroj reflect how the Bhadala view moral hierarchy and the grades of validity in religious practice as discussed in Chapter 2 (p. 74), with different forms of thought and practice found among Muslims being ranked above the general category of Hinduism. This also reflects, on the one hand, a temporal trajectory in which they describe themselves as passing from Hinduism, to confused forms of Islam before becoming good Muslims. On the other hand, this has a more contemporaneous and spatial form because, on one river bank, drumming and drunkenness accompany the Hindu sailors on their visit to a colourful deity in human form sitting on a fish; on the opposite side of the estuary the good Muslims sit together to remember Allah. Leaving aside those in attendance at Apu Pir, there was also another set of ritual performances for Nava Naroj that fell between the extremes of practice. Coconut milk flowed and incense also burned over the graves nestling against the compound wall of the Dariyalal Temple. A number of times in Salaya, I was told that they were the graves of dead Bhadala, dating from the days when they went to the site to venerate Dariyapir. These abandoned tombs have been given a renewed lease of life as new custodians have come forward, claiming miracles from the deceased, in order to counter the encroachment of the temple. Who were the braves who came to offer resistance to the appropriation of Dariyapir's stomping grounds by Hindus? They were certainly not the Bhadala because I never saw any one of them near the site; rather, they were the apprentices from the Bhadala's shipyards and their families who through flattery and necessity were attempting to curry favour with their employees by adopting their masters' enemies as their own.

Political Hindu nationalism in Gujarat

Given this background, it is unsurprising that the marginalisation of Muslims has taken on a renewed vigour in the last few decades. At district and state levels, the reasons behind the process and the mechanisms through which this occurs may vary but the signs, symbols and rhetoric are remarkably similar. Such signs are most apparent and salient at times when festivals coincide, religious sites are contested and when there is competition for space or resources. Muslims are being increasingly pressured into locations of secrecy and isolation, often for their own self-protection. In turn, the nationalist organisations spearheading anti-Muslim programmes then innocently protest that the reason for their mistrust of Muslims is their secrecy and isolation. In Gujarat, over the past few years, anti-Muslim rhetoric has grown noticeably more sophisticated and elaborate. Much of the literature on Hindu–Muslim relations – even that written in the 1990s – now seems outdated, if not to say naive, as the political landscape in Gujarat has changed beyond recognition and the anti-Muslim elements in the Hindu nationalist fold have been presented with the global resource of the 'war on terror' from which to draw evidence, rhetoric and justification. In October of 2002, there was already much talk of the American invasion of Iraq. Many Hindus were clearly enthusiastic about this impending attack on a Muslim country, apparently overlooking the fact that much of India's oil came from Iraq and the two countries had traditionally fostered close working relations. An acquaintance stressed to me a number of times that this really was going to be 'one in the eye for Muslims' and that America had finally realised, as 'India' had been saying all along, that 'Muslims' were the real problem. The bombs exploding on Baghdad and Fallujah were somehow going to lessen the problems Hindus faced in India. As we sat over tea in his fine new house in suburban Mandvi, he explained that his housing society had everything: good water, a healthy breeze, electricity supply and roads. There was, however, one problem: the Muslims. Adjacent to the housing society is a somewhat ramshackle settlement inhabited by 'Muslims', originally an illegal encroachment on government land. The settlement had been there many years, much longer than the housing society, and had recently been regularised; electricity ran to the houses and a standpipe had been installed by the municipality. Later, after further investigation, it emerged that only around four out of five of the inhabitants were Muslim; the remaining twenty per cent were Harijans (former Untouchables). It was, however, irrelevant to my friend that they legally owned the land, were not all Muslim and had moved to the site many years ago when it was considered to be waste ground. He patiently explained:

> it is the same process, the terrorism of September 11th, the hostility of Muslims to the United States, and the encroachment of this land. They are all the same thing. These people want to expand to own everything; they live here like animals, with pigs, dirty with rubbish and our Government protects them! We tried to get them removed but the Government said they were entitled to the land.

Even our own Hindu politicians protect these Muslims! There will be nothing left for us! . . . At least now America is with us and we will crush them.

I have known this man since 1997, and like many middle-class Hindus in the town his political ideas have hardened considerably in the last few years and his frustration and fascination with politics has clearly grown – as has his loyalty to the BJP. He is not considered to be a political extremist or an agitator and his writing as a journalist is seen as reflecting the opinions of the middle-of-the-road Hindu majority who read the newspaper he writes for.

Against much of the literature on Hindu nationalism, which treats this political trend as if it were a singular ideology with a shared genealogy of ideas (Hansen 1999; van der Veer 1994), I suggest that in Gujarat 'Hindutva' is a series of similar but different (like cars or flowers) and competing philosophies. At one level, we might say there is a spectrum of political Hindutva as there are Democratic and Republican agendas in America and there once was a 'left' and a 'right' in British politics, and in the Indian case this is best thought of as 'moderate' and 'hard line'. We can also observe that within moderate and hard-line forms of 'Hindutva' there is a series of rival ideologies that are firmly rooted in their sociological and historical peculiarities (see Simpson 2004). The comparison of such agendas may reveal different images of the nation reliant on different geographies and histories or, indeed, that the nation itself is ideally the exclusive property of, or best governed by, particular castes, deities and certain charismatic leaders. I also want to suggest that certain aspects of the nationalist agenda can no longer be exclusively associated with a single political party – if, indeed, behind all of the hype and fine theory, Hindu nationalism was ever really the sole property of the BJP. It seems to me that these careful analytical distinctions are important not simply because some of the previous literature has contributed to creating the sense that Hindutva is a thing with consistent and clearly identifiable properties but because we have to know exactly what currents of political intrigue Muslims are caught up in so that we may empirically analyse what it is they are responding to.

Contemporary Hindu nationalism has claimed legitimacy and power in ways well understood by politicians of the previous decades. The Indian state has expanded in new ways in recent years and it is through such expansion that it has incorporated the Sangh parivar (the family of nationalist organisations) into its fold. This family's origins can be crudely traced back to a primogenitor, the Rashtriya Swayamsevak Sangh (RSS), who begot the rebellious Vishwa Hindu Parishad (VHP) and together they gave birth to a kinder progeny to represent it on the political platform in the form of the BJP; below this triumvirate there are tiers of lesser cousins who voice regional or more specific concerns (for example, Jaffrelot 1996; Lochtefeld 1996; Smith 2003: 181–198). This genealogical model is compelling, as is the division of labour it implies: the RSS, formed in 1925, instils moral value in the population and produces suitable leaders for renascent Hindu India; the VHP, founded in 1964, campaigns for the revival of the ancient signs of Hindu might and amity. The BJP, under whose rule both the state and Hindu nationalism have flourished, was formed in the 1980s to represent the political interests of the Hindu fold.

The party's initial successes in Gujarat came from opposing the Congress Party's coalition of low-status groups dubbed 'KHAM' (Kshatriya, Harijan, Adavasi and Muslim). Resistance to this pact came primarily from high castes, namely urban and semi-urban Brahmins, Jains and other Hindu mercantile castes and the conglomeration of rural agricultural castes known generically as Patidars. The BJP capitalised on their resentment through a series of agitations against reserved quotas for the employment of low castes in the government sectors (Breman 2004: 287; Prakash 2003: 1601); this was followed by a shift in the BJP's electioneering strategies to mobilise subaltern castes for electoral gain by playing an anti-Muslim card (Breman 2004: 226–227). By the early 1990s, the BJP was a credible force and the contenders for leadership presented the party with an either/or choice between RSS or non-RSS candidates. The party won the elections of 1995 and 1998. During his reign as Chief Minister (CM), Keshubhai Patel expanded the cabinet to win favour and sideline his critics; he also reformed advisery committees and government boards including the Police Advisery Committee and the Social Justice Committee and packed them with those sympathetic to the Sangh parivar (Sondhi and Mukarji 2002: 253–254). Through these and a raft of other measures, by the end of the 1990s the BJP had changed complexion; the non-RSS faction was sidelined and the choice of leader was between RSS candidates, each with a support base rooted in particular caste affinities.

At this time, the RSS was forbidden to government employees following its involvement in the violence of the anti-reservation riots. In January of 2000, Patel removed the ban and paved the way for the government to legitimately integrate the concerns of the nationalist organisation into its fold. Within the year, Union Home Minister L.K. Advani, who represents the Gandhinagar (the capital of Gujarat) constituency, had been photographed sitting with the CM at a gathering of RSS cadres; Patel was dressed in the hallmark khaki shorts of the organisation, despite the Union Government ordering the ban to be re-imposed just two months after it had been lifted.

According to veterans of government service, twenty years ago the RSS and VHP were regarded as fringe and fanatical organisations. Today, they have taken centre stage and at the time of the violence in 2002 the CM and

President were closely associated with the RSS and the then state-level Home Minister, Gordhan Zadaphiya, was a well-known VHP activist. The VHP claims to have a presence in around 60 per cent of the state's 18,000 or so villages, to have sent 50,000 people to Ayodhya in 2002 (the highest number from any state in the country) and to run more than 3,000 of its special schools (*ekal vidyalaya*), mostly in rural and semi-rural areas. Taken as a whole, the organisational networks of the administrative service, elected politicians and the BJP are largely indistinguishable from those of the VHP and RSS who congeal the interests of governance with local tiers of temple and pilgrimage committees, local political and educational initiatives, philanthropic trusts, newspapers and other forms of media. While there is nothing particularly unique about this, in Gujarat it has opened the way for new coalitions and alliances that have been accompanied by changes to the general legislature.

Narendra Modi is widely regarded as the architect of the BJP's success in Gujarat and the victory of the RSS within the party. By 2001, Patel's government was beginning to waver. Troubled by corruption allegations and the poor handling of post-earthquake relief, the party also lost a local election within the boundaries of Advani's constituency. Modi – never having faced an election or served as an MLA – replaced Patel as CM and became the first RSS *pracharak* (volunteer to the cause) to hold such a post in India (Sarkar 2002: 2873). Only a few months later, the Sabarmati Express came to a halt outside Godhra, a sleeper carriage ablaze. Fifty-eight Hindu passengers were killed in the fire in a sleeper coach. Despite several investigations, reports remain highly sketchy as to why this happened and who was responsible, although in 2005 a committee led by the former Supreme Court judge U.C. Banerjee released its findings on the Godhra incident and concluded the disaster was caused by an 'accidental fire'. At the time, however, some sections of the media and the political elite clearly stated that it was an orchestrated attack by Muslims on the *kar sevaks* returning from Ayodhya. What happened in the following days and throughout March is also highly disputed, but between one and two thousand Muslims were killed. Many of them lost their lives in horrific ways to well-armed and highly organised mobs.

The scale and ferocity of the violence surpassed anything the state had seen during the troubled decades of the 1960s and 1980s. In the aftermath, there have been substantiated claims of police and political involvement in the killing. Numerous panels of inquiry were established to determine what had happened during those terrible weeks and to what extent the government was culpable. The National Human Rights Commission reported that levels of death and destruction were directly related to the government's poor handling of the situation.[3] Another report, written and researched by highly distinguished citizens, states: 'the post-Godhra carnage in Gujarat was an organised crime perpetrated by the State's chief minister and his government.'[4] They indicate that the then BJP president Rajendrasinh Rana immediately announced state support of the *bandh* called by the VHP in response to the Godhra incident and both Rana and Modi used the kinds of language that would only have enflamed passions, when it was their duty to quash them. The police were also accused of deliberate inaction and, worse, complicity in the violence. The same report also lists a significant number of senior police officials in the state who have personal relationships with Pravin Todagia, the hard-line international secretary of the VHP. Furthermore, it was widely observed that some of the mobs used government revenue and sales tax records and electoral rolls and databases from private businesses to identify property owned by Muslims.

Under pressure, the Gujarat Legislative Assembly was dissolved in July, some six months prematurely. By September, Modi had launched the BJP's election campaign with mass rallies throughout the state. In the same month, Muslim gunmen entered the Swaminarayan sect's temple in Gandhinagar and killed more than thirty people. Amid the unrest, the Election Committee scheduled new elections for December. The BJP–VHP–RSS combine presented the election as a referendum on the BJP Government's post-Godhra stance and attempted to mobilise the electorate along religious lines. The choice they presented was a simple one: Hindu–BJP–Gujarat–prosperity versus Muslim–Congress–Pakistan–stagnation. Leading members of the RSS and VHP played roles in the BJP's campaign. Pravin Togadia made around sixty speeches, stressing that votes should be placed on the basis of religion so the 'offspring of Mushraf', the President of Pakistan, would not come to power. He lambasted liberals for 'barking' about the violence of March 2002 and condemned Muslims, secularists and rival political parties as the evils facing Gujarat.[5] In the election, the BJP returned to power with a two-thirds majority – gaining most in areas affected by the violence (Prakash 2003: 1604–1605). Modi was again sworn in as CM. Speaking at the occasion, the president of the party, M. Venkaiah Naidu, stressed that: 'the victory was a mandate for the ideology . . . in Gujarat we have . . . proved . . . collective work is the key to success . . . Gujarat was not a mere political victory; it was a mandate for the ideology.'[6]

The events of March 2002 were dramatic as they were terrible and have created a climate of fear and mistrust throughout Gujarat among Muslims and a rather conspicuous conceit among those behind the politics of nationalism. Kachchh was spared the brunt of the violence in part, it seems, because of the competence of the then District Superintendent of Police who took swift action against a number of those intent upon stirring up trouble. In two incidents, tensions developed in response to the highly improbable story that a mentally deranged Muslim had been paid by a Kashmiri separatist to deface an image of Hanuman. These rumours aside, although the worst of the violence was far away from Kachchh, its longer-term effects have been no less felt in the District as patterns of trade and transport have been disrupted. Unsurprisingly, what happened in 2002 now dominates the ways in which communal relations are understood and described in Mandvi, largely eclipsing the grammar of hostility in the late 1990s. Furthermore, it seems to me that the explanations of what happened during 2002 are no less relevant for my informants in Kachchh than they are for those living in the big cities to the East.

A number of well-informed scholars have commented on the causes of the violence, the implications for federal politics and the duplicity of the 'state'. The prevailing view seems to be that the new inequalities caused by globalisation have been mirrored by a political crisis because the political system has not been able to respond equitably to changing economic conditions and this has led to increasing class polarisation and authoritarianism on the part of the government (Ahmad 2002; Banerjee 2002; Gupta 2002; Nandy 2002; Shah 2002a, 2002b). Jan Breman has suggested the conditions for violence emerged from the promotion of a political economy that seeks to keep the working classes fragmented and in a state of dependency in order to reduce the price of their labour to the lowest possible level (2004: 288). Therefore, it is the working class who end up throwing stones and gas canisters at one another under the spell of manufactured communal hatred. In contrast, Achyut Yagnik and Suchitra Sheth (2002) emphasise the significance of the burgeoning and socially disenfranchised middle class. They suggest the loss of traditional markers of status to urbanisation and industrialisation (also Mehta 2003: 191) has led to a quest for identity that has come to rest upon Hindu nationalist politics and it is, therefore, they who encourage the subalterns to throw stones and gas canisters at one another. Arguably combining these positions, Girish Patel (2002) suggests the religious divide has been intensified by the strong class/caste divisions created by the recruitment patterns in the post-Independence Nehruvian government and perpetuated by the unequal distribution of benefits from economic liberalisation. These conditions retarded the development of an alternative radical polity such as the anti-Brahmin movement in the South of India or the 'Mandalised' movements (those in support of reserved quotas in the public sector for low caste-people) of Gangetic Plains. Thus, in Gujarat in the 1970s and early 1980s party politics stagnated around the concerns of the middle class bolstered by the vote of the lower classes (Breman 2004; Prakash 2003).

My own view accords for the most part with Aseem Prakash's account of majoritarian polity in Gujarat in which he suggests that the organisations of Hindu nationalism have embarked on a project of 're-imagining the state' (2003: 1601). This involves creating a 'Hindu' community on the back of neo-liberal reforms at the expense of the minorities, and most obviously Muslims, for the purposes of cultural supremacy and electoral gain under the banner of 'Hindutva' or Hindu-ness (also Shah 1998;

Simpson 2004). Prakash suggests the 're-imagined state' thus sanctions 'certain castes/class[es] to own and control productive assets and sustain existing hierarchy in social relationships through the control of state apparatus' (2003: 1602; also Patel 2002), in a rather similar form to what Stuart Corbridge and John Harriss have dubbed a 'revolt of the elites' (2003: 235). However, it appears to me that what is really being re-imagined in Prakash's account are the structures of what he calls 'civil society' (where the votes are garnered, nepotistic networks formed and phantasmagoric images incubated), the relationships between its constitutive parts and the rhetoric of party politics. In his account, as with much of the literature cited above, the 'state' essentially remains unscathed, merely absorbing the various hues of Hindutva into the tried and tested institutions and methods of governance. To my mind, however, the Sangh parivar have gone further and have set about 're-imagining the state' by edging power away from formal office through the privatisation of state authority and the simultaneous outsourcing of state functions. This is something they have both planned and been allowed to do by broader structural economic and governmental transformations.

In Kachchh the violence affected election results, the relationship between Hindus and Muslims and the focus of the Bhadala's constituency-building activities. The violence in Gujarat was incited on the basis of the kinds of instrumental attitudes discussed earlier in this chapter (pp. 72–73): that Muslims are a unified community, have conspired from the outset for the ruination of Hinduism and are loyal to foreign elements such as Pakistan. The material in this chapter and the previous one has shown significant sectarian, political and class differences among Muslims and their various loyalties towards India. The events of 2002 have initiated a search by some Muslims for ways in which to build bridges to unite their divided ranks. Occasionally, one gets the impression that this process is to oppose the politics of Hindu nationalism but mostly it seems to be about creating a sense of security in a distinctly hostile environment.

What happened in Mandvi during 2002 is atypical of trends in Gujarat. It does, however, point to the fact that even the most deliberate forms of action, such as burning Muslims for political expediency, can have rather unexpected consequences. In Chapter 2, I discussed the negative attitude towards Moharam of many of the Bhadala during my fieldwork in the late 1990s. In 2004, a marked shift in attitude was apparent. Those who had previously been utterly dismissive (I have interview transcripts) of the festivities, were now outside their houses offering sherbet drinks and words of encouragement to those carrying the *tazias* through the streets. Most of the processions of a few years ago confined themselves to Mandvi; today, all make the trip across the river and through the village of Salaya, symbolically linking the Muslim areas of the two settlements. Therefore, for now at least, the Bhadala have put aside their high-minded attitudes towards the festival in order to foster a sense of unity through its practice. Elsewhere in Kachchh, the spectre of violence has brought rival reformist organisations into dialogue with one another. In these new circumstances, the Bhadala are attempting to play a pivotal and paternalistic role by organising unity through frequent meetings of different social and religious leaders, charity events and discussions with Muslims in neighbouring towns, to whom they were hostile in the recent past.

In Chapter 2, I quoted Daud explaining to his workforce how, in the run up to the state-level elections of 1998, the Bhadala were supporting the BJP candidate because he had promised them funds towards improving the water supply to Salaya. In that election campaign the winning candidate appeared on the political stage with the senior-most Bhadala men when he spoke in Mandvi. The strategy was effective: Muslims voted for the candidate en masse, he retained his seat and the water supply to Salaya was improved as he had promised. Even back then, however, there was dissent against the policies of the BJP at the state level. Daud had spoken against the Hindu ideas lurking in school curricula and the BJP's wilful neglect of secular ideals. After the attack on the train at Godhra, and one key election later, many of my informants were angry and disillusioned that the 'fanatics' had come to government. As I stood with Mohammed on top of the massive walls he was constructing in front of his house to prevent intruders gaining access from the river estuary, he told me the government had gone too far; they were just creating problems for themselves by denying 'human rights', he used the term, to Muslims. He said 'when Modi talks of actions and reactions he does not seem to realise that we too may have to react. Do they just think we lie down while they burn our homes and force us out?' He did not say more, perhaps sensing he had already said too much. He, like many others, has become increasingly politicised, speaking with a new vocabulary against the injustices of democracy and the way the state interprets the secular constitution. Others quite correctly feel that Muslims have been left with power that amounts to little more than tactical voting in the absence of a party with any chance of success to represent their interests. Muslims talk openly about their political isolation much more now than they did in the late 1990s. Since that time, I have also observed changes in their behaviour and, although the following examples are largely impressionistic, I think they are representative of broader processes. A few years ago, it was common to find popular Gujarati newspapers such as *Sandesh* and *Gujarat Samachar* in the homes and shops of Muslims. Both publications were accused of biased and irresponsible journalism during the violence of 2002 and the latter informally became known as 'Hindu Samachar' among some of my informants. These days it is more common to find *Gujarat Today* in Muslim households, a newspaper owned by Muslims and distributed from Ahmedabad. I also started to notice hefty sticks appearing under the counters of

Muslim-owned shops to ward off trouble should the need arise. A friend of mine who had spent a few seasons at sea before deciding that the life was not for him had invested a considerable sum of money in creating a passage between his and his brother's house so his family could escape to safety if need be. But for me, the most telling change between the late 1990s and 2005 was the expansion of Salaya. After the earthquake of 2001 and the violence of 2002 many Muslims from other parts of Kachchh had come to settle in the village, and the teashops, which had once been empty during the sailing season, were now crowded. They had come, perhaps they had been invited I cannot be sure, to settle in the village to swell the population and to make it and their own lives more secure.

As the BJP romped to a resounding victory in the 2002 state elections, it lost four of the six seats in Kachchh. In the previous election, the party polled just under half of the votes cast and won five of the seats, narrowly losing the border constituency of Abdasa to the Congress. In 2002, they won Abdasa and retained Mundra, but lost in Mandvi, Bhuj, Anjar and Rapar (by very small margins from less than 600 in the case of Mandvi, to 9,800 in Abdasa). A number of newspapers carried the story that the BJP candidate had retained his Mandvi seat; small retractions were printed some days later when it became apparent that he had, in fact, lost it. The turn out in Kachchh was higher at 62.3 per cent than the 59.3 per cent of 2002. Muslims in Mandvi and other constituencies, notably in nearby Bhuj, voted for Congress following concerted campaigning through formal and informal networks *against* a vote for the BJP, under whose watchful eye the atrocities of earlier in the year had been undertaken. The Congress's victory in these seats has paradoxically compounded the problems faced by some Muslims and points to some of the subtleties and consequences of elections hidden by percentage point analysis. The former Bhuj member of the Gujarat Legislative Assembly had spent a portion of his budget on providing tons of grass to Muslim pastoralists in the North of his constituency. The new candidate had no interest in pursing this policy and many lost their herds to starvation. Similarly, in Mandvi, Muslims cast their vote not explicitly against the incumbent BJP candidate but against the BJP. By doing so they deprived themselves of a sympathetic parliamentary representative. In my view, the battle for the Mandvi seat in the 2002 elections reflects perfectly the conflict, discussed above (pp. 132–133), within the BJP and the political trends of the state in a more general sense. The loser won the vote of the urban high castes and the BJP stalwarts such as the Kharvas; his rival, a Hindu Patel (the dominant caste of rural landowners), won the seat with the support of the rural majority of the same caste and, paradoxically, with the protest vote of Muslims; paradoxically because the victorious candidate, despite standing on a Congress ticket, expounds a harder communal line than the BJP candidate he replaced. In Mandvi, the BJP were not defeated because of the 'Hindutva' mandate of the state-level party but because of the battle for control of the party on the basis of caste. The Muslims unwittingly cemented the victory for non-BJP Hindutva on a Congress ticket. Rather than the BJP losing control in the future to the traditional values of secularism in the name of the Congress, it appears more likely that caste will defeat the BJP.

The recent history of the BJP in Gujarat strongly resembles patterns of high-caste politics in the state and the various battles in which they have engaged for the sizeable subaltern and minority vote. The violent nationalist turn in Gujarat was not simply the product of an ideological or economic conspiracy among the Hindu elite or a spontaneous uprising of the poor and oppressed. In the terms of party politics at least, the battle for control in Gujarat has not been between the BJP and the Congress but between factions within the BJP pursuing different nationalist agendas. Thus far each side has been reluctant to accuse the other of heresy or self-interest for fear of breaking the party's hold on power. Each side turned to the old favourites, on which all for now can agree, such as Pakistan, Muslims and, more recently, international terrorism, to disguise the fissures in the party and Hindu society. Muslims have thus been the victims of competition between Hindu elites, most visible at the level of party politics but reflective of real divisions in the fabric of society in Gujarat. Arguably, the party's success (and inevitably its eventual decline) among many voters is because the squabbles within the party enchantingly mirror the dominant conflicts of everyday life. As it becomes impossible for a single political party to claim a monopoly on the nationalist agenda in Gujarat, the old divisions between the elite urban and rural castes are once again coming to the fore. This is reflected in new disputes over the reduced subsidies for agricultural electricity and the unequal distribution of water from the Narmada Dam (a controversial mega engineering project); such organised protest movements, however, might also indicate the return to a politics of issues rather than the continuing symbolic elaboration of the Ramayana. One way out of the Muslim predicament, although not altogether satisfactory, is that one side or the other will plot to take control of state politics and will call upon the Muslim vote to do so.

Conclusion

With no one there to care for him at his last, it is difficult to say exactly when Dariyapir disappeared. He may well have vanished long before the 1980s, perhaps when the Bhadala started to move across the river earlier in the century; no one could tell me with any certainty. The Bhadala somewhat narcissistically turned to their village, to the construction of mosques and a larger constituency; the Kharva turned to temple building, Sanskritisation and, perhaps as the latest mode of social upliftment among Hindus in Gujarat, nationalism. Despite the deity's disappearance his name is still evoked. The Muslims living around the Dariyalal Temple, many of whom work on Bhadala's ships, are aware that the site was once shared and that the perimeter boundaries of the temple are encroaching on the cemetery. Returning now to 1998, I sat with some of the seafarers in the evening of Nava Naroj outside their houses to watch the crowds making their way to the temple. They were dismissive of the air of frivolity but enjoyed meeting the eyes of passing women. Our conversations gradually moved to the Bhadala's celebration of Nava Naroj. Very few of the sailors had been invited to attend, despite the fact that many of them worked on Salaya's fleet. Sitting some distance away were some high-ranking Muslims unconnected with the shipping business. Overhearing our conversation, they suggested the Bhadala were ignorant folk who had spent the day praying to the sea. One man characterised what he imagined them to have been doing with a sarcastic clapping of his hands and a swaying of his body accompanied by the chant of 'Oh Dariyapir, Oh Dariyapir'. Thus, in his absence, Dariyapir has become a sign of the past in which low status sailors prayed to a syncretic god, unaware of the heterodox nature of their actions. Although until recently the violence of 1983 was the starting point for narratives about religious divisions, I doubt that it was anything more than a visible sign of processes that had already developed a fully operational logic of their own, related as much to structural shifts in economy and polity as to the morality of illicit trade.

There are broad similarities between the communal geography of Mandvi and Salaya and the partitioned sub-continent, with Ayodhya as the epicentre of political aspiration for Hindu India. In Kachchh, a river divides a Muslim village from a larger heterogeneous population striving to establish itself within the political traditions of India; in the town, a controversial Hindu temple rises from amid the gravestones of an ancient Muslim cemetery. Perhaps this structural resemblance gives political nationalism its life as local issues have come to reflect national events and vice versa. It may well be the case that towns and villages all over India have their own Babri Masjids through which the story of religious polarisation is told, rule established and a demonised 'other' counter-posed and condemned. However, from the perspective of western India this highly politicised metaphor also reveals one of the central problems my informants face with being Indian and Muslim today.

Representations of Pakistan, or 'Napakistan' (land of the impure) as some sections of the Kachchh media describe the country, are often highly distorted and fanciful. As I have discussed (p. 126), many Muslims from Kachchh have crossed the border into the rival country and returned, happy to be back on Indian soil. This experience is however denied them by broader public discourses because they have no influence in the mainstream media; their opinions are not solicited and they continue to hear from those who have no firsthand experience of conditions in the country that the

Muslims of Kachchh are loyal to the interests of Pakistan. The same unequal pattern is evident at the level of the state and in relations between Mandvi and Salaya. Muslims form around 18 per cent of the total population of just over fifty million in Gujarat. Arguably, since the times when Congress held sway in the land, they have been under-represented in state-level institutions; however, in the absence of affirmative reservation policies as there are for other marginal groups, the degree of under-representation has increased. Today, in the Gujarat Legislative Assembly, there is a single Muslim representative, identifiable by name at least, out of the 183 seats; there are no more than a handful of Muslims in the position of Collector, Deputy Superintendent of Police or principle Government Secretary. The impression of a Hindu government evoked by Daud is not far from the mark. While this may discourage Muslims from approaching the state, further animating the belief they are isolationist, many Muslims remain dependent on the state for resources. If one of my Muslim informants from Salaya wants to buy a stamp, pay an electricity bill, obtain customs clearance for his vessel or lodge a police complaint against an errant timber merchant, he must go to Mandvi and deal with Hindu government officials to do so. In local schools, students learn from a curriculum designed from the perspective and in the idioms of the majority community; in newspapers, given the absence of alternative sources of local news, Muslims can read of their world through Hindu eyes (*Gujarat Today* does not cover local news for Kachchh). Through such unequal relationships, Muslims, not unlike minorities elsewhere, generally know much more about the ways of the majority than the majority know about them. While some find their lack of voice hurtful, for most people it is just the way of things, which, one day, due to as yet unknown causes, will change for the better. For the Bhadala, acrimonious relationships with Hindus provided some of the inertia for their reforming activities and some of its direction. In Chapter 2, the parodies I described Mohamed performing before his workforce of Hindu belief and action are only possible given his exposure to such ideas through school and engagement in a wider society. His knowledge allows him to construct a hierarchy of religious thought in which the polytheism and hierarchy of Hinduism can only appear as primitive precursors to rational forms of Islam. One of the outcomes of the violence of the early 1980s was that the Bhadala restricted their interactions with Mandvi and created demons out of Hindus and other Muslims whose practices they deemed corrupt, the latter also being those who did not come to their rescue during the troubles. They strengthened their position by reproducing the old class inequalities between merchants and sailors. This violence also led to some of them going to Christian schools in faraway places, which, in conjunction with their rapidly expanding fortunes, led them to challenge the prevailing Muslim orthodoxy that individual propensities were given by the corporeal conditions of birth.

Today, the moral and organisational heart of the state is determined by the principles of political Hinduism and supported by a self-created and prejudicial representation of political aims, objectives and actions of the Muslim minority. Legislative and empirical shifts in patterns of governance have created sets of relationships whereby political elites can mobilise anti-Muslim violence for their own purposes, while simultaneously disavowing any connection and thus appearing merely supine in the bloodshed. The state offers protection for the majority against the minority of its own making and description. Given the impression of danger, Hindus shun inter-actions with Muslims and occasionally threaten violence. Muslims sensibly avoid situations of potential conflict and group together for safety, and thus appear to be secretive and isolationist. Therefore, the Bhadala partially reneged on their pact against populism, but not hierolatry, and started to search for avenues that would engender unity among Muslims of Kachchh. Arguably, unlike the rather more straightforward case of communal violence described in the first part of this chapter, political Hindu nationalism is so successful because its demons are actively made all the more terrifying by the process itself.

5

IMAGINATION, EXCHANGE
AND VALUE

The previous chapters of this study have narrated the tale of twentieth-century migration from Kachchh, which gradually dissolved the links between Bhadala sailors and the Muslim merchants of old. Vulnerable, the Bhadala set up camp in Salaya, fortuitously prospering from various kinds of shadowy trade, largely from Dubai. Their Hindu rivals maintained links with mercantile patrons and were thus able to draw upon a wider set of conceptual and symbolic resources when trouble came. In the early 1980s, the Bhadala's success, and some of the activities on which this success was based, brought them into violent conflict with Kharvas. In the aftermath, the Bhadala invested heavily in Islamic monuments, both as competitive signs of their wealth and of the greater emphasis they began to place upon religious piety. The violence also had another effect, which was to create a rhetorical Kharva 'other' as a symbol of social and moral corruption. The Bhadala also saw that, despite their successes, within the Muslim population they continued to be low-ranking because of their mixed-blood ancestry. They went about attacking the logic of the order on which their subservience was based by drawing upon ideas firmly established in the wider Muslim world. Yet, the Bhadala's influence is felt in the old town most acutely through the actions of those employed on their vessels as the aggressive Hindu nationalist has become the Hindu sailor with whom they used to compete and with whom Rasheed now fights; the wayward Muslim has become the hierarchy to which they were subordinate in the past and about whom Rasheed argues relentlessly with his family. Together, these processes give shape to the patterns of practice and language among the Bhadala.

Looking into the past, despite the hesitancy I expressed in Chapter 1, there is a vaguely discernible pattern of mercantile communities waxing and waning, which is suggestive of the grand pendulum swings Ernest Gellner had in mind. This pattern suggests resources are brought from the 'outside' (such as elite forms of Hinduism, Islam, print media, wealth and so forth) to intersect almost cyclically with 'domestic' resources such as land, military power, autochthony and historical depth. Over the last few centuries, various communities attaining positions of mercantile prowess have drawn upon the external resources they have encountered or imagined overseas in an attempt to consolidate and domesticate their status in Kachchh, which, in turn, made them vulnerable to fragmentation and decline. This cyclical pattern obviously bears some resemblance to the macro processes behind the rise and fall of urban dynasties I discussed in the Introduction to this study (pp. 14–18). According to Gellner (1970: 239), the pendulum swings between the countryside and the city every four generations (also Ibn Khaldun 1967; Marchand 2001: 139), a time span comparable to the century approximated by Friedrich Engels (1990: 448). Interestingly, my informants in Kachchh also told me that wealth remained within families for three generations after the death of the original patriarch.

It is possible that this narrative also made its way to Kachchh from the dusty library of the Asiatic Society. However, informants were often very clear on what they saw as a paradox of wealth. They told me that merchants pursue wealth but this wealth is, in turn, the cause of their family's demise and fragmentation. The death of the patriarch and the ensuing division of property reduces the operational potential of capital and, as people contest the inheritance of architectural gems or ships, once cooperative relationships tend to sour. In Mandvi, I lived on the same street as a Jain man who was the sole inhabitant of a beautiful but decaying mansion dating back to the late nineteenth century. His ancestors had been highly successful commodity brokers in Bombay and had invested some of their wealth in this architectural gem. The man was widely thought to be as mad as a hatter and did nothing to disabuse people of this impression by sitting on the street for hours at a time loudly grinding his teeth. Another neighbour pragmatically explained that his condition was the result of having too much ancestral money, as a consequence of which he had been well educated but because he had never done a stroke of work in his life he had gradually been eaten away by his underutilised knowledge. Needless to say, the teeth grinder had lost or been cheated of his inheritance and lived in abject poverty. Others also told me that wealth ultimately led to decadence and, in the absence of meaningful pursuits, to vice and eccentricity, a set of ideas also controversially applied to the Parsis of Bombay (Luhrmann 1996).

I hesitate to make too much of this, but it is clear that successive waves of commercial migration from Kachchh have created geographically dispersed networks and ensured the constant circulation of people and thus goods and ideas. These networks varied in their size and in the distribution of their nodes but each provided a loose structure though which ships, men (occasionally women), credit, ideas and trade goods moved across the Indian Ocean. For the most part, these networks were centred upon Mandvi, where the merchants maintained property, families and offices. However, Kachchhi merchants have tended to expand commercially in a horizontal direction, opening additional branches in other locations. This may have led to the creation of sub-cultures within particular mercantile networks and to schisms occurring within previously unified caste organisations. Crudely put, a group would begin to succeed in trade, establish a centralised caste organisation or elaborate an existing one, adopt an exclusive form of religion with a private priesthood, and in time the social and religious organisations would become more-or-less coterminous (also see Dobbin 1996: 109–125). For the most part, it was too expensive for normal individuals to break the moral codes of behaviour established by the organisation (although wealthier and more powerful members did on occasion make challenges against their leaders). Later, however, a serious dispute would occur, usually revolving around allegations of moral or financial corruption levelled at the community leadership, which would, in turn, lead to the devolution of such organisations into smaller networks of trust and information, which often dissected family interests.[1] Those making or backing the challenge were typically successful merchants supported by capital reserves and significant networks, which may have been formed primarily of caste members but were not dependent solely on the caste's centralised authority for cohesion. It is, of course, possible that the decline of these communities coincided with the passing of every four generations. For these nineteenth-century merchants, the decaying grandeur of Mandvi's temples and rest houses illustrates that as they grew wealthy a new enthusiasm for their faith emerged. Defining purity as exclusivity and separation, which eventually found its way into quasi-legalistic community codes, they defined elaborate membership criteria and systems of taxation to fund the construction of monuments allowing them private access to their deities. In time, disputes were voiced in the courts and ports of the Indian Ocean and decadence and accusations of decadence tore them apart. Those remaining in Mandvi also grew increasingly precious about their rites and privileges and factionalism became rife. The Bhadala are perhaps the latest in a long line of such communities to have come to the fore in commerce.

In the Introduction to this study I outlined Gellner's model of dynamic religious change and the structural patterns on which such change is based. I identified three problems with this model. First, it appeared to operate in a vacuum in which the concerns of the outside world had no place. Second, I noted that Gellner's account of the rise and fall of urban elites was functional in its approach and modelled on the mechanical qualities of a pendulum. Third, at the point Gellner parted company with Hume he seemed to assume that the role and status of the intermediary in Islam was an intrinsic and unchanging part of the system rather than being a sociological variable equally susceptible to the vagaries and shifting winds of social change. In response to the first problem, in the four preceding chapters I have spelled out the context in which the Bhadala are attempting to change patterns of social and religious practices. With regard to the second, Chapter 2 presented the problems apprentices are faced with as they labour and Chapters 3 and 4 elaborated those problems, in effect outlining the tiny but substantive moving parts that allow the pendulum to swing and thus permit Gellner's model to work. I have thus far focused on the short-term cycles of exchange as seen in apprenticeship, learning and seafaring, which underpin the longer-term patterns of exchange concerned with the reproduction and transformation of the social and cosmic orders. I have been careful to stress that, although the Bhadala clearly draw on ideas conventionally associated with formal reformist movements, there is nothing generic in the content of the ideas and practices transmitted from master to apprentice. I have also shown how the content and direction of the reform processes are products of relationships between the protagonists, capital, patterns of material exchange, Hindus and other Muslims, and these things too can be seen very clearly in the biographies of individuals. I have suggested that the twin parts of Gellner's dualism are not clearly attached to particular groups (it might have been tempting to say Mandvi's Muslims and the Bhadala for example) but exist as tendencies that are disciplined within the bodies of individuals and appear differently in economic, ritual and political relationships with kin, non-kin, strangers, friends and enemies. However, although shipyard apprenticeship is brutal and the process dichotomises the potential actions of apprentices, there is to my mind still something missing from the process and this is where we return to Hume in order to explain what prompted marginal sailors to put aside their differences, create new patterns of religious and social legitimacy and march upon the city walls.

For Gellner, as we have seen, it fell to a particularly charismatic individual to unite the peripheral tribe under the banner of religion and take the city (or at least to construct a new one). In our case, this explanation falls short in the absence of an individual leader uniquely concerned with religious matters. It seems to me that a better explanation can be found precisely at the point at which Gellner parted company with Hume. In Hume's view, the increasingly powerful individuals came to represent the deity they patronised until they, themselves, in turn, became transcendental. This formula seems to fit my data more precisely, as worldly power clearly precedes the selection and patronage of a deity and, in a sense, it is not the nature of the deity (because the deity is beyond man's rationality) that is in dispute but the channels of legitimate access to that deity. To put this simply, the Bhadala became wealthy and turned to religion to consolidate their status and not vice versa. They built mosques and told their constituents that the only way to have a legitimate relationship with Allah was through these structures and not the shrines of the corrupt over which they had little control. However, even by reordering events thus, we are still unable to offer an alternative to the rather functionalist explanation Gellner offers for the rise of a new power under a charismatic leader in order to realise their desires for wealth and power. Where does the impetus come from to unite under the banner of Islam?

In the literature on Indian Muslims there are two starkly contrasting solutions to the first question (and others that fall between the two camps). J. Benson argues that among the Muslims of the Telangana region of Andhra Pradesh the growing intensity of Islamic 'identity' is a consequence of the loss of Muslim power and social status in a wider system of a Hindu-dominated society (1983: 42–43). In contrast, Mattison Mines has argued that among Muslims in Tamil Nadu 'ethnicity' and 'Islamisation' are expressions of status competition *between* Muslims in the struggle to define legitimate orthopraxis (1975: 404). In the first instance, Islam presents a set of conceptual resources that challenge others' sets of conceptual resources precisely because they are different; in Mines' case, however, the conceptual resources offered by Islam can be used to compete with other Muslims because all parties know the rules of the game. In sum, both conditions apply to the Bhadala as they attempt to override the historical conditions that placed them in positions of subservience in relation to other Muslims as well as trying to form a stronger political constituency through institutionalised apprenticeship to protect themselves from Hindu predations. This double opposition can be clearly seen in the examples of informal reformist rhetoric I discussed in Chapter 2. Likewise, in Chapter 3, I described the mechanisms and the logic behind the Bhadala's activities as an expression of status competition between Muslims; and, in Chapter 4, I turned to examine the influences of recent episodes of violence with Hindus on the content of their rhetoric. However, for the Bhadala, at least in the late 1990s, their opposition to Hindus and other Muslims did not form separate conceptual activities; rather, it was combined in a persuasive model of time and progress in which the Bhadala themselves were at the pinnacle, Hindus were at the bottom and other Muslims were somewhere in between. After 2002, it seems as if the Bhadala have begun to separate the images of those they oppose in response to changing political conditions.

For sociologists following Max Weber, social force and power are underpinned by the ways in which they are made to appear legitimate, which is in part given by the constituents of the power coming to understand it through ascribing its purpose to their most mundane activities. This process was legitimised through traditional, charismatic and legal (rational) modes of domination (Eisenstadt 1968: 46). Leaving aside the legalistic, the traditional forms of authority rest on habitual attitudes and beliefs in the legitimacy of standardised and sanctified practices. Charismatic domination is characterised by obedience, not to rules or traditions, but to a person of imputed holiness, heroism or some other extraordinary quality (Shils 1965: 199–203). Charismatic enterprise necessarily involves the creation of new obligations, ideas and social relationships. In this sense, charisma challenges the existing order and creates new institutions and social formations, through which extraordinary charisma is made routine and mundane. Charismatic enterprise emerges during periods of rapid social change, such as the shifting economic and social relationships structured around the shipping industry, in which traditional Muslim sailors became merchants and other traditionally higher-ranking Muslims have become sailors on Bhadala ships. But charismatic enterprise also crucially depends on disciples adopting the social values of their leader. Why are these values enchanting?

For Gellner, the charismatic leader had to be puritanical, extreme and universal in his appeal as he preached to those covetous of the wealth of the urban decadents. In the Kachchh case (as I mentioned above) wealth appears to be the catalyst for the circulation of elites and religious values, but not the sole aim. This is so because, as I described in Chapter 3 (pp. 89, 92 and 108), within the dominant patterns of Muslim social hierarchy power is not equal to status and status is seemingly harder to come by than power or wealth. Weber's own explanation for the enchantment of charisma seems to depend on an elective affinity between the 'ideal' features of charisma and the sociologically generated 'material' interests of social classes and status groups. Or, in the words of the sociologist Bryan Turner: 'The relationship which emerges, between leader and followers is not so much a discipleship relation but a patron–client pattern in which a leader supplies booty in return for adherence (1974: 24–25). In the following sections I turn to show how booty and adherence might equate and in what kind of imaginative framework status and power can be brought together. I suggest that the appeal of the ship owners is derived from the inseparability of their religious message and the ways in which they exchange booty for loyalty.

In Chapter 2, I described the labour of apprentices in the mud of the estuary. The allure of the wealth and opportunities represented by older men such as Rasheed (the hero of my Introduction) sustains them through these brutal times. As their years at sea pass, they grow wealthier and develop the swaggering confidence with which Rasheed himself would pass through the crowded bazaars. In time, the material transactions of returning sailors laden with booty increasingly mirror the logic of the social divisions impressed upon them in the shipyards. These transactions further the constituency-building activities of the masters, create separate realms of exchange and contact between themselves and the Hindu population, indebt non-seafaring Muslims to seafarers and divorce Saiyeds and their cults from meaningful patterns of constituency-building. The fact of elective affinity between the demands of masters and the aspirations of the apprentices thus finds firm expression in the logic of material exchange. I do not wish to suggest, however, that the logic of material gain is simply the underlying reason for religious reform; rather, I wish to suggest that both are aspects of the same kind of practical reasoning. This correlation is confirmed not only in the obvious parallels and corresponding webs of influence but also by the fact that at a certain point trade in religious goods is restricted for precisely the same reason that the flow of profane items is allowed to pass unchecked.

Before the winds associated with the monsoon whip up the sea, the fleet returns home to the excited chatter of townsfolk. Most sailors come laden with new goods and fashions such as soaps, perfumes, clothing, electrical items, cassettes, watches and cameras they have purchased in the Emirates. These goods are clearly valued for reasons other than their utility because such things are increasingly available in India. As I discuss below, such items are public representations of less tangible forms of wealth and display an individual's power to extract booty from the world economic system. Therefore, it seems that the 'worth' of these kinds of goods is not to be found in the cash cost but rather in other kinds of qualities, such as the origin of the goods, which, in turn, represents an individual's largesse and their power to procure and distribute such goods. The exchanges of sailors also echo the imaginative frameworks I discussed in Chapter 1 (pp. 34, 42 and 53–54) as travellers return with foreign wealth and integrate it into local society as a source of prestige that is legitimised, in this case, by the spatial and temporal narratives of Islam. The goods sailors return with are destined for personal use and display, for 'gifts' to relatives, friends and neighbours, and for sale to individuals and to independent wholesalers. Leaving aside the personal use and accumulation of these goods (which often later become items of exchange), the following sections examine the types of transaction involved in exchanging goods, which variously become what I am going to term 'gifts', 'commodified gifts' and 'transactable commodities'. All three types of exchange actualise and modify social relations. My discussion is confined to goods, but similar hierarchical patterns of exchange are also built up through the brokerage of contacts and employment prospects and, in some cases, through cash.

In Christopher Gregory's (1982) well-known argument on the separation of gifts and commodities, the former appear as an exchange of inalienable objects between interdependent transactors, while commodity exchange occurs when independent transactors exchange alienable objects. Similarly, here 'gifts' are valued because they have a biography and a social life – albeit moving from the unknown bazaar into familiar relationships – and because they entail obligation and interest. However, unlike Gregory I see that when such goods are exchanged for cash they can also embody qualities similar to 'gifts', depending on the relation between the donor and the recipient. It is when commodities are exchanged for cash with an independent broker that the qualities dissolve that made them good 'gifts' of either kind. Goods presented as 'gifts' to kin, non-kin, strangers, friends and enemies create relations of debt and power. From the sailor's perspective, giving away consumer items is a way of acquiring status among his kin group and within a wider social network, but is also a way of maintaining control over the goods and the people to whom they have been entrusted. Receiving goods creates a greater sense of relatedness to the donor than giving establishes a sense of relatedness to the recipient. Such material presentations are met with public displays of respect for the donor. For the sailor, such donations entail an element of calculation because of the limited supply of goods at their disposal. Presenting a watch to another man creates a tie between giver and recipient, but the efficacy of this relationship can dwindle if it is not refreshed with similar gifts in subsequent seasons. Thus, most gifts represent escalating long-term investments in the loyalty of particular constituents. In short, the more the sailor or ship owner gives, the more status he attracts but the more he will be obliged to give in the future. Sensibly, therefore, most sailors are at pains to draw a fragile line and not to give away all they have accrued or to make copious donations that are impossible to sustain in the long term. By doing this they are directly emulating the patronage of their employers, who, in turn, are conforming to pervasive rules of status and constituency-building that run throughout Muslim society in littoral Kachchh.

This kind of prestigious consumption has also been discussed by others (Osella and Osella 2000; Stiratt 1995; Strathern 1992), as has the form of polity to emerge from hierarchical structures of patronage and emulation. Mines, for example, argues that 'big men' in South India are quintessentially hierarchical figures who hold individual 'statuses of eminence' among their circle of supporters (1994). The 'big man' creates and defines his constituencies by redistributing resources and acting as an altruistic benefactor. In this formulation, the roles of institutions (temples or caste associations) are key to attaining and maintaining big-men's status (Mines and Gourishankar 1990: 762–763). Similarly, Thomas Blom Hansen identifies a form of 'big-manship' in Bombay known as 'dadaism', a form of maverick, non-institutional, political and social power maintained through a multitude of local, self-made networks (1996: 158; 2001: 180–181). While Mines focuses primarily on the flows of patronage from the apex of the heap, Hansen suggests that hierarchy is supported by the emulation of the *dadas* by those lower in the hierarchy and often the stories that swirl around those held in highest esteem are mythologised. I would like to develop these ideas and suggest that the model of patronage, exemplified by both 'big man' and *dada*, applies to all transactions conducted by sailors and ship owners alike. Simply, all men, unless they are the biggest of 'big men', are suppliant to other 'big men'.

Returning now to the terms of my own ethnography, each fleet is headed by an apical figure, under whom there are other successive tiers of lesser 'big men' (the grades of crew outlined in Chapter 2), the highest orders of which are often part of the kin group of the apical figure. Below them are further ranks stretching down to the lowest sailor, who also appears as a 'big man', if only in relations with non-seafarers. Each man is, at times, at the pinnacle of his own pyramid of transactions, while simultaneously being in the lower orders of others. Each segmented pyramid is presided over by an apical 'big man' who maintains client relationships, which, as I have suggested, are not so much based on discipleship but patron–client relations in which a leader supplies booty in return for support. In essence, the 'big man' is at liberty to design his own political and religious constituencies, although the structure and numbers of his constituents are dictated primarily by the size of his fleet or by his ability to present goods or favours to his clients.

Sailors not only meet the demands of relatives and friends for goods. Equally important, as they aim to become 'big men', are objects resold within client networks and potential client networks. Typically, these are smaller items that are not sold openly in the bazaar but by judiciously seeking out buyers through networks of kinship and friendship. In this instance, the body, networks and reputation of the sailor stand as the guarantee for the 'commodified gift' (the second method for disposing of booty) and its prestigious origins. Despite the fact that money is exchanged in these transactions, the new owners will describe goods in terms of the procuring sailor because this attests to their all-important power. Tracing the migration routes of commodities through the biographies of sailors affirms their authenticity; without such a biography the qualities imbued in the transaction are diminished. Here, the exchange is one of cash for booty, but the good does not become a disembodied commodity because part of its identity remains dependent on its biography (Kopytoff 2000: 66–68; cf. Gregory 1982) and on the figure (the sailor) who guarantees its authenticity. Even through cash transactions, the qualities of the donor remain inherent in the commodified gift. Access to such goods also reflects positively on the recipient's reputation because it attests to his ability to procure scarce and worthy goods and it makes no difference that he parts with cash in return for the booty. In this form of transaction the sailor acts as a patron and the recipient becomes beholden to the giver. Through such transactions sailors also gradually become bigger 'big men'. Their status increases as the seasons pass as they learn how to procure more foreign goods overseas and their skills at donating them as gifts and selling them as commodified gifts improve.

The third way of disposing of booty is entirely different to the 'gifts' and 'commodified gifts' discussed previously. Some sailors sell their personal cargo directly to a wholesaler rather than relying on word of mouth and networks of personal influence. The two wholesalers in Mandvi I am familiar with are women. To see female kin of Muslim sailors on the streets is unusual; to see them freely engaging men in conversation in public is extremely unusual. These women are, however, shrewd and cunning negotiators who come into the bazaar in the evenings and improbably remove cartons of cigarettes or bottles of perfume from their clothing before prospective clients. Widely thought of as prostitutes, they are in the business of commercially transacting commodities better known as 'gifts'. They seldom handle large or expensive items, restricting themselves to soaps, perfumes, batteries, cigarettes, watches, compact discs, branded clothes and electronic toys. Procuring goods through such agents gives the good a higher value than if it had been purchased in Bombay. However, goods purchased from a specialised broker have a lesser value than those either gifted or transacted by a relative or friend. These women mediate between social realms: between both sailors and townsfolk and sea and land, buying commodities in bulk from sailors and reselling them in the town. Regarded as sinful women, their business is not based on enticing displays or on rehearsed sales banter, because the qualities clients require are afforded by the objects themselves. The improbable figure of the female mediator obfuscates the formation of a relationship between the sailor and the consumer of the good because the inversion of the conventional mercantile gender and style ensures that the biography of the good is ruptured and depersonalised.[2] By disposing of goods in this way, sailors make money in a single transaction, but by doing so they make considerably less than they would have done if they had disposed of the goods themselves through many separate transactions. Although part of the rationale behind selling goods to wholesalers is to realise a profit, sailors willingly incur a hypothetical 'loss' in order to avoid developing a cumbersome network of clients too large for them to maintain. Bottles of perfume and bars of soap could be sold in individual transactions, but as commodified gifts such transactions would necessitate further transactions in the future.

As I have suggested, landlubbers desire all three types of goods because they have prestigious origins and reflect the social standing of the owner by demonstrating the influence they have that allows them to extract goods from others. Thus, building a constituency (as with life in the shipyards) is not simply a matter of unwitting clients receiving from powerful patrons because in this galactic form of polity recipients are able to build their own lesser constituencies from the resources of their own patrons. It also follows that through these exchanges seafarers are able to exert influence over the recipients outside the realm of the exchange itself. If, for example, Rasheed ever needed to call upon others to go armed with sticks to take his revenge on some Kharva men then he could generally find volunteers from within his exchange constituency to do so.

On Rasheed's bedroom wall images of the Abraj Shopping Centre in Dubai and the Prophet's Mosque (Masjid-e-Nabvi) in Saudi Arabia hang side by side. The association of these images is also reflected to a degree in patterns of commodity exchange. Religious artefacts that clearly have little or no value outside the Muslim community in Kachchh are also imported and distributed through client networks. However, items associated with Muslims that have some explicit place in religious practices (and, indeed, I will later suggest the practices and ideas themselves) are treated as 'gifts' and 'commodified gifts' but, vitally, always fall short of becoming 'transactable commodities'. The effect is that signs of piety are controlled by the biggest of 'big men', ultimately the ship owners themselves, in order to prevent them from entering realms in which they could become freely transactable and depersonalised. Thus, the values attributed to imported artefacts and ideas are used by a relatively small group of men to enhance their own social status and, as an integral part of this process, to reform social and religious practices among their constituents.

Mandvi's fleet of country craft mainly trades from the ports of the United Arab Emirates, notably Dubai, where the majority of Mandvi's Muslim labour migrants also work. In Mandvi, the whole of the Middle East is glossed as the 'Gulf', as in 'My brother works in the Gulf', regardless of where he is actually employed. Depending somewhat on context, this reflects the way in which the region is imagined by those who have never seen it, a generality in which sailors are complicit when they are at home. Importantly, the 'Gulf' region (not explicitly Saudi Arabia) is also held to be the cradle of Islam, the location of the life of Mohammed and his successors (as reflected in the 'traditional' hierarchy discussed in Chapter 3). The area is seen as radiating power and as carrying the sacred marks of religious triumph and defeat. Thus it is that when religious goods such as skullcaps, robes, slippers, prints and rose water are imported from the 'Gulf' they, too, carry with them elevated (over indigenous products) status and efficacy. In my time in and around the shipyards and Bapu's teashop I never saw these kinds of goods being sold to commodity agents. Most commonly, the masters in the shipyards would gift and often sell (usually in advance of wages) such items to sailors and apprentices in their shipyards either for their own use or to further interests within a particular constituency. I do not think these patterns of exchange were restricted simply because the goods themselves were sacred or because it was unfitting to sell them (because they were sold within constituencies); rather, commercial intermediaries were cut out of the patterns of exchange because they had the capacity to depersonalise the biography of good and thus to mitigate the potential for actualising particular kinds of social relationship, a power the master wanted to keep for himself.

The ship owner does not, of course, have a monopoly on procuring symbols of high religious standing. Copies of the Quran, items of clothing and prestigious ways of performing rituals can be imported by any number of sailors. However, the status of the individual whose biography attests to the authenticity of the good also plays a role in the value attached to it. Simply, goods imported by men of high standing are imbued with a greater value than those brought home by humble sailors. In this sense, the inherent power of foreign goods reinforces the existing social hierarchy of the shipping industry. With a consumer item, a sailor has to decide whether to present it to X, Y or Z. It is a limited good and competition for his largesse is zero sum. If X becomes the recipient then Y and Z lose, or, alternatively, the sailor loses Y and Z. It is possible to argue that the opposite is true of prayers and rituals because X, Y and Z can all attend and benefit from a sailor's patronage without entering the ship owner's orbit of influence. However, because of the hierarchical nature of patronage, the sailor can only be sure of enticing his inferiors to participate in such prestigious events. Through this he gains further support, but does not gain extra status within the shipping hierarchy. Only the ship owners can confer the most powerful forms of status gain – in this social sphere at least. Rituals and prayers sponsored by them remain the most prestigious and efficacious in terms of status elevation. Invitations to attend prayers during public festivals are not limited goods in the strict sense, but they are severely restricted. Therefore, we see how power and the quasi-magical qualities ascribed to foreign lands and the things brought from them are not entirely divorced from the social relations and position of those who import them, but by selectively distributing such goods the rules of social hierarchy and differentiation can be transformed.

The Bhadala's transmission of knowledge and the corresponding flows of goods inside and outside the shipyards are both expressions of social aspiration and the consolidation of power. Their efforts are rewarded because their rhetorical assertions are mirrored by the control of short-term exchanges. Both sets of related activities are intended to transform the distribution of status within the long-term cycle of social reproduction. In previous chapters, I have discussed the Bhadala's selective antipathy towards local saints. I have suggested that this is an attack on a corporeal hierarchy in which the Bhadala perform poorly rather than a simple squabble over religious authenticity. It is notable that, in the tens of thousands of transactions that ultimately cascade from the ship owner's largesse, the figure of the Saiyed (here again as mystic not scholar), against whom society outside the shipyards is ideally ordered, plays no role. The effect is to create a vast domain of exchanges involving religious artefacts in which the Saiyed plays a peripheral role. Why? The Saiyed has his own local following and claims legitimacy from his genealogical inflection. He has no need of travel (because his ancestors did that when they migrated from the 'Gulf') or to present actual material wealth in exchange for loyalty. Therefore, if religious artefacts imported from the 'Gulf' were to fall to the Saiyed the status gain for those importing them would be lost. Saiyeds have the capacity to depersonalise the meritorious religious initiatives of others by absorbing them into their own religious cults. In other words, Saiyeds can consume the migration biographies of religious practices and artefacts that others have brought to Kachchh and domesticate the status this brings for their own ends; this would clearly deny merit for those taking the initiative to import such things.

Sailors return with wealth and transform this wealth into legitimate sources of local status through exchanges or through commodity brokers. The commodity broker, however, is the last resort for the sailor, to whom he turns if he needs cash when his other obligations and aspirations are fulfilled. Here, turning such goods into cash is the least valued of the sailor's options because the opportunity costs of the various transaction paths for such goods show that some things (in this case status relationships) are usually more valuable than cash. The extraordinary figure of the commodity broker renders inert the biography of the good and sets it free into the world of transactable items. From the perspective of the ship owner, the figure of the Saiyed occupies a similar liminal position to that of the commodity broker. Both figures transgress significant worldly boundaries and live outside and between the realms of normal human possibility. The commodity broker carries with her a reputation for prostitution; in the case of the Saiyed this is matched by associations with femininity and, indeed, as we have seen, with Hinduism. More importantly, however, both Saiyed and commodity broker have the capacity to disrupt the power inherent in relations of accumulative exchange. Therefore, the ship owners shepherd their religious goods along particular paths because to farm such things out to others, or to wholesale them to intermediaries, would transform them into transactable commodities, which are categorically incompatible with maintaining the types of instrumental social relationships described here. Therefore, at certain points in the lives of apprentices and sailors the challenges made to their conceptions of corporality and human potential in the shipyards begin to coincide first with the verbal content of religious reform, which gives their labour certain affective dispositions, and later these things also come to be reflected in the logic of material exchange as sailors begin to reproduce power and status in the terms of their Bhadala employers. There is nothing neat about this process and the effects are violent and provoke arguments.

The central ideas and structure of Gellner's model accord well with the material from western India. I have illustrated two points, namely the dynamic of leadership and the inadequacy of the abstract A (high) and B (low) approach, at which my material is discordant with Gellner's. Instead of the reflux (the Bhadala's reformist initiatives) belonging to the realm of human psychology (although that may be part of it) or the pendulum being encouraged to swing by conflicts between the centre and periphery (although that may also be part of it), here I have argued from the bottom up that the dualism is embodied by apprentices (and arguably most Sunni Muslims in western India) and reflected in patterns of individual exchange. In this case, changing patterns of religious thought and practice are social processes intimately related to the contingencies of individual fortune, patterns of charisma and the various consequences of migration. These factors may also, on occasion, converge with larger centrifugal forces of pan-Islamism or the South Asian reform movements, but the outcome of this convergence must not be treated simply as a generic expression of religious sentiment. Conversely, however, rather like the past, Islam is not a limitless symbolic resource that is infinitely susceptible to the whims of contemporary interest. The symbolic structures afforded by the history of Islam are also aspects of local politics that involve competition, opposition and debate, but these processes occur in particular ways that are determined by the kinds of interaction that take place between different kinds of people (Hindus and other Muslims) in different kinds of space (Salaya, Mandvi, Bombay, Dubai and the western Indian Ocean to name but a few). The grand meta-narratives of the Quran, haj and hijra are also incorporated into the lives and relationships of the Bhadala just as the movements and voyages have put distance between them and some townsfolk and brought them closer to others. Personal pilgrimages and migrations are conjoined with the structural models of Islamic history, which are, in turn, traced on to spaces of relative value within the western Indian Ocean.

I will return to the politics and spaces of relative value below; now, however, I want to return to the discussion of Rasheed's shifting attitudes towards hierolatry. It will be recalled that Rasheed's attitudes towards saints wavered between adoration and condemnation. I have also recounted how the Bhadala sponsor Saiyeds as scholars to dismiss Saiyeds as mystics and then visit Saiyeds as mystics in times of trouble, and they see no contradiction in doing so. I have argued through the example of apprenticeship in shipyards that this dual relationship settles in the bodies of apprentices as they engage with at least two groups (seafarers and non-seafarers) with different systems of political organisation and experience continuities and discontinuities as they move between the inside and outside of the shipyards. I have confidence that, had I undertaken this study in other politicised places of learning, even in the shrines themselves in Kachchh, I would have also observed the dichotomisation of Gellner's A and B in the body of the apprentice. David Parkin notes such conflicts between groups have been in existence since the emergence of Islam (2000: 11) and that such oppositions are often the basis (rather like my treatment of standard narratives in this study) of discussion of conflict, although exactly who is on which side is also a matter for disagreement. Hammond Gibb, rather like David Hume, suggested such a division was inherent in the theological construction of Islam in relation to the humanity of its adherents (1972: 38). In other words, Islam, in practice, could be defined by the tension between a transcendental god (Allah) of the Quran and immanent forms of god (also Allah) personified in saintly lineages. In contrast, what I have attempted to show in this study is that in western India the division represents two subject or social positions open to individuals; both perhaps perform different functions as relationships with the saint tend to be more intimate and personal while congregation in the mosque is the social performance of solidarity. It is true that at a given moment the actions of one group might appear more akin to either A or B of the dualism. However, by seeing relationships with saints (and what they are generally taken to represent) as embedded in other kinds of social relationships, which are, in turn, dependent on other kinds of power and instrumentality, then Rasheed's erring is much less difficult to understand. This is not to say that A or B are simply matters of individual choice but that they represent (in terms starker than they actually are in reality) options for action in broader arenas of power and status competition between Muslims in a Hindu-dominated society. In the space of just a few years, the Bhadala returned to support the Moharam processions, as considerations such as safety and resistance to political nationalism were suddenly more important than protesting against what they previously considered to be carnivalesque shams. In short, the horrendous violence of 2002 did not lead to the reinvigoration of orthodoxy as one might expect but to the popularisation of Islam – political unity clearly being more expedient than purity of practice.

The knowledge transmitted from master to apprentice in shipyards is a reinterpretation of the traditional social order and not a revolutionary new phase. If we gaze from afar on the shipyards then it becomes evident that the masters are apical, mediate between realms and are idealised figures with initiated clients of sorts. Furthermore, it is also evident that within their social hierarchy (as life is given to the fourth generation following on from the original patriarchs) there is the potential to recreate the social order they appear to be opposed to, at least in Hume's sense. In the yards, there was often speculative conversation about what would happen when the senior-most master died. Many of the religious and social monuments in the village are largely the result of his patronage and philanthropy. He is revered and respected for his wisdom and vision and, of course, for the fact that he has been blessed with abundant wealth. It is the dominant orthodoxy in Mandvi that only descendants of the Prophet have saintly potential. The dominant opinion in the shipyards is that the pre-eminent Bhadala man will be entombed in an elaborate mausoleum near the village and clients will come to seek his protection and to request auspicious blessings and his intervention in their difficulties. Obviously, if a Bhadala man is entombed as if a saint this will signal a radical break with tradition. The fact that this idea is discussed at all in shipyards suggests his success and the structures he has built to mediate public access to the transcendental god have, as Hume might have said, become the focus for devotion as both the deity and his achievements have been elevated to a level above and beyond common comprehension.

In the South Asian literature there is a barely disguised paradox that also reflects the theoretical problem of 'universalist' and 'particularist' versions of the religious tradition. This paradox can be phrased as follows. The majority of Muslims in India are indigenous converts. On one hand, the process of conversion is held to have been 'incomplete' and, somewhat hesitant in their newfound faith, they also held on to the old beliefs, only gradually putting them aside as the generations passed (as in Robinson 1983; Roy 1983). On the other hand, conversion is seen as having been abrupt and absolute and as the generations passed the forces of popular Hinduism eroded the original integrity of the faith (suggested by Ahmad 1981). The Bhadala are with Francis Robinson and Asim Roy on this issue. In their view, unknown ancestors submitted to Islam but retained Hindu names and customs. Later, they passed into a more syncretic phase before embracing the puritanism of today. Perhaps this explains why they have little interest in the past because it is the future that holds the promise. In this light, however, they are, therefore, to forever refine their faith and practice and move constantly towards an image of perfection.

This, to my mind, is a standard narrative of the first order. It might well be the case that Gellner's overarching pendulum is swinging over Kachchh or that, as Robinson suggests, Muslims in South Asia are gradually moving towards a pattern of perfection in the overarching structures of history. In the short term, however, the details and practices of the daily lives of Muslims will continue to confound and confuse unless we take a step backwards and locate their actions within a world of mundane and prosaic activities, rather than in a world composed exclusively of the slippages between texts and actions.

CONCLUSION

Anthropology, history and parochialism
in the western Indian Ocean

If, as Arnold Toynbee (1981) suggested, Greek mariners were the first to name continents and thus divide space as they experienced it, then there is some irony in the fact that the voyages of sailors are commonly used in academic theory to display the arbitrariness of geographic classifications and to suggest ways in which space can be meaningfully redefined. Spatial tropes are 'useful fictions' (Parkin 2000: 1) and it has become quite popular to suggest that the division and naming of continents, culture areas, civilisations, world regions and so on is arbitrary and discursive rather than scientific. Martin Lewis and Karen Wigen (1997), for example, trace the origin of the ways in which continents are classified from antiquity to the global legacy of self-interested European imperialism and hegemony to show that environmental determinism and 'nation state-ism' have underpinned the tendency to map cultural centrality directly on to economic centrality. They further suggest that, to properly understand spatial relationships, human practices and social institutions should be considered rather than simply focusing on political and ecological boundaries. This somewhat commonsensical approach seems to ignore the fact that political and ecological boundaries are also ideas often supported by social institutions and by international relations, which have a great deal of influence on other kinds of ideas and social practices and, indeed, on the way that the academy comes to understand them. Furthermore, as I discussed in Chapters 1 and 5, boundaries also play a highly significant role in the imaginative structures with which people interpret movement, wealth and status.

Although the national boundary between India and Pakistan veils the past, it also plays into the formation of contemporary nationalistic sentiments. As I discussed in Chapter 1, in western India, much of the rhetoric of nationalism is premised on the existence of the apparently terrifying spectre of the Muslim nation to the west. Much of the material in previous chapters straddles the boundaries of numerous nation states; however, the idea of the nation cannot simply be ignored because numerous kinds of loyalties, including that of the state and the forms of nationalism

159

that embellish it, also point to the fact that the modern western Indian Ocean is a fragmented region and not a 'world' as many historians have described it.

The nationalisation of European colonial scholarship by Kachchhis (discussed in Chapter 1) is echoed in elements of the documented history of the Indian Ocean itself. Pearson has noted a bias in the historiography of what he calls 'Greater India' that exaggerates the role of Indians in East Africa (1998a: 227–229; also Amiji 1983). He also suggests that such literature emerged in India to emphasise or create a glorious and noble history for Indian seafaring to compensate for the humiliation of British colonialism and to contribute to a sense of national pride (see, for example, Sakarai 1980, 1981). The nation state thus sits rather uncomfortably within the idea of a unified Indian Ocean: voyages transcend the national boundaries, which also obscure past voyages and criminalise others; ships and sailors are known, coloured and, perhaps, hierarchically ordered by their national origins rather than by any commonality offered by their travels in the Indian Ocean; and some decry the voyages of others as anti-national while at the same time the nation state reproduces colonial myths of ancient seafaring endeavours as evidence of its fallen prowess. The study of transnational environments such as the Indian Ocean suggests the possibility of escape from rather simplistic accounts of nation and identity by illustrating the precise ways in which ideas of nations are transcended, rejected and embraced by moving populations. Understandings of the Indian Ocean have been partially manufactured by the persistence of regional studies in the academy, such as 'The Middle East' or 'South Asia', where each subject area has its own intellectual genealogy, style and vocabulary, which contribute to the impression of the distinctiveness of a particular place or time (Fardon 1988). The nascent academic history and social science of the Indian Ocean, themselves partly a response to the dogmas of regional studies, seem to find themselves in a similar position to those regional studies, having championed a unity and diversity paradigm (see below) to the exclusion of all else.

The Indian Ocean's chronological and spatial parameters have been described in macro histories of particular eras (Das Gupta and Pearson 1987) and as general histories of 'Muslims' (Risso 1995) or 'Portuguese' (Boxer 1969) and so on. A second trend, often using similar timeframes, has been to study particular regions in depth, such as Hadhramaut (Freitag and Clarence-Smith 1997), or particular places such as Surat (Pearson 1976; Subramanian 1987) and larger areas such as the Swahili coast (Pearson 1998b). Auguste Toussaint (1966) was convinced that the best vantage point from which to understand the Indian Ocean was from the concentrated flows of people that passed through its islands, as nexuses of interchange, exchange and cultural confluence. Adriaan Prins (1965) identified an explicitly 'maritime culture' in Lamu defined by long-distance relationships of trade, shipping and fishing. In his view, Lamu was a 'little world' characterised by its changeable culture sandwiched between the 'great civilisation' of Arabia and Persia and the trading settlements of Mombasa and Zanzibar. He gave Lamu a double cultural focus reflecting two 'great civilisations' mirrored in the one glass. While both Toussaint and Prins suggested that such locations spoke volumes for wider processes at work in the Ocean, neither went as far as to suggest the Ocean was a human whole. In subsequent decades, however, the panacea for historians has been the vision of the Ocean as a unified space or 'world'.

There are three principal ways in which this world has been characterised. First, the Indian Ocean is a synthesis of overlapping or hierarchically ordered traditions or cultural zones (de Vere Allen 1980; McPherson 1984). Second, the Indian Ocean is a unity formed of diverse elements linked at various times by common tongues, trends and trades (Chaudhuri 1999). Finally, and more recently, the Indian Ocean has been characterised rather abstractly as an imaginary world woven together by voyages and images (Alpers 2002; Chaudhuri 2001). The inspiration for all three approaches can be traced back to Ferdinand Braudel's (1972) advocacy of the unity of a cultural and geographical region defined by the movements of people across the mass of water at its centre rather than by the lands around its periphery. His analysis of cultural unity and diversity in the Mediterranean showed, by using a triple analytical framework of space, time and structure, how the frontiers of physical units and human units are not coterminous. In his view, the 'Greater Mediterranean' was a place of human activity defined by the journeys, exchanges and the cultures of the merchants, sailors, traders and caravaneers that traversed its waters and lands.

In a similar vein, James de Vere Allen (1980) saw the Indian Ocean as containing three overlapping strands of unity that may or may not be present in the same location: race, culture and Islam. Kenneth McPherson (1984) also suggested the region, comprising of overlapping cultural zones, was given cohesion by the relationship between trade and certain patterns of cultural diffusion and interaction linked through the commonality of the Ocean. Kirti Chaudhuri's (1999) structural analysis suggests that the Ocean 'unites' people and places through recognised systems of exchange but it also 'divides' by distance, changing environmental conditions and cultural differences. While considerable criticism has been directed at Chaudhuri's gloss on the details of regional trade and polity (see Arasaratnam 1990), the mathematical methods he uses to categorise chronology and to identify human unity and diversity are difficult to discredit using critical logic. In his work, set theory, an encompassing mathematical approach to the infinite, is used to suggest that all actions and practices are in some fashion a sub-set of other actions or practices. The logical extension of this argument, although Chaudhuri does not explicitly push it that far, is that all people in the Indian Ocean are in some way part of sub-sets of larger sets, which may in turn form parts of sets that unify the Ocean and, ultimately, the world system. Thus, he is able to make the somewhat contrary claim that diversity is, in fact, proof of the unity of the Ocean. Focusing primarily on the technologies, sociology and mechanisms of long-distance trade, he rightly suggests that the Ocean region includes the trans Himalayan areas and the T'ien Shan as much as it does the waters of the Red Sea, the Persian Gulf and the Mozambique Channel. Travel, movements of population, climate, waves of colonisation, mastery of sea travel and, at times, Islam, give unity to the Ocean. Diversity is to be seen in social systems and cultural traditions such as food, clothing, housing and, at times, in the practices of Islam when its expansion created distinct zones of political tension.

The recourse to set theory might not be to the liking of many, but it is a powerful imaginative tool through which to emphasise the relationship between structural elements of a system. However, while such theories account for the analysis of smaller units they continue to rely on the assumption that these smaller units can be identified as being part of a galactic entity and that the types of relationships that link smaller units are equivalent to those that link them to larger units when, empirically, such relationships must be qualitatively different and, therefore, incomparable. The longevity of the unity and diversity thesis has, undoubtedly, been due to the achievements of Braudel's rigorous scholarship and his texts have become the seminal works for anyone interested in seas and oceans.

From a broader perspective, however, it is peculiar that debates on indigenous perceptions of history, social hierarchy, nationalism, learning and religious movements have been sidelined in oceanic studies when such debates are flourishing in the social science of South Asia and East Africa. It is almost as if, by taking a comparative or connected approach to interactions between the two landfalls, the activities, preoccupations and political engagements of those on the shore have been eclipsed from view. In part, this is probably due to the methodological considerations and resources available to the historian. Archives, logs and mercantile records produce an impression of the human movement on which the historian's thesis rests but only in very rare instances do we get a glimpse of what travel meant to people, how they experienced life in foreign ports and what they did with such resources upon their return home.

Struggling against this tide, Michael Pearson has proposed the history of the Indian Ocean is best approached through littoral society (1985) and that the Ocean is not bound together by some nebulous notion of common-ality (2000, 2003). He points to regionalism as one expression of this and to the bonds of similarity shared between Muslims to the exclusion of others as another. Pearson is painting with a broad brush, but, throughout this study, I have followed his lead to show in high resolution that the diversity evident in the littoral society of Kachchh is structured primarily by movement in the Ocean. However, to move beyond this position, I have also shown the gamut of social loyalties and preferences informed by movement that lie behind the simplifying mask of a regional or national identity. My thesis is that travel and migration in the Indian Ocean are more socially divisive (in terms of hierarchy, imaginative frameworks and status) than congealing, and that, rather than diversity being evidence of a tangible unity (in Chaudhuri's sense), idioms of unity such as religious value and wealth, apparently drawn from the Indian Ocean, although by no means restricted to it, are fluid and susceptible to manipulation and appropriation, which, in turn, yields diversity.

To put this in other terms, consider the ship, although the same could also be said for language, patterns of social organisation, prayer and the nomenclature of trade. Among the most cosmopolitan of things in the Indian Ocean, ship design has incorporated European, Arabian and Persian influences in a host of ways (see Hawkins 1977; Villiers 1940). Yet, the confluence of particular techniques continues to produce identifiable regional traditions, such that the form of cosmopolitanism evident in ships built by apprentice sailors in Mandvi makes them distinguishable from ships built in other ports of the western Indian seaboard. Ships, as artefacts of historical interchange, cannot empirically reveal the diversity from which they are formed, a problem well known to marine archaeologists (McGrail 2003). Furthermore, and more importantly, the persistence of regional traditions in ship construction has not been eroded by centuries of commonality. Today, in the port of Bombay or in Dubai creek, aside from national ensigns, it is possible to tell more or less where a vessel is from by its design and decoration despite the fact such vessels operate in similar environmental and economic conditions.

I have presented the perspectives my friends and informants have upon the Indian Ocean. As far as I can tell, none of them would recognise the idea that the Ocean was a unified region of any kind. The idea of spatial or human unity is an imaginative project that they do not share with the historian. For a time, I was intrigued as to how the seafarers would graphically represent the Indian Ocean. I once asked a sailor to draw what he thought the Ocean to look like. He turned his back to me and settled for the task. A part of me expected a series of fantastic images that distorted distances and divided the waters into zones of particular wave patterns, seaweeds, fishes and dragons; instead, he produced a remarkably accurate line representing the coastline between Bombay and Somalia based on this experience of using global positioning satellites. The line was punctuated with three circles labelled 'Mumbi', 'Madi' and 'Dubi' (vernacular for Bombay, Mandvi and Dubai). I have thought about this a great deal and have tried, in various ways, to assimilate it with the other things I know about the seafarers of Kachchh. The line on this piece of paper was, however, the only visual or imaginative representation of the Indian Ocean I have ever seen while in the presence of a modern seafarer, aside from the images produced under distorting influences and in response to my provocation. Therefore, when I set out to write this book, I intended it to reflect, more accurately than the line drawing, what the seafarers of Kachchh did in the stead of imaginatively or graphically representing the space of the Indian Ocean and their personal transformations within it. Religious edicts prohibiting graphic representations and the visual bias of my own education notwithstanding, the preceding chapters have discussed the past, class, rivalries, violence and the creative disruptions of travel and politics. These things are as near as I am able to come to describing the imaginative and practical frameworks through which the seafarers experience and understand the Indian Ocean and the way it bears upon their existence. Although abstract notions of space and time inevitably figure here, it is the nature of the self, elaborated with social relations with other people, which forms the base metaphor through which all else, including the Indian Ocean, is understood.

Connections at a human level, although potentially infinite, are generally rather more limited and mundane than some of the structuralist and recent postmodern literature on the Indian Ocean and, indeed, on 'globalisation' suggests. Today, as I presume was also the case throughout the nineteenth century, the goods Kachchhis trade, decorate their mansions with, and give as gifts to potential allies, might well have fantastic biographies (the chest, for example, to the left of the deck on the vessel of the front cover of this book is marked 'Made in Germany') but there were clear limits to human travel and cosmopolitanism. The networks they forged tended to be restricted, although often very geographically diverse, and, for the most part, they were highly focused on their homeland. Consequently, it seems to me the assumption that any kind of movement over ocean or land automatically signifies cosmopolitanism or leads to unity needs to be tempered. By examining loyalties (to nations, regions, languages, religions, towns, villages and so on), migration patterns and the relative values accorded to different kinds of space and experience among the seafarers of Kachchh, I have shown the following. First, that littoral society has been formed and *re*formed by the movement of people in the Indian Ocean region. Second, human movement in the Indian Ocean fragments space and divides people. Third, the values accorded to such spaces, goods and movements are not equal in their value and prestige or in their capacities to be absorbed into local society. And, finally, differential values accorded to space, place and history can be actively used or decried as people attempt to change the social order.

NOTES

INTRODUCTION

1 FO, 881/2314. 1860. *Slave-dealing and slave-holding of Kutches in Zanzibar.*

1 TEXTS, MACHINATIONS AND THE PAST

1 The regions of Kachchh and Saurashtra were the origin points for the well-known series of migrations to East Africa and later to Europe and North America. It was during the nineteenth century that Kachchhi merchants first established a dominant quadrangle of satellite communities in the Indian Ocean (see Pocock 1959; Sakarai 1980, 1981), most notably along the eastern coast of Africa between South Africa (Padayachee and Morrell 1991), Madagascar (Campbell 1981, 1989) and Zanzibar (Reda Bhacker 1992) in the south, and Aden and Muscat (Allen 1978) in the north. General accounts of the first part of this process include Coupland (1939), Dobbin (1996), Hollingsworth (1960), Mangat (1969) and Pocock (1955, 1957, 1958a, 1958b, 1960). For Asians in Uganda see Morris (1956, 1957a, 1957b, 1958, 1959) and in Kenya see Salvadori (1996). On the Khojas in East Africa see Anderson (1964) Morris (1958) and Nanji (1974) and on Bohras see Amiji (1975). On later migrations from Africa see Tinker (1977) and Bhachu (1985).

2 There is little evidence of the trade and conditions of Mandvi prior to the arrival of the British in the early nineteenth century as the port records are reported to have been devoured by white ants and the papers housed in the district administrative offices in Bhuj were burned at the time of Independence. Many of the later colonial records for Kachchh were transferred from what is now the State Archive of Maharashtra in the 1920s and 1930s to 'Kathiawad'. I looked for these files in Jamnagar, Rajkot, Amreli and Gandhinagar without success.

3 A *candie* is roughly equivalent to one third of a tonne (Prins 1965: 87).

4 *The Bombay Gazette*, 14 July 1819.

5 MSA, PD, 1863–1864. *Annual report on the administration of the Bombay Presidency.*

6 MSA, PD, 1875. Zanzibar. Vol. IV, No 2030. *Reports from Sir Bartle Frere on the slavery.*

7 Sampat, D.D. Bhai Ladha Daamji. *Phulchhaab*, 20 August 1932.

8 A similar state of affairs is reported for the Indians (mostly Vohras and Khojas) in Madagascar where they also used dual nationality to their advantage, claiming immunity from British law by virtue of their Merina citizenship and British protection to save themselves from prosecution by the Merina (Campbell 1981: 219).

9 MSA, PD, 1864. Zanzibar. Vol. 54, No. 435. *Zanzibar. Vessels belonging to natives of India but who are resident in the dominions of the Sultan of — should fly a distinguishing flag other than the ordinary red Arab flag*; PD, 1872. Zanzibar. Vol. III, No. 201, No. 1015. *Zanzibar. Notice. All vessels and boats sailing under English colours are cautioned against any attempt to conceal their nationality or papers as rendering them liable to seizure and confiscation.*

10 The ineffective 1869 treaty ordered Kachchhis to: (i) allow the British consul to adjudicate their disputes and (ii) stop bringing slaves to Kachchh. MSA, PD, 1869. Zanzibar. Slave Trade, No. 152, No. 121. *Zanzibar, Slave Trade. On the subject of traffic in slaves by Kutchees in —.*

11 MSA, PD, 1875. Zanzibar. Vol. IV, No 2030. *Reports from Sir Bartle Frere on the slavery.* Inclosures 2 & 3.

12 MSA, PD, 1874. Zanzibar. Vol. I, No. 277, No. 310. *Zanzibar. Case of Kanjee Laljee of Kutch charged with slave dealing and committed for trial before the High Court of Bombay.*

13 MSA, PD, 1873. Zanzibar. Vol. II, No. 230. *Zanzibar. Hadjee Omar. Despatches of Political Agent to Government of India and case of — convicted of slave dealing.*

14 The treaty of 1873 again instructed Kachchhis in Zanzibar to stop holding and trading slaves, and to adopt British nationality. MSA, PD, 1873. Zanzibar. Vol. IV, No. 232, No. 1906. *Zanzibar proclamations regarding the slave trade.*

2 SHIPYARD APPRENTICESHIP AND THE TRANSMISSION OF KNOWLEDGE

1 There is a rare dictionary detailing of some of this language (Mankad [Guj.] 1935) and, to a lesser degree, also see Vaidya (1945).

4 HINDU NATIONALISM AND THE MUSLIM RESPONSE

1 The 'twelve' (sixteen) villages are Aarambhada, Dwarka, Goghla, Goriyari, Jam Salaya, Jamnagar, Mandvi, Mangrol, Mundra, Okha, Porbunder, Positara, Salaya, Vanakbara, Varvala and Veraval.

2 For caste literature relating to these kinds of claim see: [Guj.] *Ahevaal*, July, 1992–1997. Mandvi: Shri Kharva Vidhotejak Mandal.

3 *'Maaro! Kaapo! Baalo!' State, society, and communalism in Gujarat.* People's Union for Democratic Rights: Delhi; 2002, Vols I and II.

4 *Crime against humanity. Vol. II. An inquiry into the carnage in Gujarat. Findings and recommendations. Concerned Citizens Tribunal*, Printed by Citizens for Justice and Peace: Mumbai, p. 75.

5 Extracts from this speech were reproduced in *The Indian Express* (*Ahmedabad City Edition* and *The Saurashtra Newsline*) 'Vote on the basis of religion: Togadia' (19 October 2002).

6 This speech was reproduced as a pamphlet for the media under the title 'Bharatiya Janata Party. National Executive Meeting. Presidential Address by Shri M. Venkaiah Naidu.'

5 IMAGINATION, EXCHANGE AND VALUE

1 In the latter part of the nineteenth century, for example, there was a high-profile court case, known as the 'Maharaj Libel Case', to settle differences between

factions of the Hindu Bhatiya mercantile community over the legitimacy and immorality of the priesthood of the Pushtimarg sect (Purandare 1997); there was also the 'The Khoja Case' in which different groups of mercantile Muslims contested the power and authority of the Aga Khan (Allen 1978: 123; Shodhan 2001). This period also saw a groundswell of dissent among the Vohras, which resulted in a number of legal cases that carried on throughout the twentieth century (see Blank 2001; Engineer 1995). In part, such disputes emerged from the dispersed nature of the communities and the resulting scope for local initiative and maverick forms of local leadership (see Masselos 1978); they also emerged as forms of protest against the centralised leadership taxing mercantile profits and as a response to changing conceptions of identity and community fostered by colonial rule.

2 In an interesting parallel to the way I have described female brokers rupturing the biographies of goods brought by men into Kachchh, Claude Markovits has recently argued that for Hindu merchants of Sind during the nineteenth century the moral perils of journeying overseas also became gendered as men passed the prohibition to women (2000: 27, 266). This prohibition was also noted in the 1870s by Richard Burton, who wrote that the Hindu merchant is a visitor to Zanzibar, not a colonist (1872: 330) and that the wives and designated priests of these merchants will not cross the sea (ibid.: 333). At about the same time, Captain Colomb, engaged with naval manumissions along the coast of Africa, noted the influx of Kachchhis to Zanzibar was of those 'permitted' to bring their wives with them rather than of those 'castes which cannot settle permanently outside Hindustan' (1873: 367). Colomb was writing during the same period I discussed in the Introduction to this study when the schisms appeared to emerge between the merchants and rulers of Kachchh and merchants left to settle permanently overseas. Less speculatively, however, it is clear that, throughout the nineteenth century, among many elite Hindu castes, a dispute raged on the morality of voyaging overseas. In a volume documenting the rise of an Indian steam navigation company, 'Nauticus' writes: 'crossing the high seas was considered a heinous sin and undergoing *prayaschitta* – ritual atonement – was considered obligatory on those who ventured abroad' (1977: 8). 'Seavoyage', as this issue became known in the colonial lexicon, was a series of prohibitions on overseas travel, supposedly derived from ancient Vedic texts (see Carroll 1979).

   At a national level, such disputes were given momentum by the need for a foreign (usually English) education to progress to the higher echelons of the Indian Civil Service. In Kachchh, however, other concerns were voiced over the activities of those who made long journeys overseas and merchants often had to pay heavily for their peccadilloes. The Hindu merchant Ladha Damji is reputed to have sold salted beef to the British Navy in Zanzibar and one of his associates was fined by a religious leader for conducting trade contrary to the precepts of the Pushtimarg movement (Burton 1872: 330). On their return to Kachchh, the merchants would make extravagant donations to their priests and undertake pilgrimage to the Vaishnava centres of Ujjain and Mathura to seek ritual atonement (Sampat [Guj.] v.s. 1995). Other critics expressed concern that life overseas jeopardised the efficacy of Hinduism once its practitioners were on foreign soils (Visanji [Guj.] 1924). Burton noted that very few Bhatiyas turned to Islam 'except those who have been perverted by Muslims in their youth, or who form connections with strange women' (1872: 333). However, in the 1860s, two Bhatiyas allegedly converted, which, Burton claimed, led their caste fellows to declare that the great destruction was drawing nigh (ibid.: 333–334). At around the same time, there appears to have been controversy surrounding the gift of a parcel of land by the Sultans to the Bhatiyas for the construction of a place of religious denomination. A small temple was apparently constructed, but this broke with Brahmanical tradition, as temples in *mleccha* (barbarian) lands were unclean and unfit for worship (Visanji [Guj.] 1924). For a number of reasons, the relationship between gender, commerce, purity and travel in the Indian Ocean has received no scholarly attention but suggests a fruitful avenue for further investigation.

BIBLIOGRAPHY

Ahmad, I. (ed.) (1978) [originally pub. 1973] *Caste and social stratification among Muslims in India*, New Delhi: Manohar.
—— (ed.) (1984) [originally pub. 1981] *Ritual and religion among Muslims in India*, New Delhi: Manohar.
—— (2002) 'The state of lies and the lies of the state. The Gujarat pogrom and the future of India', in M.L. Sondhi and A. Mukarji (eds) *The black book of Gujarat*, pp. 37–46. New Delhi: Manak.
Aitken, E.H. (1907) *Gazetteer of the province of Sind*, Karachi: The 'Mercantile' Steam Press.
Ali, H. (1978) [originally pub. 1973] 'Elements of caste among the Muslims in a district in southern Bihar', in I. Ahmad (ed.) *Caste and social stratification among Muslims in India*, pp. 19–40. New Delhi: Manohar.
Allen, C.H. (1978) *Sayyids, shets and sultans: Politics and trade in Masqat under the Al Bu Sa'id, 1715–1914*, Ph.D. dissertation, University of Washington.
Alpers, E.A. (1976) 'Gujarat and the trade of East Africa, c.1500–1800', *The International Journal of African Historical Studies*, 9.1: 22–44.
—— (2002) 'Imagining the Indian Ocean world', Opening address to the International Conference on Cultural Exchange and Transformation in the Indian Ocean World, UCLA.
Amiji, H.M. (1975) 'The Bohras of East Africa', *Journal of Religion in East Africa*, 7: 27–61.
—— (1983) 'The Asiatic bias in the historiography of the East African Coast', *Journal of African Studies*, 10: 66–72.
Anderson, J.N. (1964) 'The Ismaili Khojas of East Africa', *Middle Eastern Studies*, 11.4: 21–39.
Andrew, W.P. (1859) *The Indus and its provinces, their political and commercial importance considered in connexion with improved means of communication*, London: W.H. Allen and Co.
Appadurai, A. (1981) 'The past as a scarce resource', *Man* (n.s.), 16.2: 201–219.
Arasaratnam, S. (1990) 'Recent trends in the historiography of the Indian Ocean, 1500 to 1800', *Journal of World History*, 1–2: 225–248.
Assayag, J. (2004) *At the confluence of two rivers* (trans. L. Sahgal), New Delhi: Manohar.
Banerjee, S. (2002) 'Gujarat carnage and a cynical democracy', *Economic and Political Weekly*, 4 May: 1707–1708.

Barnett, S., L. Fruzzetti and Á. Östör (1976) 'Hierarchy purified: Notes on Dumont and his critics', *The Journal of Asian Studies*, 35.4: 627–646.

Barth, F. (1960) 'The system of social stratification in Swat, north Pakistan', in E. Leach (ed.) *Aspects of caste in India, Ceylon, and north-west Pakistan*, pp. 133–146. Cambridge: Cambridge University Press.

Basu, H. (1993) 'The Siddi and the cult of Bava Gor in Gujarat', *Journal of Indian Anthropological Society*, 28.3: 289–300.

—— (1998) 'Hierarchy and emotion: Love, joy and sorrow in a cult of black saints in Gujarat, India', in P. Werbner and H. Basu (eds) *Embodying charisma. Modernity, locality and the performance of emotion in Sufi cults*, pp. 117–139. London and New York: Routledge.

Benson, J.E. (1983) 'Politics and Muslim ethnicity in South India', *Journal of Anthropological Research*, 39.1: 42–59.

Bhachu, P. (1985) *Twice migrants. East African settlers in Britain*, London and New York: Tavistock Publications.

Blackburn, S. (2003) *Print folklore, and nationalism in colonial South India*, New Delhi: Permanent Black.

Blank, J. (2001) *Mullahs on the mainframe. Islam and modernity among the Daudi Bohras*, Chicago, IL and London: The University of Chicago Press.

Bloch, M. (1991) 'Language, anthropology and cognitive science', *Man* (n.s.), 26.1: 183–198.

—— (1992) *Prey into hunter*, Cambridge: Cambridge University Press.

—— (1998) *How we think they think. Anthropological approaches to cognition, memory and literacy*, Oxford: Westview Press.

—— and J. Parry (1995) [originally pub. 1989] 'Introduction. Money and the morality of exchange', in J. Parry and M. Bloch (eds) *Money and the morality of exchange*, pp. 1–32. Cambridge: Cambridge University Press.

Bourdieu, P. (1977) *Outline of a theory of practice* (trans. R. Nice), Cambridge: Cambridge University Press.

Boxer, C.R. (1969) *The Portuguese seaborne empire, 1415–1825*, London: Hutchinson.

Brass, P. (1997) *Theft of an idol. Text and context in the representation of collective violence*, Princeton, NJ: Princeton University Press.

Braudel, F. (1972) [originally pub. 1948] *The Mediterranean and the Mediterranean world in the age of Philip II* (Vols I and II) (trans. S. Reynolds), London: Collins.

Breman, J. (2004) *The making and unmaking of an industrial working class. Sliding down the labour hierarchy in Ahmedabad, India*, New Delhi: Oxford University Press.

Burgess, J. (1971) [originally pub. 1874–1875] *Report on the antiquities of Kathiawad and Kachh. Being a result of the second season's operations of the archaeological survey of Western India*, Varanasi: Indological Book House.

Burnes, A. (1836) 'On the maritime communications of India, as carried on by the natives, particularly from Kutch, at the mouth of the Indus', *Journal of the Royal Geographical Society*, 6: 23–29.

—— (1879) 'Appendix No. IV. Five papers on Kachh antiquities', in *Selections from the Bombay Records* (n.s.) No. 152. Bombay: Government Central Press.

Burton, R.F. (1872) *Zanzibar; city, island, and coast*, Vols I and II, London: Tinsley Brothers.

Campbell, G. (1981) 'Madagascar and the slave trade', *The Journal of African History*, 22.2: 203–227.

—— (1989) 'Madagascar and Mozambique in the slave trade of the western Indian Ocean', in W.G. Clarence-Smith (ed.) *The economics of the Indian Ocean slave trade in the nineteenth century*, pp. 166–193. London: Frank Cass.

Caplan, L. (1987) *Studies in religious fundamentalism*, London: Macmillan Press.

Carroll, L. (1979) 'The seavoyage controversy and the Kayasthas of North India, 1901–1909', *Modern Asian Studies*, 13.2: 265–299.

Chandras, A. (1961) Gujarat fairs and festivals. *Census of India*, V, Part VII, B, 228, New Delhi: Government of India Press.

Chaudhuri, K.N. (1999) [originally pub. 1985] *Trade and civilisation in the Indian Ocean: An economic history from the rise of Islam to 1750*, Cambridge: Cambridge University Press.

—— (2001) 'The Middle East & South Asia through the eyes of the beholder: An outline of a theory of equivalence', Keynote Lecture to the Conference on Comparative Studies of South Asia and the Middle East, UCSB, 2000.

Clarence-Smith, W.G. (1989) 'The economics of the Indian Ocean and Red Sea slave trades in the nineteenth century: An overview', in W.G. Clarence-Smith (ed.) *The economics of the Indian Ocean slave trade in the nineteenth century*, pp. 1–20. London: Frank Cass.

Colomb, R.N. (1873) *Slave-catching in the Indian Ocean. A record of naval experiences*, London: Longmans, Green & Co.

Connerton, P. (1995) [originally pub. 1989] *How societies remember*, Cambridge: Cambridge University Press.

Corbridge, S. and J. Harriss (2003) [originally pub. 2000] *Reinventing India. Liberalization, Hindu nationalism and popular democracy*, New Delhi: Oxford University Press.

Coser, L.A. (1992) 'Introduction: Maurice Halbwachs 1877–1945', in M. Halbwachs *On collective memory* (edited and trans. L.A. Coser), Chicago, IL: University of Chicago Press.

Coupland, R. (1939) *The exploitation of East Africa 1856–1890: The slave trade and the scramble*, London: Faber & Faber.

Coy, M.W. (1989) 'Being what we pretend to be: The usefulness of apprenticeship as a field method', in M. Coy (ed.) *Apprenticeship: From theory to method and back again*, pp. 115–136. Albany, NY: State University of New York.

Das, V. (1984) 'For a folk-theology and theological anthropology of Islam', *Contributions to Indian Sociology*, 18.2: 292–300.

Das Gupta, A. and M.N. Pearson (eds) (1987) *India and the Indian Ocean, 1500–1800*, Calcutta: Oxford University Press.

de Vere Allen, J. (1980) 'A proposal for Indian Ocean studies', in *Historical Relations Across the Indian Ocean, The General History of Africa, Studies and Documents 3*. Paris: UNESCO.

Didier, B.J. (2004) 'Conflict self-inflicted: Dispute, incivility, and the threat of violence in an Indian Muslim community', *The Journal of Asian Studies*, 63.1: 61–80.

Dirks, N. (2001) *Castes of mind: Colonialism and the making of modern India*, Princeton, NJ: Princeton University Press.

Dobbin, C. (1996) *Asian entrepreneurial minorities. Conjoint communities in the making of the world-economy, 1570–1940*, Richmond, Surrey: Curzon.

Doniger, W. (1999) 'Presidential address: "I have Scinde": Flogging a dead (white male Orientalist) horse', *The Journal of Asian Studies*, 58.4: 940–960.

Dumont, L. (1980) [revised edition, originally pub. 1966] *Homo hierarchicus. The caste system and its implications*, Chicago, IL: University of Chicago Press.

Eaton, R.M. (1978) *Sufis of Bijapur 1300–1700: Social roles of Sufis in medieval India*, Princeton, NJ: Princeton University Press.

—— (2001) [originally pub. 2000] *Essays on Islam and Indian history*, New Delhi: Oxford University Press.

Eickelman, D.F. (1976) *Moroccan Islam: Tradition and society in a pilgrimage center*, Austin, TX: University of Texas Press.

—— (1978) 'The art of memory: Islamic education and its social reproduction', *Comparative Studies in Society and History*, 20.4: 485–516.

—— (1981) *The Middle East. An anthropological approach*, Englewood Cliffs, NJ: Prentice-Hall.

—— (1982) 'The study of Islam in local contexts', *Contributions to Asian Studies*, 17: 1–16.

Eisenstadt, S.N. (ed.) (1968) *Max Weber on charisma and institution building. Selected papers*, Chicago, IL and London: University of Chicago Press.

Engels, F. (1990) [originally pub. 1894] 'On the history of early Christianity', First published in *Die Neue Zeit*, 1894–95 (trans. Institute of Marxism-Leninism, 1957).

Engineer, A.A. (1989) *The Muslim communities of Gujarat. An exploratory study of Bohras, Khojas and Memons*, Delhi: Ajanta Publications.

—— (1995) *The Bohra clergy and religion*, Bombay: Central Board of the Dawoodi Bohra Community.

—— (ed.) (2003) *The Gujarat carnage*, New Delhi: Orient Longman.

Evans-Pritchard, E.E. (1954) [originally pub. 1949] *The Sanusi of Cyrenaica*, Oxford: Clarendon Press.

Ewing, K.P. (1984) 'The Sufi as saint, curer and exorcist in Modern Pakistan', *Contributions to Asian Studies*, 18: 106–114.

—— (1988) 'Ambiguity and shari'at: A perspective on the problem of moral principles in tension', in K.P. Ewing (ed.) *Shari'at and ambiguity in South Asian Islam*, pp. 1–22. Berkeley and Los Angeles, CA: University of California Press.

Fardon, R. (ed.) (1988) *Localizing strategies: Regional traditions of ethnographic writing*, Edinburgh: Scottish Academic Press.

Freitag, U. and W.G. Clarence-Smith (eds) (1997) *Hadhrami traders, scholars and statesmen in the Indian Ocean, 1750s–1960s*, Leiden, New York and Cologne: Brill.

Gardner, K. (1993a) 'Desh-bidesh: Sylheti images of home and away', *Man* (n.s.), 28.1: 1–15.

—— (1993b) 'Mullahs, migrants, and miracles: Travel and transformation in Sylhet', *Contributions to Indian Sociology* (n.s.), 27.2: 213–235.

Geertz, C. (1968) *Islam observed: Religious development in Morocco and Indonesia*, Chicago, IL: University of Chicago Press.

Gellner, E. (1964) *Thought and change*, London: Weidenfeld & Nicolson.

—— (1969) *Saints of the Atlas*, Chicago, IL: University of Chicago Press.

—— (1970) 'A pendulum swing theory of Islam', *Philosophical Forum*, 2.2: 234–244.

—— (1981) *Muslim society*, Cambridge: Cambridge University Press.

—— (1988) *Plough, sword and book. The structure of human history*, Chicago, IL: University of Chicago Press.

—— (1992) *Postmodernism, reason and religion*, London and New York: Routledge.

Gibb, H.A.R. (1972) [originally pub. 1947] *Modern trends in Islam*, New York: Octagon Books.

Goodfriend, D.E. (1983) 'Changing concepts of caste and status among Old Delhi Muslims', in I. Ahmad (ed.) *Modernization and social change among Muslims in India*, pp. 119–152. New Delhi: Manohar.

Goody, J. (ed.) (1968) *Literacy in traditional societies*, Cambridge: Cambridge University Press.

—— and I. Watt (1968) 'The consequences of literacy', in J. Goody (ed.) *Literacy in traditional societies*, Cambridge: Cambridge University Press.

Gregory, C. (1982) *Gifts and commodities*, London: Academic Press.

Gupta, D. (2002) 'Limits of tolerance. Prospects of secularism in India after Gujarat', *Economic and Political Weekly*, 16 November, pp. 4615–4620.

Gupta, H.R. (1969) *The Kutch affair*, Delhi: U.C. Kapur & Sons.

Haas, J. (1989) 'The process of apprenticeship: Ritual ordeal and the adoption of a cloak of competence', in M. Coy (ed.) *Apprenticeship: From theory to method and back again*, pp. 87–113. Albany, NY: State University of New York.

Halbwachs, M. (1980) *The collective memory* (trans. F.J. Ditter and V.Y. Ditter), New York: Harper & Collins.

—— (1992) *On collective memory* (edited and trans. L.A. Coser), Chicago, IL: University of Chicago Press.

Hansen, T.B. (1996) 'Recuperating masculinity. Hindu nationalism, violence and the exorcism of the Muslim "other"', *Critique of Anthropology*, 16.2: 137–172.

—— (1999) *The saffron wave. Democracy and Hindu nationalism in modern India*, Princeton, NJ: Princeton University Press.

—— (2001) *Wages of violence. Naming and identity in postcolonial Bombay*, Princeton, NJ: Princeton University Press.

Hawkins, C.W. (1977) *The dhow. An illustrated history of the dhow and its world*, Lymington, Hampshire: Nautical Publishing Co.

Herzfeld, M. (2004) *The body impolitic. Artisans and artifice in the global hierarchy of value*, Chicago, IL and London: The University of Chicago Press.

Hobsbawm, E. and T. Ranger (eds) (1983) *The invention of tradition*, Cambridge: Cambridge University Press.

Hollingsworth, L.W. (1960) *The Asians of East Africa*, London: Macmillan & Co.

Hourani, G.F. (1951) *Arab seafaring in the Indian Ocean in ancient and early medieval times*, Princeton, NJ: Princeton University Press.

Howorth, H.H. (1873) 'Anthropological miscellanea. The Avares, or Eastern Huns', *Journal of the Anthropological Institute of Great Britain and Ireland*, 2: 114–127.

Hume, D. (1998) [originally pub. 1757–1779] *Dialogues and natural history of religion*, Oxford: Oxford University Press.

Hutchins, E. (1996) *Cognition in the wild*, London: The MIT Press.

Ibn Khaldun, 'abd al-R. (1967) *An introduction to history: The Muqaddimah/Ibn Khaldun* (trans. F. Rosenthal; abridged and edited N.J. Dawood), London: Routledge & Kegan Paul with Secker & Warburg.

Ingold, T. (2000) *The perception of the environment. Essays in livelihood, dwelling and skill*, London: Routledge.

Jaffrelot, C. (1996) *The Hindu nationalist movement and Indian politics, 1925 to the 1990s*, London: Hurst.

Jain, S.P. (1978) [originally pub. 1973] 'Caste stratification among Muslims in a township in Western Uttar Pradesh', in I. Ahmad (ed.) *Caste and social stratification among Muslims in India*, pp. 225–242. New Delhi: Manohar.

Jenkins, T. (1994) 'Fieldwork and the perception of everyday life', *Man* (n.s.), 29.2: 433–455.

Keller, C. and J.D. Keller (1996) *Cognition and tool use. The blacksmith at work*, Cambridge: Cambridge University Press.

Khan, A.M. (1928) *Mirat-i-Ahmadi: A history of Gujarat in Persian* (edited by S.N. Ali), Baroda: Oriental Institute.

Kondo, D.K. (1990) *Crafting selves: Power, gender and discourses of identity in a Japanese workplace*, Chicago, IL: Chicago University Press.

Kopytoff, I. (2000) [originally pub. 1986] 'The cultural biography of things: Commoditization as process', in A. Appadurai (ed.) *The social life of things. Commodities in cultural perspective*, pp. 64–91. Cambridge: Cambridge University Press.

Kramrisch, S. (1964) *Unknown India: Ritual art in tribe and village*, Philadelphia, PA: Philadelphia Museum of Art.

Lave, J. (1984) 'Introduction: Thinking and learning in a social context', in B. Rogoff and J. Lave (eds) *Everyday cognition: Its development in social context*, Cambridge, MA: Harvard University Press.

—— (1988a) *The culture of acquisition and the practice of understanding*, Palo Alto, CA: Institute for Research on Learning.

—— (1988b) *Cognition in practice. Mind, mathematics and culture in everyday life*, Cambridge: Cambridge University Press.

—— (1993) 'Introduction: The practice of learning', in S. Chaiklin and J. Lave (eds) *Understanding practice. Perspectives in activity and context*, pp. 3–34. Cambridge: Cambridge University Press.

—— and E. Wenger (1991) *Situated learning: Legitimate peripheral participation*, Cambridge: Cambridge University Press.

Lawrence, T.E. (2000) [originally pub. 1926] *Seven pillars of wisdom. A triumph*, London: Penguin Books in association with Jonathan Cape.

LeGrand, G. (1856) [originally pub. 1841] 'Historical, geographical, and statistical memoirs of the province of Kattywar', in *Selections from the Records of the Bombay Government* (n.s.), 37. Bombay: Bombay Educational Society's Press.

Lévi-Strauss, C. (1978) *Myth and meaning*, London: Routledge & Kegan Paul.

Lewis, B. (1971) *Race and color in Islam*, New York: Harper & Row.

Lewis, I.M. (1961) *A pastoral democracy. A study of pastoralism and politics among the northern Somali of the Horn of Africa*, Oxford: Oxford University Press.

Lewis, M.W. and K.E. Wigen (1997) *The myth of continents: A critical metageography*, Berkeley, CA: University of California Press.

Lindholm, C. (1986) 'Caste in Islam and the problem of deviant systems: A critique of recent theory', *Contributions to Indian Sociology* (n.s.), 20.1: 61–73.

Lochtefeld, J.G. (1996) 'New wine, old skins: The Sangh parivar and the transformation of Hinduism', *Religion*, 26.2: 101–117.

Luhrmann, T.M. (1996) *The good Parsi: The fate of a colonial elite in a postcolonial society*, Cambridge, MA: Harvard University Press.

McGilvray, D.B. (1982) 'Mukkuvar vannimai: Tamil caste and matriclan ideology in Batticaloa, Sri Lanka', in D.B. McGilvray (ed.) *Caste ideology and interaction*, pp. 34–97. Cambridge: Cambridge University Press.

McGrail, S. (ed.) (2003) *Boats of South Asia*, London: Routledge.

MacMurdo, J. (1820a) 'An account of the province of Cutch, and of the countries lying between Guzerat and the river Indus: With cursory remarks on the inhabitants, their history, manners, and state of society', in *Transactions of the Literary Society of Bombay*, 2. London: Longman, Hurst, Rees, Orme, Brown (and John Murray).

—— (1820b) 'Papers relating to the earthquake which occurred in India in 1819', in *Transactions of the Literary Society of Bombay*, 3. London: Longman, Hurst, Rees, Orme, Brown (and John Murray).

—— (1856) [originally pub. 1812] 'Memoir on the province of Kattywar: With remarks on the Runn of Kutch and the District of Okhamundal', in *Selections from the Records of the Bombay Government* (n.s.), 37. Bombay: Bombay Educational Society's Press.

McPherson, K. (1984) 'Processes of cultural interaction in the Indian Ocean: An historical perspective', *The Great Circle*, 6.2: 78–92.

—— (1995) [originally pub. 1993] *The Indian Ocean. A history of people and the sea*, Delhi: Oxford University Press.

Malinowski, B. (1922) *Argonauts of the Western Pacific*, London: Routledge & Kegan Paul.

Mangat, J.S. (1969) *The history of Asians in East Africa c.1886–1945*, Oxford: Clarendon Press.

Manjhu, S. ibn M. (1961) *The Mirat-i-Sikandari: A history of Gujarat* (edited S.C. Misra), Baroda: Maharaja Sayajirao University of Baroda.

Marchand, T.H.J. (2001) *Minaret building and apprenticeship in Yemen*, Richmond, Surrey: Curzon.

Markovits, C. (2000) *The global world of Indian merchants, 1750–1947*, Cambridge: Cambridge University Press.

Marriott, M. (1976) 'Hindu transactions: Diversity without dualism', in B. Kapferer (ed.) *Transactions and meaning. Directions in the anthropology of exchange and symbolic behaviour*, pp. 109–142. ASA Essays in Social Anthropology 1. Philadelphia, PA: ISHI.

—— and R.B. Inden (1977) 'Toward an ethnosociology of South Asian caste systems', in K. David (ed.) *The new wind: Changing identities in South Asia*, pp. 227–238. The Hague and Paris: Mouton.

Masselos, J.C. (1978) [originally pub. 1973] 'The Khojas of Bombay: The defining of formal membership criteria during the nineteenth century', in I. Ahmad (ed.) *Caste and social stratification among Muslims in India*, pp. 97–116. New Delhi: Manohar.

—— (1996) [originally pub. 1995] 'Migration and urban identity: Bombay's famine refugees in the nineteenth century', in S. Patel and A. Thorner (eds) *Bombay. Mosaic of modern culture*, pp. 25–58. Bombay: Oxford University Press.

Masud, M.K. (1990) 'The obligation to migrate: The doctrine of *hijra* in Islamic law', in D.F. Eickelman and J. Piscatori (eds) *Muslim travellers. Pilgrimage, migration, and the religious imagination*, pp. 29–49. London: Routledge.

Mehta, U. (2003) 'The Gujarat genocide. A sociological approach', in A.A. Engineer (ed.) *The Gujarat carnage*, pp. 186–197. New Delhi: Orient Longman.

Messick, B. (1993) *The calligraphic state. Textual domination and history in a Muslim society*, Berkeley and Los Angeles, CA: University of California Press.

Metcalf, B.D. (ed.) (1984) *Moral conduct and authority. The place of* adab *in South Asian Islam*, Berkeley and Los Angeles, CA: University of California Press.

—— (1990) 'The pilgrimage remembered: South Asian accounts of the *hajj*', in D.F. Eickelman and J. Piscatori (eds) *Muslim travellers. Pilgrimage, migration, and the religious imagination*, pp. 85–110. London: Routledge.

—— (2004) *Islamic contestations. Essays on Muslims in India and Pakistan*, New Delhi: Oxford University Press.

—— (2005) [originally pub. 1982] *Islamic revival in British India: Deoband, 1860–1900*, New Delhi: Oxford University Press.

Miller, B.S. (1991) 'Presidential address: Contending narratives – the political life of the Indian epics', *The Journal of Asian Studies*, 50.4: 783–792.

Mines, M. (1975) 'Islamisation and Muslim ethnicity in South India', *Man* (n.s.), 10.3: 404–419.

—— (1994) *Public faces, private lives. Community and individuality in south India*, Berkeley and Los Angeles, CA: University of California Press.

—— and V. Gourishankar (1990) 'Leadership and individuality in South Asia: The case of the South Indian big-man', *The Journal of South Asian Studies*, 49.4: 761–786.

Misra, S.C. (1964) *Muslim communities in Gujarat. Preliminary studies in their history and social organisation*, London: Asia Publishing House.

Morris, H.S. (1956) 'Indians in East Africa: A study of a plural society', *British Journal of Sociology*, 7.3: 194–211.

—— (1957a) 'Communal rivalry among Indians in Uganda', *British Journal of Sociology*, 8.4: 306–317.

—— (1957b) 'The plural society', *Man*, 57: 124–125.

—— (1958) 'The divine kingship of the Aga Khan', *Southwestern Journal of Anthropology*, 14.4: 454–472.

—— (1959) 'The Indian family in Uganda', *American Anthropologist*, 61: 779–789.

Nandy, A. (2002) 'Obituary of a culture', *Seminar*, 513: 15–18.

Nanji, A. (1974) 'Modernization and change in the Nizari Ismaili community in East Africa – a perspective', *Journal of Religion in Africa*, 6.2: 123–139.

'Nauticus' (1977) 'A profile', in N.G. Jog (ed.) *Narotam Morarjee. Architect of modern shipping*, pp. 7–40. Bombay: The Scindia Steam Navigation Company Limited.

Osella, F. and C. Osella (2000) 'Migration, money and masculinity in Kerela', *The Journal of the Royal Anthropological Institute*, 6.1: 117–133.

Padayachee, V. and R. Morrell (1991) 'Indian merchants and Dukawallahs in the Natal economy, c.1875–1914', *Journal of Southern African Studies*, 17.1: 71–102.

Pálsson, G. (1994) 'Enskillment at sea', *Man* (n.s.), 29.4: 901–927.

Parkin, D. (1980) 'The creativity of abuse', *Man* (n.s.), 15.1: 45–64.

—— (2000) 'Inside and outside the mosque: A master trope', in D. Parkin and S.C. Headley (eds) *Islamic prayer across the Indian Ocean. Inside and outside the mosque*, pp. 1–22. Richmond, Surrey: Curzon.

Parry, J.P. (1994) *Death in Banares*, Cambridge: Cambridge University Press.

Patel, G. (2002) 'Narendra Modi's one-day cricket. What and why?', *Economic and Political Weekly*, 30 November, pp. 4826–4837.

Peabody, N. (2001) 'Cents, sense, census: Human inventories in late precolonial and early colonial India', *Comparative Studies in Society and History*, 43.4: 819–850.

Pearson, M.N. (1976) *Merchants and rulers in Gujarat: The response to the Portuguese in the sixteenth century*, Berkeley, CA: University of California Press.

—— (1985) 'Littoral society: The case for the coast', *The Great Circle*, 7.1: 1–8.

—— (1998a) 'Indians in East Africa: The early modern period', in R. Mukherjee and L. Subramanian (eds) *Politics and trade in the Indian Ocean world: Essays in honour of Ashin Das Gupta*, pp. 227–249. Delhi: Oxford University Press.

—— (1998b) *Port cities and intruders: The Swahili coast, India and Portugal in the early modern era*, Baltimore, MD: Johns Hopkins University Press.

—— (2000) 'Consolidating the faith: Muslim travellers in the Indian Ocean world', *UTS Quarterly: Cultural Studies and New Writing*, 6.2: 6–13.

—— (2003) *The Indian Ocean*, New York: Routledge.

Pickthall, M.M. (1930) *The meaning of the glorious Qur'ān. An explanatory translation*, London: Ta-Ha Publishers.

Pocock, D.F. (1955) 'The role of Indians in East Africa', *Times British Colonies Review*, Autumn, pp. 23–24.

—— (1957) 'Difference in East Africa: A study of caste and religion in modern Indian society', *Southwestern Journal of Anthropology*, 13.4: 289–300.

—— (1958a) 'Indians in East Africa', *Economic Weekly*, pp. 863–864.

—— (1958b) 'Race and racism in East Africa', *Economic Weekly*, pp. 999–1004.

—— (1959) 'Slavery and Indo-Arab relations in nineteenth century Zanzibar', *Economic Weekly*, pp. 165–172.

—— (1960) 'Generations in East Africa', *Economic Weekly*, pp. 153–162.

—— (1972) *Kanbi and Patidar: A study of the Patidar community of Gujarat*, Oxford: Clarendon.

Pollock, S. (1993) 'Ramayana and political imagination in India', *The Journal of Asian Studies*, 52.2: 261–297.

Postans, M. (1839) *Cutch; or, random sketches, taken during a residence in one of the northern provinces of Western India; interspersed with legends and traditions*, London: Smith, Elder & Co., Cornhill.

Postans, T. (1839–40) 'Some account of the present state of the trade between the port of Mandavie in Cutch, and the eastern coast of Africa', *Transactions of the Bombay Geographical Society*, 3: 169–176.

Prakash, A. (2003) Re-imagination of the state and Gujarat's electoral verdict, *Economic and Political Weekly*, 19 April, pp. 1601–1610.

Prins, A.H.J. (1965) *Sailing from Lamu. A study of maritime culture in Islamic East Africa*, Assen: van Gorcum & Comp. N.V.

Purandare, M.B. (1997) *A case study of the Bhatia community (a history)*, Ph.D. dissertation, University of Mumbai.

Reda Bhacker, M. (1992) *Trade and empire in Muscat and Zanzibar. Roots of British domination*, London: Routledge.

Risso, P. (1995) *Merchants and faith: Muslim commerce and culture in the Indian Ocean*, Boulder, CO: Westview Press.

Robb, P. (1995) 'Introduction: South Asia and the concept of race', in P. Robb (ed.) *The concept of race in South Asia*, pp. 1–76. Delhi: Oxford University Press.

Robertson, J. (1889) 'Introduction', in D. Hume *The natural history of religion*, pp. v–xxiv. London: Fleethought Publishing Company.

Robinson, F. (1983) 'Islam and Muslim society in South Asia', *Contributions to Indian Sociology* (n.s.), 17.2: 185–203.

—— (2003) [originally pub. 2000] *Islam and Muslim history in South Asia*, New Delhi: Oxford University Press.

Roy, A. (1983) *The Islamic syncretistic tradition in Bengal*, Princeton, NJ: Princeton University Press.

Rushbrook Williams, L.F. (1958) *The black hills. Kutch in history and legend: A study in local Indian loyalties*, London: Weidenfeld & Nicolson.

Sahlins, M. (1985) *Historical metaphors and mythical realities. Structure in the early history of the Sandwich Islands kingdom*, Ann Arbor, MI: The University of Michigan Press.

—— (1996) 'The sadness of sweetness. The native anthropology of western cosmology', *Current Anthropology*, 37.3: 395–415.

—— (1999) 'Two or three things that I know about culture', *Journal of the Royal Anthropological Institute* (n.s.), 5.3: 399–421.

Sakarai, L.J. (1980) 'Indian merchants in East Africa part one: The triangular trade and the slave economy', *Slavery and Abolition*, 1.3: 292–338.

—— (1981) 'Indian merchants in East Africa part two: British Imperialism and the transformation of the slave economy', *Slavery and Abolition*, 2.1: 2–30.

Salvadori, C. (1996) *We came in dhows: Stories of the Indian pioneers in Kenya* (Vols I–III), Nairobi: Paperchase Kenya.

Sarkar, T. (2002) 'Semiotics of terror. Muslims, children and women in Hindu Rashtra', *Economic and Political Weekly*, 13 July, pp. 2872–2876.

Schoff, W.H. (1912) *The Periplus of the Erythræan Sea*, New York: Longmans & Co.

Shah, G. (1998) 'The BJP's riddle in Gujarat: Caste, factionalism and Hindutva', in T.B. Hansen and C. Jaffrelot (eds) *The BJP and the compulsions of politics in India*, pp. 243–266. New Delhi: Oxford University Press.

—— (2002a) 'Contestation and negotiations. Hindutva sentiments and temporal interests in Gujarat elections', *Economic and Political Weekly*, 30 November, pp. 4838–4843.

—— (2002b) 'Caste, Hindutva and hideousness', *Economic and Political Weekly*, 13 April, pp. 1391–1393.

Shepard, W.E. (1987) 'Islam and ideology: Towards a typology', *International Journal of Middle East Studies*, 19.3: 307–335.

Sheriff, A. (1989) 'Localisation and social composition of the East African slave trade', in W.G. Clarence-Smith (ed.) *The economics of the Indian Ocean slave trade in the nineteenth century*, pp. 131–145. London: Frank Cass.

Shils, E. (1965) 'Charisma, order, and status', *American Sociological Review*, 30.2: 199–213.

Shodhan, A. (2001) *A question of community, religious groups and colonial law*, Calcutta: Samya.

Siddiqui, M.K.A. (1978) [originally pub. 1973] 'Caste amongst the Muslims of Calcutta', in I. Ahmad (ed.) *Caste and social stratification among Muslims in India*, pp. 243–268. New Delhi: Manohar.

Simpson, E. (2003) 'Migration and Islamic reform in a port town of western India', *Contributions to Indian Sociology*, 37.1&2: 83–108.

—— (2004) '"Hindutva" as a rural planning paradigm in post-earthquake Gujarat', in J. Zavos, A.Wyatt and V. Hewitt (eds) *Cultural mobilisation and the fragmentation of the nation in modern India*, pp. 136–165. New Delhi: Oxford University Press.

—— (2006) 'Shipyard apprenticeship in western India', *Journal of the Royal Anthropological Institute*, 12.1.

Smith, B. (2003) *Hinduism and modernity*, Oxford: Blackwell Publishing.

Sondhi, M.L. and A. Mukarji (eds) (2002) *The black book of Gujarat*, New Delhi: Manak.

Speke, J.H. (1864) *What led to the discovery of the source of the Nile*, London: Blackwood.

Starrett, G. (1995) 'The hexis of Interpretation: Islam and the body in the Egyptian popular school', *American Ethnologist*, 22.4: 953–969.

Stirrat, J. (1995) [originally pub. 1989] 'Money, men and women', in J. Parry and M. Bloch (eds) *Money and the morality of exchange*, pp. 94–116. Cambridge: Cambridge University Press.

Strathern, M. (1992) 'Qualified value: The perspective of gift exchange', in C. Humphrey and S. Hugh-Jones (eds) *Barter, exchange and value. An anthropological approach*, pp. 169–191. Cambridge: Cambridge University Press.

Subramanian, L. (1987) 'Banias and the British: The role of indigenous credit in the process of imperial expansion in western India in the second half of the eighteenth century', *Modern Asian Studies*, 21.3: 473–510.

Tambiah, S.J. (1996) *Levelling crowds. Ethnonationalist conflicts and collective violence in South Asia*, Berkeley and Los Angeles, CA: University of California Press.

Tinker, H. (1977) *The banyan tree: Overseas emigrants from India, Pakistan, and Bangladesh*, Oxford: Oxford University Press.

Tominaga, C. (1996) 'Indian immigrants and the East African slave trade', in S. Sato and E. Kurimot (eds) *Essays in Northeast African Studies* (Senri Ethnological Studies 43), pp. 295–317. Osaka, Japan: National Museum of Ethnology.

Toussaint, A. (1966) *History of the Indian Ocean*, London: Routledge & Kegan Paul.

Toynbee, A.J. (1981) *The Greeks and their heritages*, Oxford: Oxford University Press.

Turner, B.S. (1974) *Weber and Islam. A critical study*, London: Routledge & Kegan Paul.

Turner, V.W. (1969) *The ritual process: Structure and anti-structure*, London: Routledge & Kegan Paul.

Vaidya, K.B. (1945) *The sailing vessel traffic on the West Coast of India and its future*, Bombay: The Popular Book Depot.

van der Veer, P. (1992) 'Playing or praying: A Sufi saint's day in Surat', *The Journal of Asian Studies*, 51.3: 545–564.

—— (1994) *Religious nationalism. Hindus and Muslims in India*, Berkeley and Los Angeles, CA: University of California Press.

Varadarajan, L. (1991) 'Perspectives on maritime activity in Gujarat', in A. Gupta (ed.) *Minorities on India's West Coast. History and society*, pp. 1–16. Delhi: Kalinga Publishers.

179

Varadarajan, S. (ed.) (2002) *Gujarat. The making of a tragedy*, New Delhi: Penguin.

Vatuk, S. (1996) 'Identity and difference or equality and inequality in South Asian Muslim society', in C. Fuller (ed.) *Caste today*, pp. 227–262. New Delhi: Oxford University Press.

Villiers, A. (1940) *Sons of Sinbad: An account of sailing with the Arabs in their dhows, in the Red Sea, around the coasts of Arabia, and to Zanzibar and Tanganyika: pearling in the Persian Gulf: and the life of the shipmasters, the mariners and merchants of Kuwait*, New York: C. Scribner's Sons.

Vincent, D.D. (1805) *The Periplus of the Erythrean Sea* (Parts 1–3), London: A. Straham for T. Cadwell Jr and W. Davies.

vom Bruck, G. (2005) 'The imagined "consumer democracy" and elite (re)production in Yemen', *Journal of the Royal Anthropological Institute* (n.s.), 11.1: 255–275.

Werbner, P. (1989) 'The ranking of brotherhoods: The dialectics of Muslim caste amongst overseas Pakistanis', *Contributions to Indian Sociology* (n.s.), 23.2: 285–315.

—— and H. Basu (eds) (1998) *Modernity, locality and the performance of emotion in Sufi cults*, London and New York: Routledge.

Yagnik, A. and S. Sheth (2002) 'Whither Gujarat? Violence and after', *Economic and Political Weekly*, 16 March, pp. 1009–1011.

Yusuf Ali, A.A. (1934) *The Holy Qur'an: Translation and commentary*, Lahore: Shaikh Muhammad Ashraf.

Zaman, M.Q. (1999a) 'Commentaries, print and patronage: "Hadith" and the madrasas in modern South Asia', *Bulletin of the School of Oriental and African Studies, University of London*, 62.1: 60–81.

—— (1999b) 'Religious education and the rhetoric of reform: The madrasa in British India and Pakistan', *Comparative Studies in Society and History*, 41.2: 294–323.

GOVERNMENT PUBLICATIONS

Gazetteer of the Bombay Presidency (1880) *Cutch, Pâlanpur, and Mahi Kântha*, Vol. V, Bombay: Government Central Press.

—— (1884) *Katiawar*, Vol. VIII, Bombay: Government Central Press.

—— (1896) *History of Gujarat*, Vol. I, Part I, Bombay: Government Central Press.

—— (1899) *Gujarat population: Musalmans and Parsis*, Vol. IX, Part II, Bombay: Government Central Press.

—— (1901) *Gujarât population: Hindus*, Vol. IX, Part I, Bombay: Government Central Press.

Gujarat State Gazetteer (1989) Part 1, Gandhinagar: Government of Gujarat.

Linguistic Survey of India (1908) *Indo-Aryan family. Central group. Specimens of the Rajasthani and Gujarati*, Vol. IX, Part II, Calcutta: Superintendent Government Printing, India.

—— (1919) *Indo-Aryan family. North-western group. Specimens of Sindhi and Lahnda*, Vol. VIII, Part I, Calcutta: Superintendent Government Printing, India.

People of India (2003) *Gujarat*, Part One, Vol. XXII, Anthropological Survey of India, Mumbai: Popular Prakashan.

GUJARATI BIBLIOGRAPHY

Karani, D. (1972) *Kachchhni rasadhar* (Vols I–IV), Ahmedabad: Gujarat Grantharatna Karyalaya.

—— (1988a) *Kachchh kaladhar* (Vols I and II), Bombay: Suman Prakashan.

—— (1988b) *Kachchhna santo ane kavio* (Vols 1 and II), Bombay: Suman Prakashan.

Maharaj, H. and V.P. Dwivedi (v.s. 2003) *Shri Uderaalaal aakyaan*, Mumbai: Vichaarshil Prakaashan.

Mankad, H.R. (1935) *Vahaanni paribhasha*, Ahmedabad: Gujarat Vernacular Society.

Neygandhi, J.J. (v.s. 1993) 'Seth Dharamsinh Vallabdas. Ek adars purush', *Bhaatiya Yuvak*, Chaitra, pp. 368–374.

Pandhi, M.B. (1976–1977) 'Naukashastra, nauka sthapatya-no prachin gauravanvit itihas dharavtun – Kachchn-nun vahanvatun', in S.K. Bhowmik (ed.) *Museum Bulletin. Special issue to honour the centenary celebrations of Kutch Museum*, pp. 141–172. Museum and Picture Gallery: The Department of Museums, Gujarat State.

Sampat, D.D. (v.s. 1995) 'Seth Liladhar Morrarji Bhimani', *Bhaatiya Yuvak*, Divali, pp. 131–132.

—— (1935) *Kachchhnu vepari tantra*, publisher unknown.

—— (1940) *Saagar kathaao*, Bombay: R.R. Sethni Company.

—— (1943) *Kachchhni lokvaartaa*, Ahmedabad: T.K. Thakkar.

—— (1950) *Shahshik sodaagaro*, Bombay: Bhaarati Shaahitya.

Visanji, T.N. (1924) *Jangbar ane Kachchio*, Ahmedabad: publisher unknown.

INDEX

adab 74, 87, 96, 98
Aga Khan, the 32
Ahl-e-Hadith 107
Ahmad, I. 89
Ahmedabad 23, 30, 39, 43, 137
Appadurai, A. 35–6, 54
apprentice(-s/ship) i, ix, 10, 13, 19,
    20–4, 41–2, 64, 83, 84, 85, 86, 108,
    109, 112, 129, 146, 147, 148, 153,
    155, 156, 157, 163; and rites of
    passage 8; anthropological theories
    of 8, 55–7, 78–80; descriptions of
    7–9, 58–63, 80; language and
    thought 65–77
Arab 1, 27, 36, 47, 71, 76; history 91–2,
    94–5
Arabic (language) xi, 3, 13, 37, 52,
    66–7, 109
Assayag, J. 90, 101
Ayodhya 23, 111, 133, 140

Babri Masjid *see* Ayodhya
Barnett, S. 92, 103
Bhadala 2; and apprenticeship 7, 12–13,
    56, 59, 67, 83, 154; and Hindu
    nationalism 23–4, 53, 69–70, 111,
    112, 128, 136, 142, 147; and
    charisma 22; and football 127;
    history of 27, 29, 51, 52, 81;
    individuals among 68, 69, 76–7;
    lineages among 96; Nava Naroj 113,
    114, 129, 139–40; relationship with
    Mandvi 18, 22, 23, 52, 73, 86, 87,
    113, 114, 116, 118–19, 126, 129,
    139, 141, 143, 147; and religious

reform 12, 22, 52, 73–4, 77, 83,
    103–9, 136, 137, 143, 145, 146;
    reputation of 4, 82, 88, 124, 125–26,
    128, 140, 143; and saints (Saiyeds)
    71, 75, 83, 84, 103–9, 154, 156;
    textual references to 27, 52
Bhatiya(-s) 30, 31, 39, 44, 46, 48, 116,
    117, 121; caste journal of 35
BJP 23; electoral performance in
    Kachchh 69, 137, 138–9; growth
    in Gujarat 132–6, 138; internal
    schisms 131, 132, 139
Bloch, M. 8, 56
body, the 23, 24, 60, 63, 65, 80, 83,
    84, 90, 93, 96, 108, 109, 151, 156;
    and social hierarchy 22, 82–3;
    anthropological theories of 21–2,
    79, 81–2; as a metaphor 24, 164;
    dichotomisation of 85, 156; Muslim
    conceptions of 22, 81–2, 85–6,
    98–9
Bombay 1, 3, 4, 5, 6, 27, 28, 29, 32,
    34, 37, 38, 40, 43, 44, 45, 46, 47,
    48, 50, 51, 68, 69, 75, 76, 94, 122,
    126, 127, 128, 144, 150, 152,
    156, 163; renamed as Mumbai
    xi–xii
border(-s) and boundary 32, 126;
    theories of 159–60; with Pakistan
    27, 126, 140 (*see also* Partition);
    social 32, 46, 70, 96, 97, 103, 125
Bourdieu, P. 8, 79
Brass, P. 118
Braudel, F. 29, 42, 161, 162
Breman, J. 135

183